The World Bank

RETHINKING BRETTON WOODS

Series Editors:
Jo Marie Griesgraber and Bernhard G. Gunter

This series of five books explores a broad range of proposals for achieving more equitable, sustainable and participatory development, particularly through the international financial institutions. The task of the series is to offer the activist and political communities insights into effecting genuine institutional reform over the next 10 to 15 years.

THE WORLD BANK

Lending on a Global Scale

Edited by
Jo Marie Griesgraber and Bernhard G. Gunter

Pluto  **Press**
LONDON • CHICAGO, IL.
with
Center of Concern WASHINGTON, DC

First published 1996 by Pluto Press
345 Archway Road, London N6 5AA
and 1486 West Randolph, Chicago, Illinois 60607, USA

British Library Cataloguing in Publication Data
A catalogue record for this book is available from the
British Library

ISBN 0 7453 1050 8 hbk

Library of Congress Cataloging in Publication Data
The World Bank : lending on a global scale / edited by Jo Marie
    Griesgraber and Bernhard G. Gunter.
        p.   cm. — (Rethinking Bretton Woods : v.3)
    Includes bibliographical references and index.
    ISBN 0–7453–1050–8 (hc)
    1. World Bank 2. International finance—History. 3. Economic
development—History. I. Griesgraber, Jo Marie. II. Gunter,
Bernhard G., 1964–   . III. Series.
HG3881.R418 1996   vol. 3
[HG3881.5.W57]
332.1'532—dc20   95–53123
                                                            CIP

Designed, typeset and produced for Pluto Press by
Chase Production Service, Chipping Norton, OX7 5QR
Printed in the EC by T. J. Press, Padstow

Contents

LIST OF TABLES

This volume is dedicated to
THE GRAMEEN BANK OF BANGLADESH

Preface

To explore a broad range of proposals for achieving more equitable, sustainable and participatory development, particularly through the international financial institutions, the Center of Concern convened a conference in Washington, DC, from June 12–17, 1994. The conference was a part of the Rethinking Bretton Woods project, which marked the fiftieth anniversary of the Bretton Woods, New Hampshire, meeting that created the World Bank and the International Monetary Fund (IMF) and laid the groundwork for the General Agreement on Tariffs and Trade (GATT), succeeded by the World Trade Organization (WTO) in 1995.

Conference participants came from 27 countries in Africa, Asia, Australia, Europe, and North and South America, and included economists, historians, sociologists, lawyers, businesspeople, political scientists, theologians and representatives of the Bretton Woods institutions (BWIs). Their papers and discussions focused on roles for the BWIs – the World Bank, the IMF and the soon-to-be-established WTO – in initiating, assisting and sustaining such development. This series of books originated as the preparatory papers for that conference.

The project's 23 sponsors include people from academic and non-governmental institutions in 18 countries; an advisory group has members from nine countries. The lead organization, the Center of Concern, is a Washington, DC-based social justice research center founded in 1971 to analyze, educate and advocate on issues of international development. Louis Goodman, Dean of the School of International Service at The American University, a project adviser and sponsor, hosted the conference.

This book is the result of the hard work and generosity of many: the advisers and sponsors of Rethinking Bretton Woods;

the funders, the John D. and Catherine T. MacArthur Foundation, the Ford Foundation, the C.S. Mott Foundation, the World Council of Churches, CEBEMO, Trocaire and CAFOD, and their very competent staffs; the staff and interns of the Center of Concern; the style editors Joan Leibman and Jane Deren; the staff at Pluto Press, Roger van Zwanenberg, *et al.*; but especially the intelligent and persistent John Walsh, who pulled it all together. The editors appreciate deeply the support and good humor of families: Shaw, Andrea, Stanley, David and Jesmin.

Jo Marie Griesgraber
Bernhard G. Gunter
Washington, DC
August 1995

List of Acronymns

ACP	African, Caribbean and Pacific (countries)
AfDB	African Development Bank
ANC	African National Congress
APPER	African Priorty Program for Economic Recovery
ADB	Asian Development Bank
BWI	Bretton Woods institution
CPE	centrally planned economy
EBRD	European Bank for Reconstruction and Development
ECOSOC	Economic and Social Council
ECOWAS	Economic Community of West African States
EC	European Community
ED	executive director
EEC	European Economic Community
EFF	Extended Fund Facility
EIA	environmental impact assessment
ERP	Economic Reform and Recovery Programme
FAO	Food and Agriculture Organization
FDI	foreign direct investment
G-7	Group of Seven
G-24	Group of Twenty-four
GATT	General Agreement on Tariffs and Trade
GDP	Gross Domestic Product
GEF	Global Environment Facility
GNP	Gross National Product
GRO	grass-roots organization
GSP	Generalized System of Preferences
HDI	Human Development Index
IBRD	International Bank for Reconstruction and Development

IDA	International Development Association
IDB	Inter-American Development Bank
IFAD	International Fund for Agricultural Development
IFC	International Finance Corporation
IFI	international financial institution
IMF	International Monetary Fund
ILO	International Labour Organisation
ITO	International Trade Organization
LDC	less developed country
MDB	multilateral development bank
MIGA	Multilateral Investment Guarantee Agency
NAFTA	North American Free Trade Agreement
NGO	non-governmental organization
NIC	newly industrialized country
OAS	Organization of American States
OAU	Organization of African Unity
ODA	official development assistance
OECD	Organization for Economic Cooperation and Development
RBM	Richard Bay Minerals
RDP	Reconstruction and Development Programme
SAL	structural adjustment loan
SAP	structural adjustment program
SDR	Special Drawing Right
SECAL	sectoral adjustment loan
SIA	social impact assessment
SIF	Social Investment Fund
SOE	state-owned enterprise
SPA	Special Programme of Assistance
SSA	Sub-Saharan Africa
TNC	transnational corporation
UNCTAD	United Nations Conference on Trade and Development
UNDP	United Nations Development Programme
UNECA	United Nations Economic Commission for Africa
UNEP	United Nations Environment Programme
UNESCO	United Nations Educational, Scientific and Cultural Organization
UNICEF	United Nations International Children's Emergency Fund
WFP	World Food Programme
WHO	World Health Organization
WTO	World Trade Organization

Introduction

The current understanding of development extends far beyond economic growth, encompassing issues of quality of life within a finite ecosystem. What does this mean for the lending programs of the international financial institutions (IFIs), particularly the World Bank, and the conditions attached to their lending programs? What methodologies should be used to design project and program lending that incorporate the social and political dimensions so integral to development, without violating the Bank's mandate to avoid considering political criteria when making loan decisions? Agreement on the need does not result automatically in agreement on the means. But where broad consensus does exist is on the need for fundamental overhaul of policy-based lending, known as structural adjustment programs (SAPs). The authors in this volume criticize SAPs but also offer alternative approaches to policy-based lending.

The volume's underlying theme is increasing the effectiveness of the World Bank's lending program, effectiveness being understood here as more equitable, sustainable and participatory development. Because the evaluation and replacement of the Bank's standard package of SAPs is essential to increased effectiveness, a few preliminary words on structural adjustment policies are warranted. SAPs are the long-term loans of IFIs which are supposed to restore equilibrium and especially economic growth. The original rationale for SAPs was that sound projects were not possible in an unsound policy environment. The World Bank introduced SAPs in the early 1980s and they were adopted soon thereafter by the regional development banks as well. For the IFIs, a new instrument to influence policies at the macro-economic level was needed because existing loan instruments could only influence policies at the project or sector (agriculture, finance, transportation, etc.) level.

The theoretical basis for SAPs was a return to orthodox neoclassical economics, *laissez-faire* and free trade, which today goes by the name of 'neoliberalism'. To make this move, the World Bank provides structural adjustment loans (SALs), which run eight to ten years. The provision of sectoral adjustment loans (SECALs), which target policy reforms at the sectoral level, have also been conditioned on implementing SAPs. In many cases, SAPs have been preceded by and depended on stabilization programs with the International Monetary Fund (IMF). Stabilization programs differ from SAPs in that the former are short-term loans with policy conditions to correct short-term balance-of-payment problems. The two main components of stabilization programs are expenditure-reducing policies (especially fiscal, or budget, contractions) and expenditure-changing policies (especially devaluation).

SAPs have seven basic elements:

- exchange rate liberalization,

- trade liberalization,

- fiscal policy reform,

- the closing or privatization of state owned enterprises (SOEs),

- reform of the financial sector,

- opening the economy to foreign investment; and

- sectoral reforms of agriculture, industry and social sectors.

The main critique of SAPs is that they are often ineffective, inequitable and adopted in an unfair manner. They are often ineffective because countries are expected to adjust as if they could do so in a vacuum. Most of the developing countries are highly vulnerable to external factors beyond their control and beyond the reach of adjustment policies. SAPs are often ineffective because they neglect the asymmetry in the international adjustment process and include severe contractionary prescriptions. As a result, structural adjustment impedes the country's ability to grow in an environmentally sustainable manner, meet the needs of its people and service its debts.

SAPs are inequitable, in part, because they open the markets of adjusting countries prematurely to an increase in imports, especially of consumer goods meant for higher-income groups, without giving sufficient time for the capacity to pay to catch up. They do not create sufficient room for long-term investments, especially in infrastructure and human capital necessary for long-term economic health, as well as short-term help for the poor. This inequity is accentuated by the very heavy burdens which, in practice, fall on already poor or vulnerable groups.

SAPs are unfair because they do not take into consideration the concerns and voices of all the groups affected, particularly the poor, and the resources available through the Bank and the Fund are inadequate to the task of restructuring simultaneously the more than 40 economies that have accepted SAPs. In addition, weighted voting in the Bank and the Fund ensures that the countries with the greatest say in setting institutional priorities are not the ones that will need to follow those policies.

There are many alternatives to SAPs; it is convenient to cluster them in three groups. Each group is represented within this volume. The first group suggests simple additions to the current approach of structural adjustment and is represented in this volume by authors de Vries, Cock and Webster, and Gillies. They argue that structural adjustment is basically correct, but needs to take into account other aspects such as social and environmental dimensions as well as human rights. The second group agrees with the first that structural adjustment is necessary, but stresses that SAPs must be modified fundamentally. Three authors of this volume – Teriba, Chandrasekhar and Milder – represent this second group. A core critique of the second group is that it has been a fundamental error to make the *laissez-faire* doctrine central to structural adjustment. A third group sees no good in structural adjustment and suggests that structural adjustment be replaced by grass-roots development projects. Milder describes and evaluates the position of the third group, which is articulated by a wide range of Northern non-governmental organizations (NGOs).

The editors of this volume propose that no single alternative to structural adjustment will be sufficient. Some policies should be added to the standard structural adjustment package, some aspects of the package need modification, and still others should be abandoned. Structural adjustment is basically correct in requiring a realistic exchange rate and domestic price liberalizations. Modifications of SAPs are necessary in the way the government cuts its budget. Until recently, the IFIs did not care where the government cuts its expenditures, which particularly harmed the poor who are supposed to benefit most from development. Further modifications are also necessary in the broader social and environmental aspects of SAPs, which can be done with social and environmental impact assessments, as proposed by Cock and Webster. While the World Bank has taken the lead in integrating social and environmental aspects into its adjustment programs, its efforts still fall short of providing adequate protection for the poor and the environment.

Current structural adjustment policy must be modified fundamentally in its theoretical underpinnings. SAPs have been based on the neoliberal approach to government activity which is based on the formula: the less government the better the result. Experience over the last several years has demonstrated that correct government activity is crucial for successful economic restructuring. The debates now rage over what is correct government activity. As a general rule, governments should not be involved in strictly business ventures but play a crucial role in providing infrastructure: 'Governments have done too much of the things they cannot do well – regulating markets and producing ordinary goods – and too little of the things they must do well – maintaining macroeconomic stability and making necessary public investments.'[1] Chandrasekhar concludes that the correct kind of state intervention is a crucial prerequisite for human development. Milder reviews the political history and lessons of SAPs and concludes that an activist role for government is central for successful economic restructuring, understood as equitable, sustainable and participatory development. He encourages the Bank to actively use its catalytic abilities to promote participation and cross-class coalitions.

Structural adjustment is inappropriate and should be abandoned in areas involved with the development of micro-businesses and the informal sector. A strategy which provides access to credit for the poor, following the Grameen Bank model, is crucial. SAPs cannot deal with these aspects. NGOs have the comparative advantage within these areas and funds should be made available to NGOs to work on the development of micro-businesses and the informal sector. The recent experiences of the Inter-American Development Bank (IDB) support this view and enjoy the strong backing of IDB's President Enrique Iglesias.

Recent plans by the World Bank to increase participation through regional participation action plans and its more extensive general participation agenda are essential for the success of its development agenda. There is also a growing consensus within the Bank that the correct sequencing of reform policies has received inadequate attention.

Volume III contains six chapters. In Chapter 1, 'The Challenge of Africa's Socioeconomic Transformation', Dr Owodunni Teriba examines the efficacy of the intellectual, financial and institutional contributions of the Fund and the Bank to Africa's development process; the challenges that participating in Africa's socioeconomic transformation pose to these institutions; and the institutions' general mandates and objectives. Given his experience as Chief of the Socio-Economic Research and Planning Division of the UN Economic Commission for Africa (UNECA) in Addis Ababa, Ethiopia, his critique of the Bank's effectiveness in Africa is thoroughgoing, and he calls for substantial increases in development assistance funds with dramatic reduction in conditions applied. He cautions the Bank and Fund as they become engaged in issues of 'democracy' and 'governance', arguing the need for 'universally agreed parameters' within a UN-administered framework. Otherwise the Bank especially risks 'incrementally taking on political functions that are both unnecessary and unrelated to its basic functions and general mandate'.

In Chapter 2, 'An Alternative to Structural Adjustment', C.P. Chandrasekhar, Associate Professor at the Centre for Economic Studies and Planning, Jawaharlal Nehru University, New Delhi, India, levels a devastating critique at the standard package of SAP, as applied to India, for failing to reduce poverty and facilitate growth of the domestic productive economy. His unequivocal conclusion and recommendation is that economic growth with social welfare requires an interventionist state – contrary to the standard SAP-mandated policy changes. He arrives at this conclusion by observing that a nation's or state's level of GDP per capita does not always correlate with development. For example, the social well-being of all the people, including the poor, is better in Sri Lanka and the Indian state of Kerala than in relatively wealthier polities. The difference is the state's intervention. Chandrasekhar's economic analysis of economic policies brings him to the same conclusion as Milder's political analysis: an active government is crucial for development.

Barend A. de Vries brings nearly 40 years' experience at the World Bank and the IMF to his analysis of 'The World Bank's Focus on Poverty' in Chapter 3. The Bank's own internal evaluation of SAPs found that the best performers were those able to export manufactures, such as Brazil, Korea, Morocco, the Philippines, Thailand, Uruguay and Yugoslavia, unlike the African reality that Teriba deals with. De Vries acknowledges that neither poverty eradication nor alleviation has been a goal of SAPs; indeed, implementation of SAPs entailed a set-back for the poor. De Vries finds that structural adjustment loans 'were redesigned to make sure they would not adversely affect the poor'. His critique stops short of challenging the basic assumptions under-girding SAPs, as do Teriba, Chandrasekhar and Milder. He asserts the need for growth as well as explicit anti-poverty programs, strongly shaped by local people's input. He finds the Bank's overall strategy for poverty reduction severely lacking. He calls for greater specialization and decentralization of World Bank staff so that they know well the countries where they work. Like Teriba, he calls for mobilizing far greater resources for poverty reduction.

In Chapter 4, 'Environmental and Social Impact Assessments', Jacklyn Cock and E.C. Webster define and recommend the use of social and environmental impact assessments (SIAs and EIAs) in all development loans. SIAs would address the problems that most development projects neglect – the social and political impacts of their interventions and inadequate levels of local public participa-tion. There is considerable verbiage afloat about the need for 'par-ticipation'. Cock and Webster operationalize the concept, providing high standards for incorporating local participation into social and environmental impact assessments of project and program loans. Cock and Webster are eminent South African sociologists from the University of the Witswatersrand and activists who have used their academic base to promote change in South Africa – in human rights, feminism, environment and anti-militarism in the case of Cock, and in labor rights and organizing in the case of Webster.

In Chapter 5, 'Human Rights, Democracy and Good Govern-ance: Stretching the World Bank's Policy Frontiers', David Gillies, Policy Coordinator at the International Centre for Human Rights and Democratic Development in Montreal, Canada, explores the need and the means to incorporate human rights criteria into operations of IFIs, especially the World Bank. His recommenda-tions differ from those of Teriba and of Tomasevski in Volume I of this series, yet all agree on the centrality of human rights to genuine development.

Finally, in Chapter 6, 'Foreign Assistance as Catalyst for Domestic Coalition Building', Daniel Milder shares the fruits of his extensive dissertation research, positing that not only is the Bank currently engaged in the domestic politics of its borrowers, but its political engagement has been overtly and deliberately anti-democratic. Instead, Milder would have all donors recognize the inherently political nature of development, and that for development to succeed, cross-class coalitions must be nurtured. Exclusionary tactics are wrong and do not work.

This volume applies to the World Bank the principles and paradigms articulated in Volume II of this series. Those principles and paradigms will be applied to the International Monetary Fund in Volume IV, *The International Monetary System: Toward Stability and Sustainability in the Twenty-first Century*, and to the World Trade Organization in Volume V, *World Trade: Toward Fair and Free Trade in the Twenty-first Century*.

Note

1   Lawrence H. Summers and Vinod Thomas, 'Recent Lessons of Development' in *World Bank Research Observer*, vol. 8, no. 2 (July 1993) p. 249.

1 The Challenge of Africa's Socioeconomic Transformation

Owodunni Teriba

INTRODUCTION

The central challenge for the international economic system is to achieve higher rates of global output while ensuring the equitable distribution of growth's benefits in the context of an improved world economic and social order. Are existing international monetary, trade and financial arrangements adequate to this task at a time of rapid globalization of the world economy; the onset of prolonged recession into a world with grossly uneven distribution of global income and development opportunities; increased deployment of regional trading blocs and economic and monetary unions; and changes in the relative power and economic status of various countries and groups of nations, including continued retrogression in certain Third World countries?

This chapter has a limited focus and scope. It will examine the efficacy of the intellectual, financial and institutional contributions of the Bretton Woods institutions (the IMF and the World Bank) to Africa's development process; the challenges that participating in Africa's socioeconomic transformation pose to the Bretton Woods institutions (BWIs), and the institutions' general mandate and objectives. As the last development frontier and the only region of the world that has yet to generate an agrarian revolution or achieve a reasonable measure of food security, Africa poses the greatest development test in our world today. Containing most of the world's poorest and least developed countries – 32 out of 47 – the problems Africa faces are enormous.

As the second largest continent in the world, harboring almost one-fifth of the world's land mass and natural resource endowments, with a fast-growing population estimated at more than 650 million, Africa does not lack development potential, provided it receives top priority in terms of international support for endogenous development and structural transformation. African economies are linked to the developed countries through trade, aid, investment and migration. The question to be explored is whether those links, together with the rules and arrangements governing them, can be more democratically managed through an accountable, participatory and transparent system of global governance. There is no better way to address this question than by taking a close look at the performance of the BWIs in promoting socioeconomic development in Africa.

The second section discusses the general mandate and objectives of the IMF and the World Bank in relation to Africa's chronic underdevelopment and economic backwardness. The third examines the record of the World Bank and the IMF in the context of their poor social and economic performance in Africa, especially during the lost decade of the 1980s. It will also elaborate on the policies and programs designed or brokered by the Bretton Woods twins, and their results. Finally, in the last section, new roles are proposed for the Fund and the Bank in the light of the daunting challenges of Africa's socioeconomic transformation and evolving global economic relations.

THE BWIs AND AFRICA'S CHRONIC UNDERDEVELOPMENT

The IMF and World Bank were created at the end of World War II to fulfill two separate but related functions considered crucial to world economic recovery and growth: full employment and the re-establishment of order and stability in a post-war economy.[1]

The IMF was to occupy the center of an international monetary mechanism, a stable exchange-rate system, and a balance-of-payments adjustment system. In order to maintain monetary stability, the IMF was to implement a system of fixed exchange rates in which only narrow fluctuations would be permitted, except in countries certified as suffering chronic and fundamental disequilibrium in their balance of payments. The focus of adjustment was (a) to center on the use of reserves (including temporary funds from the IMF itself), (b) to limit the use of exchange restrictions, and (c) to remove capital flow controls and trade restrictions.[2] Thus, the IMF was to rid the new post-war world

2

economy of the chronic monetary instability, currency disorders, competitive devaluations, excessive protectionism, exchange restrictions, barter deals and widespread 'beggar-thy-neighbor' policies that had paralyzed the inter-war world economy. It was to function as a 'lender of last resort' to member countries experiencing temporary balance-of-payments difficulties, and to ensure, through specific ground rules on the conduct of international finance, that payment imbalances would be equitably resolved and the burden of adjustment shared by both the surplus and deficit countries.

The World Bank, for its part, was set up to provide capital for reconstruction and development in the world economy. Apart from spearheading the reconstruction of war-torn Europe, the Bank was to focus on long-term project lending in the developing countries. At the time of its establishment, there was no thought of the Bank ever getting into policy conditionality as a basis for its lending programs, and indeed, this was never the case in western European countries which were the first beneficiaries of the Bank's lending programs. The main source of development finance provided by the World Bank was supposed to be rich, industrialized nations and their capital markets, from whom the Bank would borrow funds for on-lending to poor nations. The Bank was thus expected to function as the intermediary and machinery for recycling surplus resources between global capital markets and underdeveloped countries.

How relevant the original mandate and basic objectives of the BWIs are to the development problems of the African continent with its large number of national economies (now numbering 52), is a question that needs to be explored. As stated in Africa's Submission to the Special Session of the General Assembly on Africa's Economic and Social Crisis, the fundamental problem of Africa is:

> insufficient structural transformation and the economic diversification that are required to move the continent away from inherited colonial structures, typified by a vicious interaction between excruciating poverty and abysmally low levels of productivity in an environment characterized by serious deficiencies in basic infrastructure, most especially the physical, capital, research capabilities, technological know-how and human resources development, that are all indispensable to an integrated and dynamic economy.[3]

Since its establishment, the World Bank has been involved in mobilizing resources for financing development. But the quality and quantity of its lending, its resource mobilization capability, and its willingness to take risks have all, in time, been found wanting in the very poor countries of Africa. At first, the Bank financed government-guaranteed development projects and programs through sector and project loans, but later it began to shift to policy lending predicated on an intricate web of conditionalities.[4]

World Bank lending is principally accomplished through two tools: the traditional non-concessional window, and the concessional window of its affiliate, the International Development Association (IDA), established in 1960.[5] Given the lending terms of the two windows, IDA's assistance is obviously more suited to the needs of the poor African countries. But IDA's resources have generally accounted for less than 30 per cent of World Bank lending globally, and it was not until the mid-1980s that most Sub-Saharan African countries became eligible for IDA loans.

IMF policies, for their part, have reflected a practical preoccupation with three main objectives: fiscal balance, free trade and inflation control. In pursuit of these objectives, the IMF has become a highly specialized, purely economistic institution, focusing on short-term aggregative fiscal-monetary issues in spite of the broader macroeconomic objectives and purposes spelled out in Article 1 of its Articles of Agreement.[6] It is not surprising that the Fund's embrace of monetarist economics has engendered global deflation and economic slow-down. The main element of its general mandate, of crucial importance to developing countries, is the very one the Fund has gradually drifted away from: namely, the equitable management of the global monetary system through the creation of ample liquidity, and the timely provision of balance-of-payments finance to tide member countries, especially those facing the threat of import strangulation, over shortfalls in their export earnings.

The overall liquidity under control of the IMF has diminished to the point where it is now equal to no more than 2 per cent of world imports. And the developing countries now bear the main burden of trade and balance-of-payments adjustment even though they are responsible for less than 10 per cent of global liquidity.[7] Contrary to its mandate, the Fund has transformed itself into an institution that exerts monetary discipline on developing countries (but not on the more powerful industrial countries) through the enforceable obligations of its balance-of-payments adjustment loans.

The Fund has been able neither to issue its own currency nor to expand appreciably the liquidity and stock of available concessional finance as envisaged by the founders of the BWIs. The botched experiments with limited issues of special drawing rights (SDRs) were a poor and distant approximation to the original idea of an international reserve currency, and SDRs were far from being a new source of foreign exchange for the developing countries that most needed it. The SDRs, which formally came into existence on August 6, 1969, were created to

> meet the long-term global need, as and when it arises for a supplement to existing reserve assets in such a manner as will promote the attainment of its purposes and will avoid economic stagnation and deflation as well as excess demand and inflation in the world.[8]

However, the SDRs actually issued were dwarfed in importance by continuing US dollar deficits, the growing role of short-term financing in international commercial bank lending, and the increase in the price of gold. After an initial distribution in 1969 of $12 billion, the second distribution of $12 billion was not started until 1979, and accounted for less than 5 per cent of official reserves. The share of SDR holdings in global reserves has fallen steadily to below 3 per cent, even though the objective enshrined in the IMF's Articles of Agreement was to make the SDR the principal reserve asset of the international monetary system. Without access to gold reserves and lacking in credit-worthiness for commercial bank borrowing, the poor African countries lose the most from the lack of concessional short-term finance and balance-of-payments support from the Fund.

The two BWIs have diverged from other aspects of their original mandates and objectives as well. For instance, the system was supposed to avoid the instability experienced under the gold standard by ensuring exchange-rate stability without restrictions on the money supply, thereby providing adequate time for balance-of-payments adjustment.[9] However, having convinced themselves that inflation was the main problem in the world economy, and that its cause was the fiscal and monetary policies pursued in member states, the Fund and the Bank seized upon national budgets, which had to be brought into greater balance, even at the expense of growth and employment, as instruments of economic management. This largely contradicted the recommendations of many eminent economists who had hoped for a Fund that could provide international liquidity to avoid global deflation. Also, as noted in a study sponsored by the European Union, the

Fund and the Bank have misunderstood some Keynesian ideas when formulating elements of their ideological monetarism. While Keynes recommended devaluation only as an alternative to deflation, the institutions have made devaluation the centerpiece of their policy requirements in developing countries, often combining it with deflation.[10]

Not only do the Bank and the Fund now work in close consultation with each other, using the same approach and mutually agreed policies and requirements, but they are both moving towards the same conditionalities. Conditionality, as originally conceived by the BWIs, is the configuration of macro and microeconomic policies that recipient governments are required to implement, although they may have had little or no role in designing them. Some macroeconomic adjustment, as Frances Stewart has pointed out, is normally necessary for countries suffering severe imbalances, whether derived from domestic policies or external factors, so long as the deterioration in circumstances is likely to be long-lasting and/or cannot be financed. But it does not follow that conditionality of the sort pursued by the Bank and the Fund is the proper way to bring about macroeconomic adjustment; not only because of the content of the programs but because of the politics of adjustment. For programs to be effective, governments must have a genuine commitment to them, which is easily negated by the process of conditionality.[11]

Given the perpetual and difficult negotiations with the BWIs that African governments have been forced to engage in over economic policies, debt terms, and provision of aid as a result of the linkage of conditionality with financial disbursements, the relationship of African debt-distressed countries with the IMF and the World Bank has become akin to that between colonial power and colony.[12] Never since the time of colonial governors has so much foreign power and policy leverage been exercised in Africa. In the process, structural adjustment programs (SAPs) often become of questionable worth, as does government commitment to their implementation, because they are viewed as imposed from the outside.

Criticisms of the development paradigm underlying the operations of the IMF and the World Bank are manifold and span economic, political and social concerns. More specifically, they include the threat that the policies of the BWIs pose to democratic processes; their impact on poverty and equity; the ineffectiveness of devaluation as an instrument of trade policy in the

African setting; the deflationary bias of SAPs, and the exclusively economistic focus and overemphasis of the Bank and IMF on liberalization.[13]

The overall objective of the Bretton Woods system is to help member states to avoid measures destructive to national and international prosperity. However, lacking the mechanism for liquidity creation or automatic replenishment of capital, neither the Bank nor the Fund has been able to muster resources needed to sustain the vast increases in net credits or reserves required by developing countries. In an increasingly unstable and uncertain global environment, it is doubtful that the two institutions are competent to moderate the extreme cycles of unregulated financial markets and speculation in any meaningful way. Even though Africa's membership has risen from four African states out of a total membership of 25 countries in 1945 to 52 African out of a total of 178 countries in 1994 – the total number of developing countries in the Fund is now almost 130 – it is doubtful whether the Fund in particular is a suitable agency for tackling Africa's long-term structural and balance-of-payments problems.

The extensive involvement of the BWIs and their misplaced orientation towards Africa's development objectives and strategies[14] have generated great controversy on the continent about their role in reducing poverty and promoting economic growth. Moreover, their activities and effectiveness, especially those of the Fund, have been questioned in other parts of the world. As Gerald K. Helleiner has pointed out:

> The International Monetary Fund has never been popular in the developing countries. In Latin America, in particular, the IMF has for years been seen as the villain in innumerable disputes between nationalist or populist governments and the [forces of Western reaction].... There have also been substantive and analytical reasons for concern about the role of the IMF in the developing countries, especially in Latin America. No matter how vigorously the IMF now defends its pragmatism and flexibility, its missions have not always been above analytical approach. Stabilization programs have been imposed on member countries with rather more confidence in their efficacy than subsequent events or the limitations of economic science could justify. The conditionality of much IMF lending has given the IMF an opportunity to promote its staff's own point of view. In particular, the IMF has been attacked for its overemphasis on demand management, blunt

monetary-policy instruments and [shock] treatment to reduce or eliminate inflation and balance-of-payments disequilibria; its relative neglect of supply-side policies, longer-term development, and income distribution; and its traditional aversion to controls.[15]

AFRICA'S LOST DECADE AND THE RECORD OF THE BWIs

Prior to the 1970s and the onset of economic decline and social crisis in the African countries, the World Bank and the IMF were far less prominent there, either in advisory roles or in development and balance-of-payments finance. Apart from the Union of South Africa, there were only three independent African countries (Egypt, Ethiopia and Liberia) represented at the United Nations Monetary and Financial Conference at Bretton Woods in 1944 who subsequently became 'original' members, and there was little involvement of the Bank and the Fund in Africa in the 1950s and 1960s. The Bank's involvement came mainly in the form of sectoral economic research and country case studies, and only ten of the 43 developing countries that actually utilized IMF stand-by arrangements between 1963 and 1972 were from Africa.

Beginning in the 1970s, however, both the IMF and the Bank became more actively involved in Africa: the Fund by providing short-term balance-of-payments finance, the Bank by providing project loans and conducting extensive research. Between 1973 and 1980, the average African share in total IMF net credit outstanding to non-oil, developing countries rose to 23 per cent. The relationship of the BWIs with the African countries was rather uneventful and uncontroversial. The turning point for both institutions came in 1974 when the Fund introduced a new policy instrument, the Extended Fund Facility (EFF). In addition to the usual demand management criteria, many new conditionalities were imposed under the Extended Fund Facility. The addition of supply-side conditionalities intensified with the Bank's introduction of sectoral adjustment loans (SECALs) in 1979, and structural adjustment loans (SALs) in 1980.

The 1980s are generally regarded as a lost decade, and a disaster for development in Africa – a period in which the continent was engulfed in a series of unprecedented social, economic and political crises. Plagued by debilitating environmental degradation, bludgeoned by the collapse of commodity prices, and strangulated by debt and development finance crunch, the African economy faced its most severe crisis in history. Most of the countries, especially those of Sub-Saharan Africa (SSA), which constitute the weakest link in the chain of African under-development, experienced continuous deterioration in significant indicators of economic and social development.

It is instructive to consider the convergent views of the United Nations Economic Commission for Africa (UNECA) and the World Bank on Africa's deepening crisis of the 1980s. In a unique commentary in 1989, the World Bank concluded that:

> Sub-Saharan Africa has now witnessed almost a decade of fall-ing per capita incomes and accelerating ecological degradation. Per capita food production first fell, then rose, but remains lower than in 1980. Africa has lost a substantial part of its share in the world market for its exports. Some African coun-tries have surrendered some of the gains they made earlier in human resource development – notably in school enrollments. Open urban unemployment is a growing problem in many countries. In the past decade six countries – Equatorial Guinea, Ghana, Liberia, Nigeria, Sao Tome and Principle, and Zambia – have slipped from the middle-income to the low-income group (as classified in the World Bank's *World Development Report*). If overvalued exchange rates were taken into account, more would have slipped. Thirteen African countries – account-ing for a third of the region's population – are actually poorer in per capita terms today than they were at independence.[16]

UNECA, for its part, maintained that:

> During this period [the 1980s] ... the region lapsed into wide-spread and precipitous economic and social decline at the domestic level, and suffered further marginalization externally. There was a general deterioration in the main macroeconomic indicators, widespread disintegration of the productive and infrastructural facilities, a rapid worsening in the social scene, repeated droughts and accelerating environmental degradation. The unending crisis did not only affect the current well-being of the average African; it threatened the long-term development prospects of the region as a whole ... Incomes per capita fell by 1.7 per cent yearly, against rises of 3 per cent and 2.4 per cent yearly in the preceding decades, respectively, while the invest-ment ratio crumbled from 24.5 per cent of GDP at the end of

the 1970s to only 15.5 per cent of GDP by 1989, hardly a sufficient amount to compensate for depreciation and the widespread capital decumulation.[17]

The socioeconomic crisis was beginning by the early 1970s, first as a result of the oil price shock of 1973 which prompted many African countries to borrow from external sources in order to sustain import levels, and later as a result of the Great African Drought of 1983–5 which left in its wake huge losses in productive capacity, livestock and human life. These set in motion a major process of environmental degradation and social dislocation. Furthermore, the interaction of at least five external trends brought the already weak and dependent African economies to inevitable crises of debt and unsustainable balance-of-payments deficits. These external trends, which came together at a time of the continent's highest vulnerability, included:

- terms of trade deteriorations associated with rising import prices, along with the collapse in export commodity prices of most African countries;

- stagnation and decline in Official Development Assistance (ODA);

- unprecedented high interest rates that substantially increased the cost of borrowed capital, made the servicing of existing external debt impossible, and consequently led to debt accumulation;

- the shift to a period of sharply fluctuating exchange rates; and

- increased protectionism in the developed countries.

All this occurred in addition to the damaging impact of inappropriate domestic economic policy, economic mismanagement and bureaucratic inefficiency in many African countries.[18]

The depth and severity of the crisis gave birth to a number of reform programs and new policy approaches to economic management in Africa. The most significant were the African Priority Programme for Economic Recovery (APPER) 1985–90, which was adopted by the heads of state and government of the Organisation of African Unity (OAU) in 1985; the United Nations Programme of Action for Africa's Economic Recovery and Development (UN-PAAERD) in 1986;[19] and the series of national Economic Reform and Recovery Programmes (ERPs).

As the crisis worsened, African countries began putting stabilization programs in place and, from 1980 on, deployed the SAPs championed by the BWIs. Between 1980 and 1988, 33 African countries had concluded IMF Stand-By Arrangements, 12 had agreements under the Fund's Extended Fund Facility, and 15 had structural adjustment loans from the World Bank. In all, over 240 such programs were implemented between 1980 and 1990, with multiple programs deployed in many countries.

The general aim of the SAPs drawn up by the BWIs was to eliminate economic distortions and improve efficiency of resource allocation and utilization through:

- stabilization measures to compress domestic demand to the reduced level of available external resources;

- measures to bring about changes in relative prices; and

- institutional reforms.

Underlying the SAPs was the neoclassical paradigm of static comparative advantage and perfect factor mobility, and the implied economic ideology of *laissez-faire* and free functioning markets in which the role of the state is drastically curtailed. Anchored to a liberal economic philosophy, SAPs generally require economic, financial and trade liberalization measures; decontrolled, free-market pricing; large cuts in government expenditures; persistent devaluation of currency through floating exchange rates; deflationary trends through drastic budget cuts and high interest rates; credit squeeze; removal of domestic subsidies on production and consumption; and deregulation and privatization of public enterprises. Conventional wisdom held that adoption of these reform measures would bring about economic turnaround and growth in the 'adjusting' countries, and that once implementation started, the process of adjustment would be generously financed and funded by the BWIs and by the donors who gave aid conditional upon acceptance of SAPs. That at least was the promise, the thrust of the institutional thinking, and the prevalent philosophy in the IMF and the World Bank concerning Africa.

Various studies that have since been made of Bank and Fund-supported SAPs reveal that in practice they left much to be desired. The standard adjustment measures did not contribute to the attainment of Africa's central objectives of development and socioeconomic transformation. Only a handful of adjusting countries have been able to record any appreciable growth, even after nearly a decade and a half of 'adjustment' and austerity. The SAPs have not corrected the basic imbalances in any African country while maintaining output, nor have they generated the fundamental conditions needed for economic recovery and sustainable growth. Rather, because of their narrow focus on macroeconomic aggregates within a limited time perspective, and a mechanical stance that demands an unvarying approach to the design of adjustment programs, the SAPs have depressed the incomes of a wide range of groups, most especially those in the poorest sectors.

Because SAPs were not designed to take into account the spill-over impact of adjustment policies on neighboring countries and on the developing countries as a whole, they may have contributed to a decline in the terms of trade of the primary commodity exporters on the basis of the 'fallacy of composition' by pushing economies into over-specialization and further dependence on primary commodities. As Hans Singer has forcibly argued:

> The pressure on terms of trade due to debt service is further intensified by the specific 'outward orientation' now pressed upon developing countries and the method of negotiating the structural adjustment needed to obtain debt-service on a country by country basis. This amounts to making the 'small country assumption', i.e. neglecting any impact on other countries and world markets. The 'small country assumption' becomes fallacious if several debtor countries exporting the same or similar commodities are being subjected towards 'outward orientation', with its full complement of devaluation, higher incentive prices to exporters, trade liberalization, etc.[20]

The lack of regional policy dimensions and coordination in SAPs not only undermined sub-regional economic cooperation and integration on the continent, it also wrought damage on programs of regional economic communities for customs unions, and on the rationalization of production structures at a regional level.[21]

While it may not be correct to say that IMF/World Bank SAPs were principally responsible for Africa's social and economic deterioration in the 1980s, the nature, content and modalities of their policy conditionality surely frustrated the process of recovery. In a sharply deteriorating external environment, characterized by depressed export markets, declining ODA flows and uncertain prospects of increased private foreign investment, the assumption that SAPs could bring about a rapid turnaround in the external payments situation through increased export earnings or induced capital inflows was extremely dubious, if not utterly misplaced. It underestimated the significance of weak export capacities and of the particular way African countries are placed in the world economy as exporters of a limited range of primary export commodities (cocoa, coffee, tea, copper, crude oil and cobalt) and importers of virtually the whole range of processed, intermediate and capital goods.

The root cause of the African crisis and, therefore, the most important issue in the continent's development strategy, as already pointed out, lies in the weak infrastructure that prevents effective supply response across all economic sectors. This is aggravated by the uniquely difficult physical context of development and the socioeconomic circumstances that contribute to making Africa the least developed area in the world today. SAPs have been largely unsuccessful because they have ignored or underestimated these issues, and because they accorded priority to the short-term objectives of maintaining balance of payments and sound fiscal balance sheets, to the detriment of long-term development goals. Many major reforms in social sectors, education, transport, infrastructure, environment and urban development have had to be put on hold or subordinated to macroeconomic objectives and management.

The Bank's 1994 study on SAPs[22] acknowledges that of 29 adjusting countries evaluated, only six experienced a median GDP per capita growth rate of 1.8 per cent, nine had a median growth rate of 1.5 per cent, and the rest had a negative growth rate of 2.6 per cent (Table 1.1). While the Bank has attributed the disappointing performance to the failure of most countries to implement its policies seriously, some analysts have argued that it is the orientation and implementation of SAPs themselves that have aggravated the socioeconomic crisis in Africa. There is a strong belief that the social disasters accompanying SAPs are not just the results of marginal errors but the inevitable consequence of the programs' inherently faulty logic and implementation procedures.

Table 1.1: Performance of Adjusting Countries in Africa

Median change (percentage)	Period used in this study (1981–6 to 1987–91)		
	6 countries with large improvement	9 countries with small improvement	11 countries with deterioration
GDP per capita growth	1.8	1.5	–2.6
Agriculture growth	–0.2	0.3	–0.1
Industrial growth	6.1	2.8	1.7
Manufacturing	5.8	1.2	1.1
Export growth	7.9	3.0	–0.7
Gross domestic investment[a]	1.0	1.6	–3.6
Gross domestic savings	3.3	1.6	–3.3

[a] Calculations include the oil-exporting countries (Cameroon, Congo, Gabon and Nigeria).

Source: World Bank, *Adjustment in Africa: Reforms, Results and the Road Ahead* (Oxford: Oxford University Press, 1994) Table B.4.

The detrimental impact of the SAPs on human and social conditions in Africa is well documented by the ILO, UNESCO, UNICEF, UNECA and even by the BWIs themselves.[23] Studies on the broader social context of adjustment have underscored the lack of attention to the social consequences of adjustment, beyond *ex post facto* adoption of special programs, such as the social dimensions of adjustment, that were too late in coming and too little to alleviate the devastating negative impact of SAPs on the poor. Although the World Bank has recently undertaken compensatory measures like the provision of social safety nets and social action programs, now a regular feature of SAPs in the African countries, it remains unclear as yet how such remedial and special programs to alleviate poverty can succeed when the original designs of the SAPs are themselves biased against poverty alleviation.

The negative social consequences of SAPs have been so severe, especially on women, children and the poor, that UNICEF started demanding 'adjustment with a human face' toward the end of the 1980s.[24] UNECA, for its part, recognized the need for a more holistic adjustment approach and proposed an African Alternative Framework to Structural Adjustment Programmes (AAF-SAP) for Socioeconomic Recovery and Transformation.[25] In the goals of short-term adjustment, and those of medium and long-term socio-economic transformation, the AAF-SAP would be pursued in tandem through alternative policy directions and instruments. The former would lay the required solid foundation for the latter, and both would reinforce each other.

The efforts of the IMF and the World Bank to stimulate recovery and promote growth in Africa in the 1980s were flawed not only by the inappropriate approach and remedies of SAPs, but also by the mix and sequencing of prescribed policies and measures, and by the additional problems of inadequate provision of resources for successful growth and recovery. In spite of Africa's urgent need for external resources to augment its import capacity and close its balance-of-payments gaps – both crucial aspects of financing growth and development – net inflows of financial resources have declined in real terms. Although total financial flows to Africa increased in nominal terms from 1980 and 1990, the increase becomes insignificant when adjusted for inflation and exchange-rate fluctuations. In real terms, it was considerably below that required to compensate for the losses sustained from the collapse of commodity markets and the dramatic fall in export prices. In addition, reduced control of international financial institutions over exchange rates, liquidity creation and interest rates has aggravated the burden of inter-national adjustment by allowing financial and monetary systems to become more asymmetrical and volatile. It has also increased the difficulties faced by the weaker developing countries in acquiring satisfactory levels of reserves and external resources in a situation of global recession.

The actual financial assistance extended by the World Bank in response to the continent's financial difficulties and debt crisis was not particularly significant, especially in terms of net credits and transfers. As Table 1.2 shows, from 1980 to 1990, gross disbursements of the World Bank Group amounted to some $18.4 billion or a yearly average of $1.7 billion. On the other hand, debt service payments to the Bank amounted to $8 billion or an average of $727 million per annum. Excluding technical assistance, this means that net resource transfer to Africa by the Bank amounted to only $10.4 billion during that period, or an annual average of $918 million. From 1991 to 1993, net transfers averaged $850.7 million, representing .02 per cent of aggregate GDP per year and 1.1 per cent of total annual imports of the African region. More than 70 per cent of these credits were from IDA concessional lending, which rose from about $400 million in 1980 to almost $2 billion in 1990,[26] basically reflecting an increase in the number of eligible African countries. But the real amount in per capita terms was on the decrease.

Table 1.2: World Bank lending and net transfers to Africa (US$ million)

	Gross Commitments (IBRD and IDA)	*Gross Disbursements*	*Net Transfer*
1980	2,027	1,357.7	1,136.9
1981	1,631.6	1,153.1	893.8
1982	1,721.9	1,167.5	875.2
1983	1,700.6	1,167.5	826.5
1984	1,631.6	1,153.1	875.2
1985	1,597.3	1,483.9	854.3
1986	2,054.5	1,695.7	879.1
1987	2,097.7	2,364.3	1,278.3
1988	2,928.7	1,873.4	582.4
1989	3,924.7	2,256.2	876.7
1990	3,932.9	2,703.5	1,263.9
1991	3,394	2,848	895
1992	3,974	2,550	783
1993	2,817	2,620	874

Source: World Bank, *Annual Report*, various years.

Table 1.3: IMF Net Transfers to Africa

IMF Financial Year	Net Transfers to developing Africa (US $ million)	Net Transfers to Sub-Saharan Africa (US $ million)
1980	818	612
1981	1,493	1,303
1982	926	594
1983	890	773
1984	–18	–29
1980–4 average	822	651
1985	–519	–394
1986	–1,245	–932
1987	–949	–849
1988	–700	–460
1989	–362	–719
1990	–947	–454
1985–90 average	–787	–635
1991	–195	–261
1992	–491	–186
1993	–576	–189

Source: World Bank, *World Debt Tables*, 1993–4.

The situation regarding the Fund was even more paradoxical and perplexing (see Table 1.3). The IMF has been a net recipient of resources from Africa since 1984, notwithstanding the Structural Adjustment Facility (SAF) and the Enhanced Structural Adjustment Facility (ESAF) established to provide assistance on more concessional terms. Because of the restrictive conditionalities of SAPs, only 15 African countries were able to access the Fund's enhanced and compensatory facilities by 1992. Net transfers, which had averaged a positive $519 million or 0.7 per cent of total regional imports per year from 1980 to 1985, were transformed into an average deficit of $841 million per year in the 1985–90 period. With total Fund purchases amounting to $6.6 billion from 1985 to 1990 in contrast to total Fund repurchases and charges of

$11.4 billion, there was a reverse flow of resources from Africa to the IMF of $4.8 billion during the period – a complete negation of the *raison d'être* of the Bretton Woods system. The above statistics indicate that efforts of the BWIs to support Africa's development in the 1980s were too little and too late to effectively redress inadequate financial flows. Not only was the IMF slow in establishing SAF and ESAF resources, it was also slow disbursing them.

It was not until 1988 that the World Bank organized the Special Program of Assistance (SPA) as part of its resource mobilization and aid coordination for poor, debt-distressed countries in SSA. But actual disbursements of adjustment assistance and debt relief under SPA I averaged less than $2 billion per year from 1988 to 1991. Furthermore, most of this aid was probably not over and above existing programs. In addition, the Bank mobilized $2 billion non-project aid and joint financing of SAPs from mid-1985 to 1988. Besides its very slow disbursements of low-concessionality aid, the World Bank has been criticized for consistently understating and underestimating the magnitude of Africa's medium-term finance requirements. This has led to a strong suspicion that the principal preoccupation of the Bank is to generate aid targets considered politically acceptable by the major industrial countries that are Africa's partners-in-development.[27]

The conclusion by Oxfam that international financial institutions, the IMF in particular, have used 'the wrong resources and the wrong approach' in Africa should not come as a surprise. It is based on a report which found that in spite of IMF and World Bank programs, Africa's share in world trade is declining from 4 per cent in 1960 to 1 per cent in the 1990s, with a foreign direct investment inflow of less than 1 per cent of the world total. The number of African poor will increase to 300 million by the year 2000. Oxfam asserts that the Fund has failed and calls for its reform or extrication from Africa.[28]

MANAGING AFRICA'S SOCIOECONOMIC TRANSFORMATION: NEW ROLES FOR THE BWIs

The emerging consensus at the beginning of the 1990s was that African development would be a long-term fundamental process of transformation.[29] African countries have long shown their collective commitment to change by adopting seminal documents and policy blueprints such as the following:

- Lagos Plan of Action and the Final Act of Lagos (1980);

18

- African Priority Programme for Economic Recovery (APPER) for 1985–90;

- United Nations Programme of Action for Africa's Economic Recovery and Development (UN-PAAERD) (1986);

- African Alternative Framework to Structural Adjustment Programmes (AAF–SAP) (1989);

- African Charter on Popular Participation (1990); and

- Abuja Treaty for the establishment of the African Economic Community (1991).

The primary aim of all of these documents is to address fundamental weaknesses in the African economies and to clear the way for rapid, self-sustaining growth and development. However, the African governments have failed to implement their own plans and programs effectively. This will have to change if persistent economic and social deterioration is to be arrested, and the foundation for an internally generated process of development is to be laid. Five specific obstacles that must be overcome in order to transform the African economy are:

- dualism and internal socioeconomic disarticulation at almost all levels of economic activity, creating the paradox of commodities produced mainly for export, side by side with heavy importation of goods for local consumption;

- weak, undiversified export base and capabilities, confined to a narrow band of primary agricultural and mineral commodities;

- extreme dependence on external inputs and markets;

- fragmented product markets, and

- weak endogenous human, physical, institutional and technological capacities and deficient infrastructure.

The objectives and goals for Africa's development and socioeconomic transformation were first articulated in the Lagos Plan of Action and the Final Act of Lagos. They included self-reliant and self-sustaining growth, regional food security and self-sufficiency, and satisfaction of the people's basic needs for health care, safe drinking water, education, housing, clothing and transport. These goals were reaffirmed in the regional reform efforts and programs of the 1980s, and more recently in the context of shared responsibility in the New Agenda for Africa's Development in the 1990s. In these plans, the basic approach to Africa's long-term development and socioeconomic transformation centers on regional and subregional self-reliance, internalization of the engine of growth, and restructuring of the African production base. So conceived, it is a pragmatic approach that necessarily focuses on human beings as the means and the target of development. Viewed against this background, the role of the World Bank and IMF on the continent in the 1990s and beyond can be examined in respect to its involvement in three inextricably linked areas: external resource mobilization, debt relief, and economic management and reform within Africa.

Resource Flows

If African countries are to pull themselves up to self-sustaining development by their own bootstraps, it is imperative that the current low levels of domestic savings and investment rates be increased and efficiency in the utilization of resources raised. After all, the African people and their institutions must bear primary responsibility for their own economic recovery and development. But the contemporary reality is that domestic savings have been extremely low and are likely to remain so in the light of the current stagnation and decline in output growth rates; the narrow tax base with its limited revenue generation; and the relatively underdeveloped nature of domestic financial structures and intermediation processes. Added to these problems are a multitude of external factors beyond Africa's control. As the socioeconomic crisis has deepened, the task of mobilizing resources for development has become ever more difficult and elusive. Most African countries remain in the grip of slow economic growth and deteriorating terms of trade.

Financing of development has been made even more difficult by stagnation of external financial flows. Net real flows to Africa have been on the decline since 1990, falling by 15.9 per cent in 1991, and again by 5.7 per cent in 1992. Africa now accounts for a mere 3 per cent of the additional net flows to developing countries as a whole. Although it has come to depend on ODA for two-thirds of its external resource flows, bilateral ODA flows have been falling in recent years, a situation that has left Africa

even more dependent on multilateral ODA flows. The requirements for external development finance in Africa are enormous,
based on the following estimates from the World Bank, UNECA
and the African Development Bank (AfDB), respectively:[30]

- $28 to $29 billion (in 1988 dollars) of gross external financing
  are required annually throughout the 1990s by the 36 countries
  in SSA to enable them to raise the growth rate of output to 5
  per cent by the year 2000. This includes the countries'
  scheduled debt service payments amounting to about $16
  billion annually;[31]

- an annual average of $61.4 billion (in 1990 dollars) of external
  resources, net of debt service payments, is required by African
  countries to attain a regional average growth rate of 5 per cent
  over the period 1992-2001;[32]

- $460 billion of net external transfers (in 1990 dollars) are
  required by African countries to achieve the growth target of 6
  per cent in GDP over the period 1993–2005, as estimated by
  the United Nations New Agenda for the Development of Africa
  (UNNADAF). Another $490 billion would be required to meet
  external debt service obligations over the 13-year period.[33]

The differences among the three sources are primarily due to
varying assumptions regarding the progress of economic recovery,
the feasible pace of macro- and microeconomic reform, and the
evolution of external trade elasticities. What is common to them
is the clear sense that financial inflows from external official
transfers must be significantly increased and sustained at the
higher level for the rest of the decade and beyond. The bottom
line is that they all call for an increase in resource flows to Africa
on the scale of a Marshall Aid program.

Meeting that challenge calls for a substantial proportional
increase in the share of IDA flows in the World Bank's overall
lending to Africa. It necessitates a review of IDA eligibility
criteria so that all countries in SSA will be accommodated by
IDA rather than non-concessional resources. If the Bank is to
provide Africa with the credits needed for socioeconomic transformation, it will be necessary to devote a lion's share of IDA
resources to its long-term development for the next decade or
two, just as was done for Asia in the first 25 years of IDA's
existence. In this respect, several proposals have been made for

the creation of a third type of loan/assistance facility, somewhere between the non-concessional window and IDA concessional window, for other developing countries that have better internal structures in place, in order to free up IDA resources for the African countries.

The World Bank will also need to intensify and diversify its catalytic role in the mobilization and coordination of external financial assistance. So far the Bank has attempted to do this through such fora as the Consultative Groups and the Special Program of Assistance (SPA). This represents a major innovation for the Bank, and is certainly an advance in collaborative efforts towards African development. African countries pursuing economic reforms have obtained adjustment assistance and debt relief from multilateral and bilateral donors through these fora, but the total amount has fallen far short of its massive external development finance needs.

The problem of lagging disbursements has continued to plague the SPA even though it is primarily intended to act as a concessional, quick distribution system of development finance. As of the end of December 1992, the average ratio of actual disbursements to allocations was less than 50 per cent. Some delays were due to the difficulties of obtaining the required stamp of approval from the World Bank itself. Further, not all the debt relief promised by the SPA actually materialized: for example, the former Soviet Union and other non-members of the Paris Club did not provide debt relief under this arrangement. By the end of 1992 only 26 countries in SSA were receiving funds from the SPA, and less than half of the total amount of resources pledged for co-financing under the SPA could be considered additional to existing aid programs.

The overall undisbursed level of committed external resources for Africa rose from $42.9 billion in 1985 to an average of $57.4 billion from 1990 to 1992, or about 20 per cent of the aggregate debt stock. Much of that – an average of $44.2 billion from 1990 to 1993 – is from official creditors, although undisbursed resources from private creditors are quite substantial for the North Africa subregion. The level of undisbursed debt increased from $9.6 billion in 1985 to an average of $16 billion from 1990 to 1993. This amount, as pointed out by the Bank's vice-president for the Africa region, is equivalent to one IDA replenishment. Tranches of adjustment disbursements are routinely held up by the Bank and the Fund whenever they consider that macroeconomic performance targets and conditionalities are not met by 'adjusting' countries.

There is need for the World Bank to review its overall coordinating role in the context of the SPA and similar schemes to achieve a more comprehensive and rationalized coverage of the development finance needs of the African countries. It must be based on revamped eligibility criteria for balance-of-payments gaps and debt relief needs. For the SPA and other forms of lending it is imperative to delink development resource flows and debt relief from the present conditionalities and negotiating processes of SAPs. As discussed above, SAP conditionalities have serious detrimental effects on employment, per capita incomes, and poverty alleviation. Moreover, they have made it almost impossible for the African countries to couple adjustment with sustained growth. Since a large part of SPA disbursements is currently earmarked for debt relief, greater efforts towards mobilizing fresh money and new ODA flows for investment is imperative.

However, with every aid donor demanding conditionalities over and above the performance criteria of the BWIs, there is the real danger of the continent's limited management and advisory capacity being overwhelmed. This expansion of conditionalities now encompasses political as well as human rights criteria and is seen by many in Africa as nothing more than a ploy to curtail resource flows. What is most urgently needed is not more conditionality, but a thorough revamping of conditionality in the direction of less deflationary policies that will take full cognizance of the exogenous difficulties facing Africa, and will, above all, focus on a reorientation of domestic resource use towards growth-oriented adjustment.

For countries emerging from the ravages of civil conflicts and the accompanying human tragedy – there may have been ten to fifteen countries in Africa in this category by the end of 1995 – and those hard hit by natural and environmental disasters, it is clear that neither traditional SAPs nor standard Economic Reform and Recovery Programmes (ERPs) are sufficient. For such countries, where much of the already limited stock of human, physical and financial resources has been dissipated in unproductive ways, assistance and support from the international community is required for rehabilitation and resumption of socioeconomic development. Eligibility criteria for financial assistance must be clearly linked to institutional capacity building and overall resource requirements for reconstruction of plants and infrastructure.

The BWIs must take the lead in improving the quality and effectiveness of development aid for Africa, as well as increasing the magnitude of resource flows. More than a quarter of ODA resource flows to Africa continue to be absorbed by expensive foreign technical assistance, even though its effectiveness has been seriously questioned in the light of the prevailing brain drain and gross under-utilization of qualified and experienced indigenous personnel. Much of the technical assistance remains supply-driven and unrelated to the capacity of recipient countries to absorb it. Often it is tied to specific bilateral donors and is not as fungible as financial aid: its salutary impact on management or professional capacity in recipient countries is minimal at best.

It is a good omen that in their current 'introspection' the World Bank and the Fund are reconsidering some of their own operational principles and past practices, even though the primary focus of attention has been on the institutions' internal effectiveness rather than the continued relevance of their basic objectives and roles. Some progress has been shown in increased questioning of concepts such as 'technical assistance' and 'imposed management of projects and programs' as viable bases for furthering African development. In a speech at the African-American Institute in May 1993, the World Bank vice-president for Africa highlighted the new resolve of the World Bank to:

- discontinue its past practice of directly writing reform plans for the African countries instead of acknowledging indigenous capacity and expertise;

- seek collaborative arrangements with local experts in the economic and sector work of the Bank; and

- use government ministries rather than World Bank project management units on World Bank financed projects.[34]

African member states and many critics of the BWIs would welcome the 'ownership' of reform and development programs resulting from such an ongoing process. The BWIs would then be in a better position to persuade major donors to give support. In this way, the professional capacity of African governments, NGOs and the private sector would be strengthened, and bilateral/multilateral technical assistance would become more focused and fungible *vis-à-vis* financial aid.[35]

Africa has not been able to obtain any significant amount of capital flow from foreign private investment. For instance, total foreign direct investment (FDI) in the region is estimated at less than $.5 billion annually since 1990, and it is sometimes even negative as a result of disinvestment. Indications are that FDI fell precipitously in all sectors in the 1980s, with the possible exception of a few oil and mineral-exporting countries. The general perception of Africa as a continent characterized by political instability and a hostile investment and business environment, coupled with its increasingly unsustainable debt burden and its lack of infrastructure, has reduced its attractiveness for foreign capital inflows. To the extent that the macroeconomic uncertainties induced by SAPs are part of the disenabling environment for foreign private investment, both the World Bank and the Fund are in a position to enhance investor confidence and attract global resources by overhauling the present conditionalities. This would be in addition to the current positive influence that the World Bank exerts through the activities of the International Finance Corporation (IFC), which focuses exclusively on private sector development, and the Multilateral Investment Guarantee Agency (MIGA), which promotes foreign investment by providing political risk insurance to investors and advisory services to governments.

Africa's Debt Problems and Debt Relief

The international economy has been altered by the accelerating globalization of economic transactions and by phenomenal technological innovations. Consequently, there has been a rapid restructuring of the international division of labor favoring economies that are adaptable to economic and technological innovations, but discriminating against those that produce primary commodities and raw materials. As a consequence of the diminishing export earnings and mounting indebtedness, full debt-service obligations now exceed 50 per cent of export revenues for a number of African countries.[36] The debt overhang thus retains a stranglehold on the region's recovery efforts as many countries, unable to service their debt, find it increasingly difficult to attract fresh capital inflows because they are considered high risk. It has also resulted in major reductions in spending on education, health, sanitation, employment creation, etc. The debt burden continues to weigh heavily on export revenues which might otherwise be channeled into financing the imports required for development. By the end of 1993, the total stock of Africa's external debt was $285.4 billion and amounted to 95.9 per cent of regional GDP. The situation in SSA is even more precarious, with external debt amounting to over 110 per cent of GNP and 340 per cent of exports.

The debt owed to multilateral institutions (principally the BWIs) has been a major source of debt-servicing difficulties. It has also proved the most difficult to manage as it has not been eligible for rescheduling or reduction through cancellation or swapping arrangements. Indeed, the amount of multilateral debt in Africa's aggregate external debt has increased steadily to 21 per cent in 1993.

The fact that the sources of Africa's external debt and ODA flows are concentrated among a handful of industrialized countries – France, Germany, the United States, Japan, Great Britain and Italy – has great significance for the prospects of resolving the resource flow problems of the continent. Nearly 60 per cent of the region's external debt is owed to the key members of the OECD and the influential Group of Seven (G–7) industrialized nations which, as a UNDP report puts it, 'represents the closest approximation to governance of the global economy'.[37] These countries dominate the international economic system and the international institutions of trade, money and finance. They form the core of the Paris Club which manages world bilateral debt, and are the principal markets for Africa's exports and its source of imports. Thus, they have it in their power, provided there is the political will, to assist Africa's socioeconomic transformation by implementing measures to relieve African countries of their crushing debt burden and external resource crunch. Such assistance could take the form of sustained bilateral flows, guarantees and inducements that would enable African countries to gain access to new money. In addition, some assistance could take the form of rescheduling and reducing commercial debt-service obligations of countries like Nigeria, Côte d'Ivoire and Morocco to commercial banks and other private creditors in G–7 countries.

Since debt servicing draws on scarce financial resources that could otherwise be used for investment in development, the debt overhang of the African countries has severely constrained the region's recovery. There are two essential aspects to any comprehensive strategy for resolving the African debt problem. One takes the form of immediate massive reductions in debt stock and debt-servicing obligations: the other, a more medium and long-term strategy, is the diversification and transformation of African economies so as to squarely address the commodity problem of which the debt crisis is primarily a by-product. The countries themselves must improve their choice and use of debt financing for development projects, moving external finance away from consumption and expenditures on projects with low socio-economic return and little relation to capacity building.

In the past, debt strategy centered largely on the need to protect the international banking system and the creditor countries, hence the emphasis on rescheduling of debt and debt-service obligations, with only some token reduction of ODA debt. It is now apparent that debt reschedulings are a mere palliative that only postpone the debt burden into an uncertain future. Africa's external debt crisis is not just a manageable and temporary *liquidity* problem; it is a *solvency* problem. Hence, the need is for a substantial reduction in external debt to a point that will restore confidence in future prospects and bring private foreign investment back. Most debt-relief initiatives have been designed principally to benefit low-income African countries, and do not adequately address the acute debt problems of middle-income countries. For example, under the Enhanced Toronto Terms, which are clearly a step in the right direction, just twelve African countries have benefited so far, with total consolidated amounts estimated at about only $2–5 billion. In short, while the concessionality of debt relief has increased somewhat, it has not increased sufficiently to solve the acute problem of Africa's debt overhang.

A large number of proposals have been made to relieve the debt burden by swapping existing external liabilities for local assets – physical or financial. Examples include swapping debt for equity, debt for environmental upgrading, or debt for development projects in education and public health. Current debt reduction strategies under the Paris and London Clubs include the possibility of a wide range of debt and debt-service swaps. Unfortunately, the use of these arrangements has been neither very widespread nor highly successful, essentially because of doubts about their potential applicability to African realities. A case in point is the debt-for-equity swap which, in principle, could be extremely helpful, but which has been used only sparingly in a limited number of countries (such as Nigeria), due to a perceived lack of investment opportunities and developed markets.

Direct efforts by the World Bank and IMF to deal with Africa's debt problems have had limited effect, confined as they are to the promotion of debt relief through:

- Brady-type operations, aimed at commercial debt reduction for major developing countries;

- the World Bank's Debt Reduction Program[38] for the commercial bank debt of IDA-only countries, and

- IMF's Rights Accumulation Program.[39]

27

In view of the large number of African countries that need to secure access to these programs, there is an immediate need to broaden their scope and to provide them with more resources. For example, only three African countries – Niger, Mozambique and Uganda – have thus far derived any relief from the World Bank's Debt Reduction Program.

As the most important multilateral financial institutions, the World Bank and the IMF have a large role to play both in addressing Africa's debt problem – multilateral, bilateral and commercial – and in external resource mobilization. The starting point in becoming effective in Africa's debt management is for the Bretton Woods twins to adopt a long-term perspective, in which solutions will be perceived in the context of securing fresh and adequate resources for socioeconomic development and transformation. Therefore, the Bank and Fund should begin to reschedule, reduce and convert some of the overdue interest and capital payments on their own loans as an essential first step in lobbying and convincing others to do likewise. It is paradoxical that other creditors, whose policies are dependent on the approval provided by the lending programs of the BWIs, should be undertaking their own debt revision when the Bank and the Fund do not themselves do so on any meaningful scale.

Although the BWIs have recently begun to voice the need for debt forgiveness, they continue to demonstrate a primary concern for debt repayment even when it proves a great detriment to economic and social conditions in Africa. By continually maintaining a case-by-case approach to the debt problem instead of creating fresh policies, they have undermined their own effectiveness. There is little doubt that if the Fund and the Bank were to resolve the contradictions in their own broader policies, and if they were to have enough conviction to function as debt management rather than debt collection agencies, they would be able to work effectively with Africa's creditors. This would result in consolidating and renegotiating national debts at much lower interest rates.

In the light of the African Common Position on Debt formulated in 1987 along with more recent developments, the following proposals can be made regarding the solution of Africa's persistent debt problems:

• Commitment by all creditors to substantially reduce debt stock, arrears on debt servicing, and interest rates. In this mode, the Pronk Proposal suggests forgiveness of bilateral official debt owed by less developed countries (LDCs) that are severely debt-distressed, and by other low-income countries pursuing strong economic reform programs. The Naples Terms should be enhanced to accommodate reduction of the full stock of official bilateral debt in SSA.

• Agreement by the G–7 countries to remove restrictions on resource flows that arise out of linking debt relief to the implementation of IMF/World Bank SAPs. This should be followed by G–7 acceptance of non-BWI adjustment programs and policy reforms that are voluntarily implemented in African countries as adequate preconditions for new debt relief programs.

• Recognition of the need to adopt comprehensive measures to resolve Africa's debt crisis involving the linkage between external debt relief, enhancement of export sector performance – especially in primary commodities – and increased resource flows. These measures should be tied to requirements for a faster rate of growth and development to ensure a human-centered process.

• Agreement between creditors and African countries to limit debt service to no more than 10 to 15 per cent of export earnings in any one year where 100 per cent debt reduction has yet to be accomplished, and the capping of interest rates applicable to the residue of unrescheduled debt stock.

• The IMF and the World Bank should make larger resources available under the ESAF and the Debt Reduction Program to countries with overdue debt service obligations to them, so that repurchase of debt can be undertaken with the advantage of the relief inherent in those facilities: larger grant elements, longer grace periods and greater concessionality.

• Creation of new SDRs by the IMF, some of which would be specifically earmarked for eligible African countries to enable them to repay debt arrears owed to the IMF, the World Bank, the AfDB and other multilateral banks.

• Conversion by the IFC of debt owed to the World Bank by low-income African countries into equity, and making it fungible either through privatization or new investment loans.

• Sale of gold by the IMF to be used to clear arrears of payment to it by African countries.

Economic Reforms in Africa: Challenges for the BWIs

Both the World Bank and the IMF, as we have seen from the preceding analysis, have wielded tremendous influence on the direction and pace of economic management in Africa since the late 1970s. This is nowhere more evident than in the SAPs that the institutions have prescribed and continue to implement. The Bretton Woods twins have not only influenced the orientation and thrust of Africa's economies, they have also generally determined the overall attitude of the international community toward Africa. For the past 15 years, donor countries have made the BWIs the designers of economic reform policies, and the overseers of a country's behavior in respect to them. Virtually all external support has been linked to the award by the BWIs of a 'certificate of good behavior' or 'stamp of approval', dependent on strict adherence to the SAP conditionalities.

It needs to be pointed out, however, that the concept of policy conditionality, as invented by the BWIs, has expanded to the potential detriment of the reputation of the institutions themselves. A good illustration is the growing donor attitude of conditioning aid on democratic reforms, and equating democracy with good governance. Good governance, viewed as encompassing several broad categories such as accountability, transparency of information and policy making, administrative and bureaucratic consistency, and the rule of law, is admittedly an end in itself. To the extent that it fosters efficient economic management, it is also a means to an end. Nevertheless, it is possible for a system of democratic governance not to meet some of the criteria of good governance while some of the elements of good governance may thrive without a popularly elected government. So, for donors and the BWIs to insist, as they now do, that democratic governance is the key to good governance and efficient economic management, even when the available evidence is patchy at best – given democracies with hopelessly poor records of economic management – the overall effect is to undermine the very concept of 'good governance'. Good governance is a dynamic process which does not easily lend itself to quantifiable assessment. Thus, in order to prevent the BWIs and donors from coming up with differing criteria of good governance and/or a selectivity of application, there is need for universally agreed parameters, say within a multilateral framework such as the United Nations, against which progress could be measured. Only in this way can the World Bank avoid the risk it now runs, albeit unwittingly, of incrementally taking on political functions that are both unnecessary and unrelated to its basic functions and general mandate.

Flexibility and adaptability require that, after more than a decade of implementing certain policies in Africa with little or no positive results, the BWIs now seriously review those policies. They should consider alternative strategies set forth in the large body of literature on the subject, also reviewing the major African documents and decisions of the UN General Assembly and its Economic and Social Council over the last 15 years. For Africa to resume the path towards sustainable development, the BWIs must implement far-reaching economic reforms that transcend the narrow confines of short-term macroeconomic and financial balance goals; embrace and integrate growth restoration and poverty alleviation as objective concerns; and imply a departure from relying solely on compensatory social safety nets, social action programs and funds to mitigate the adverse consequences and social costs of adjustment on the poor. Such recovery plans must take into account, among other things, the African socioeconomic milieu and the centrality of human and social dimensions in development policies. Above all, these programs must involve the massive domestic investment in human resources and infrastructure that will promote long-term economic growth. They must also be supported by well-coordinated, comprehensive actions at the international level aimed at resolving Africa's interlocked problems of external debt overhang, declining commodity prices and inadequate resource flows.

The BWIs must embrace the African position that what is needed is 'adjustment with transformation'. They need to concentrate on a pragmatic, non-ideological development paradigm anchored on a human-centered strategy in which people's welfare is seen as the main focus of the development process. Such an approach to development will generate faster sustainable increases in the rate of economic growth, reduce poverty and build capacity in its widest context – infrastructural, human, institutional and technological. It will have to address not only fiscal imbalances, but inefficiencies in capacity building and utilization. These measures are crucial to the enhancement of Africa's ability to respond flexibly to external and internal shocks, and to participate more meaningfully in the global economy.

In order to be more effective in meeting the challenge of Africa's socioeconomic transformation, the BWIs should be restructured to fulfil those original objectives envisaged by John Maynard Keynes and the British delegation at the Bretton Woods conference. So restructured, a basic element of the function of these institutions would be to assist the developing countries in overcoming the severity of their overall resource constraints, and not to hold them hostage to some outmoded development paradigm. In short, the Fund and the Bank will need to resume their non-political roles within the framework of global economic management. The Fund can do this by providing African countries with timely bridging finance and by expanding liquidity in the face of unexpected shocks and external payments difficulties. The Bank can do this by focusing on a development-oriented adjustment process and on renewed efforts to mobilize increased external resources that would complement increased domestic resource mobilization and effective utilization efforts that the African governments and people must undertake to realize the objectives, priorities and targets of such a process.

A clearer definition of mandates is called for between the BWIs and the United Nations agencies in the economic and social field, so that the responsibility for highly concessional assistance (grant and technical assistance) to the developing countries will reside principally in the UN agencies which have traditionally enjoyed a comparative advantage in this area. This would end, or at least reduce, the current encroachment of the BWIs into many areas of competence of the United Nations. What is true of the BWIs and the UN in terms of clearer division of labor is true, equally if not with greater force, of the Bretton Woods system itself; what with the Fund now duplicating the role of the Bank in the provision of IDA-type support to the African countries through funds like Structural Adjustment Facilities (SAFs) and Enhanced Structural Adjustment Facilities (ESAFs). The BWIs need additionally to work in closer liaison and complementarity with Africa's multilateral institutions, especially the AfDB, by channelling resources through the latter for on-lending in consonance with the region's objectives of development and socioeconomic transformation.

In parallel, UN technical and resource capacities need to be enhanced to assist broad-based sustainable development. Such a strengthening of the UN system would lead to the partnership with the BWIs so urgently needed for multilateral cooperation and development. The UN could also articulate operational principles for a more meaningful and acceptable BWI advisory role on economic management in Africa. Currently the United Nations, faced with major financial and staffing difficulties, is neither able to galvanize international support for the implementation of progressive development strategies that have evolved under its aegis, nor to interact meaningfully with the BWIs that have clout and resources, but are themselves unable to generate mutually agreed comprehensive frameworks for the development of the poor countries of the world. Therefore, harmonization of all parts of the global institutional system is urgently called for.

To address the above issues, the North-South Roundtable has made significant recommendations aimed at strengthening the UN system and reforming the Bretton Woods system. Its recommendations include the establishment of a World Social Charter, a Development Security Council, a New Framework for Development Cooperation and the issuance of SDRs at very low interest rates. If given the necessary support by the developed countries, such recommendations could bring great force to the new roles of the IMF and the World Bank and could generate a world economic order capable of transforming the socioeconomic milieu of the poor regions of the world.

Notes

1. The mandate of the two institutions have caused much controversy right from their creation in 1944. The most notable criticisms then, which are even more relevant today, came from the eminent British economist John Maynard Keynes. Keynes had envisaged much more effective international institutions in an increasingly interdependent world of full employment and economic growth, in which economic policy coordination would prevail in the areas of trade and employment. Therefore, he had proposed: (a) a Fund equal to 50 per cent of the value of world imports, (b) an IMF which would serve as a World Central Bank, with its own reserve currency (the bancor), (c) an International Trade Organization (ITO) for counter-cyclical coordination of trade and employment policies and (d) stable exchange rates.
2. It was indeed not until 1969 that conditionality was formally incorporated into the Articles of Agreement of the Fund, relating to a small number of demand management variables and the exchange rate.
3. UNECA/OAU, Document E/ECA/ECM/1/Rev.1 of March 31, 1986, p. 4.

4. Underlying the World Bank's advocacy of structural adjustment policies (SAPs) as the panacea for Africa's economic ills was a controversial report by the World Bank, *Accelerated Development in Sub-Saharan Africa: An Agenda for Action* (Washington, DC: World Bank, 1981).

5. There is also the International Finance Corporation (IFC), which is the third affiliate of the World Bank. It was established in 1956 as a source of direct financing for private-sector projects and activities in developing countries.

6. For an historical analysis of the IMF since its foundation, see Margaret Garritsen de Vries, *Balance of Payments Adjustment, 1945–1986: The IMF Experience* (Washington, DC: International Monetary Fund, 1987).

7. See North South Roundtable, *The United Nations and the Bretton Woods Institutions: New Challenges for the 21st Century* (New York: Society for International Development, 1993).

8. Joseph Gold, 'Special Drawing Rights: The Role of Language', *IMF Pamphlet*, No. 15 (Washington, DC: International Monetary Fund, 1971) p. 11.

9. The assumption was that the major trading countries would maintain stable costs in their tradeable goods sectors through productivity-restricted wage increases.

10. See Commission of the European Communities, *Towards a New Bretton Woods: Alternatives for the Global Economy*, Report for the FAST Programme (Brussels: Commission of the European Community, 1993).

11. Frances Stewart, 'Should Conditionality Change?' in Kjell J. Havenevik (ed.), *The IMF and the World Bank in Africa* (Uppsala: Scandinavian Institute of Africa Studies, 1987) pp. 29–45. Also see Norman Girvan, 'Empowerment for Development: From Conditionality to Partnership' in Jo Marie Griesgraber and Bernhard G. Gunter (eds), *Rethinking Bretton Woods*, Vol. I, *Promoting Development: Effective Global Institutions for the Twenty-first Century*, Chapter 2 (London: Pluto Press with the Center of Concern, 1995).

12. David Finch, *IMF Surveillance and the Group of 24: International Monetary and Financial Issues for the 1990s*, Research Papers for the Group of 24, Vol. 2 (New York: UNCTAD, 1993).

13. For an assessment of the experience with the policies of the Bretton Woods institutions, see: Dag Hammarskjold Foundation, 'The International Monetary System and the New International Order' in *Development Dialogue*, no. 2 (Uppsala: Dag Hammarskjold Foundation, 1980); Lance Taylor, *Varieties of Stabilization Experience: Towards Sensible Macroeconomics in the Third World* (Oxford: Clarendon Press, 1988); United Nations Economic Commission for Africa (UNECA), *African Alternative Framework to Structural Adjustment Programmes for Socio-Economic Recovery and Transformation* (Addis Ababa: UNECA, 1989), and Giovanni A. Cornia, Richard Jolly, and

Frances Stewart (eds), *Adjustment with a Human Face – Protecting the Vulnerable and Promoting Growth*, Volumes I and II, A UNICEF Study (Oxford: Clarendon Press, 1987).

14. According to World Bank Vice-President for the Africa Region, Mr Edward V. K. Jaycox, the Bank enjoys the dominant intellectual role on African economic issues, and is involved in 90 per cent of the analytical research on Africa.

15. Gerald K. Helleiner, 'The IMF and Africa in the 1980s', Essays in International Finance, no. 152 (July 1983) Princeton University, Department of Economics monograph series.

16. World Bank *Sub-Saharan Africa; From Crisis to Sustainable Growth: A Long Term Perspective Study* (Washington, DC: World Bank, 1989) pp. 17–18.

17. United Nations Economic Commission for Africa (UNECA) *Economic Report on Africa 1990* (Addis Ababa: UNECA, 1991) p. 3.

18. For the economic limitations imposed by external factors on the scope of independent macroeconomic policy in African countries, see Charles Soludo, *Growth Performance in Africa: Further Evidence on the External Versus Domestic Policy Debate*, Development Research Papers Services, no. 6 (Addis Ababa: UNECA, November 1993).

19. In its assessment of the United Nations Programme of Action for African Economic Recovery and Development in 1986–90, the 46th Session of the General Assembly concluded that the program had not achieved its objectives. This was why the successor program – the United Nations New Agenda for the Development of Africa in the 1990s (UN-NADAF) – was adopted, reconfirming African economic recovery as one of the five priorities of the United Nations in 1990s.

20. Hans W. Singer, 'Terms of Trade: New Wine and New Bottles' in *Development Policy Review*, vol. 9, no. 4 (1991) pp. 346–7.

21. See African Development Bank (AfDB), *African Development Report 1993*, Part III: Economic Integration and Structural Adjustment in Africa (Abidjan: African Development Bank, 1993).

22. World Bank, *Adjustment in Africa: Reforms, Results and the Road Ahead* (Oxford: Oxford University Press, 1994).

23. The most well-known publication contending that the costs of adjustment are unfairly borne by the poorest groups is Cornia, Jolly and Stewart (eds), *Adjustment With a Human Face – Protecting the Vulnerable and Promoting Growth*. The evidence in the World Bank's *Adjustment Lending Policies for Sustainable Growth*, Policy and Research Series No. 14 (Washington, DC: World Bank, 1990), admits that the twelve poorest intensely adjusting countries experienced declining levels of nutrition and declining school enrollments over time. In the World Bank's *Adjustment in Africa* (Washington, DC: World Bank, 1994), editors Ishrat Husain and Rashid Faruqee state that: 'While the early generation of these programs might not have explicitly addressed the consequences of reforms on the social sectors, the

subsequent awareness and sensitization of these issues have changed the scene.' (p. 9).

24. See Cornia, Jolly, Stewart (eds), *Adjustment with a Human Face – Protecting the Vulnerable and Promoting Growth.*
25. UNECA, Document No. E/ECA/CM.15/6/Rev.3, 1989.
26. These resources included the IDA reflows which the Bank started providing from 1988 under the 'fifth dimension' programme to help IDA-eligible countries to refinance their IBRD repayments.
27. See Gerald K. Helleiner, 'Africa's Adjustment and External Debt Problem: Issues and Options – An Unofficial View' in I.G. Patel (ed.), *Policies for African Development: From the 1980s to the 1990s* (Washington, DC: International Monetary Fund, 1992) p. 98.
28. Oxfam, *Africa, Make or Break: Action for Recovery* (London: Oxfam, 1993).
29. See United Nations Development Programme (UNDP), *Human Development Report 1992* (Oxford: Oxford University Press, 1992); United Nations Economic Commission for Africa (UNECA), *African Alternative Framework to Structural Adjustment Programmes*; World Bank, *Sub-Saharan Africa; From Crisis to Sustainable Growth*; World Bank, *World Development Report 1990* (Oxford: Oxford University Press, 1990); and the Proceedings of the Africa Conference, Maastricht, July 2–4, 1990.
30. See Jorge Culagovski, Victor Gabor, Maria Cristina Germany, and Charles P. Humphreys, *African Financing Needs in the 1990s,* Policy, Research, and External Affairs Working Papers, Technical Department, Africa Regional Office (Washington, DC: World Bank, 1991); UNECA, *Strategies of Financial Resource Mobilization for Africa's Development in the 1990s,* Document E/ECA/CM.19/5 (Addis Ababa: UNECA, April 1993); and African Development Bank (AfDB) *Group Projections on Africa's External Resource Requirements and the Bank Group: A Ten Year Perspective* (Abidjan: African Development Bank, April 1993).
31. Culagovski, Gabor, Germany, and Humphreys, *African Financing Needs in the 1990s* pp. 35–8.
32. African Development Bank (AfDB), *Group Projections on Africa's External Resource Requirements and the Bank Group.*
33. UNECA, *Strategies of Financial Resource Mobilization for Africa's Development in the 1990s.*
34. Transcript of Address by Edward V.K. Jaycox to the African-American Institute Conference on 'Capacity Building – The Missing Link in African Development', Reston, Virginia, May 20, 1993.
35. See *The Issues Paper* at Global Coalition for Africa (GCA) Meetings, Cotonou, Benin, June 9–11, 1993.
36. While the actual debt-service ratio may be no more than 25 to 35 per cent for most African countries when rescheduling agreements and unilateral debt-servicing moratoria are taken into account, for some countries this ratio still far exceeds 50 per cent.

37. United Nations Development Programme (UNDP), *Human Development Report 1992*, p. 74.
38. See World Bank Press Release of June 1, 1989, in *IMF Survey*, vol. 18, no. 12 (June 12, 1989) p. 188.
39. See IMF Press Release in *IMF Survey*, vol. 20, no. 9 (April 29, 1991) p. 138.

2 An Alternative to Structural Adjustment

C.P. Chandrasekhar

INTRODUCTION

Among the many transitions characterizing post-World War II history, one of remarkable significance is the growth in influence of the current dominant paradigm of international development. For almost three decades after World War II, developing countries as a group had believed in the need for the protection that tariffs and quantitative restrictions on imports offered, in the support and 'guidance' that an interventionist state provided, and in the role that the government could play in development. However, in recent years, these countries have opted for more open trade regimes and diluted or dismantled government controls and regulations. They are choosing strategies that put the state in retreat.

The essence of this paradigm transformation needs elaboration. The *dirigiste* regime which most developing countries adopted after World War II was informed by two perceptions: first, that a degree of isolationism and insularity was an unavoidable response to the extreme external vulnerability generated by the open economic regimes they were forced to adopt for almost a century before the Great Depression; and second, that domestic capital itself should be disciplined. It should be guided along lines that would ensure successful autonomous development, and regulated to mitigate the adverse effects its unrestricted play could have on equality within the system.

The new regime is based on a completely altered set of perceptions. The current dominant paradigm of international development now argues that the only route to efficient development in the current world order is dependence on the market, or, more euphemistically, the exploitation of interdependence through the mechanisms of the market. Any effort to reserve domestic economic space for domestic interests, to directly influence the pace and pattern of domestic development, or to alleviate the inequalities characteristic of emerging capitalism would only foreclose growth opportunities and spell stagnation. Tethering oneself to the powers that dominate the international economic order and allowing the 'animal spirits' of the private investor free play have become the main mechanisms to stimulate growth. These changed perceptions, not necessarily empirically grounded, provide the basis for the structural reforms now underway in the developing world.

The paradigm change ostensibly aims to exploit the 'benefits' of interdependence, which developing countries missed out on because of past isolationism, by encouraging the following policies:

- reducing tariff barriers to imports (having earlier done away with quantitative restrictions on them);

- allowing the market to determine exchange rates;

- doing away with restrictions on, and disincentives for, the inflow of foreign direct and portfolio investment;

- dismantling controls on production, prices and capacity creation, to provide domestic and foreign investors with the 'flexibility' needed to restructure capacity in the new environment; and finally,

- using restrictive fiscal and monetary policies as the residual device to prevent explosive volatility in the balance of payments during the transition to what is expected to become a vibrant and internationally competitive economy.

The process of implementation and consolidation of the new, 'market friendly' paradigm has been impelled by two forces. The Bretton Woods institutions (BWIs) have imposed the policy paradigm on the developing countries mainly through their structural adjustment programs (SAPs). More recently, the governments of developing countries themselves have voluntarily accepted the paradigm because of their inability to guarantee the circumstances needed to render import-substitution development strategies successful.

A CRITIQUE OF STRUCTURAL ADJUSTMENT

The Bretton Woods Mandate

The role of the Bretton Woods institutions in disciplining developing country governments and enforcing a shift toward more
market-friendly regimes is indeed surprising, because it was hardly
a part of their original mandate. That mandate was influenced by
the need to impose much-needed order in a world capitalist system
riven by the economic rivalry between the industrial nations that
culminated in World War II. This concern generated a degree of
unity among the 44 participating countries of the Bretton Woods
Conference. Since most of the world was still under colonial rule,
fewer than 30 countries were from the developing world, with just
eight from Africa, Asia and the Middle East combined. Unsurpris-
ingly, it was not the problems faced by these countries that were
dealt with in this conference.

The conference resulted in the creation of a system of fixed
exchange rates and the creation of two permanent international
bodies: the International Monetary Fund (IMF) and the International Bank for Reconstruction and Development (IBRD) or
World Bank. The IMF was assigned the task of assuring the
stability of exchange rates and their orderly adjustment when
necessary by providing balance-of-payments finance. The World
Bank was to rebuild the economies of war-torn nations and
bridge any gap that might threaten their peaceful coexistence by
providing long-term credit.

The system fashioned at Bretton Woods remained in place for
almost three decades. Those were the years of the 'great American celebration'. Under the system of fixed exchange rates, the
dollar was considered 'good as gold', enabling the US government
to finance, without concern for economic fundamentals, both the
policing of the world and the post-war boom. The spread of
development from North America to Europe to the Asian and
Pacific area was a corollary of that boom.

The collapse of the Bretton Woods fixed exchange-rate system
in the early 1970s robbed the IMF of the core of its charter.
Without the anchor of a dollar value tied to a physical quantum
of gold, systemic volatility in exchange rates became the order of
the day. And market-driven exchange rates could hardly be managed by the IMF, which was not a national, let alone world,
central bank, unless the countries involved turned to it for help.

Unfortunately for the IMF, access to finance from private sources has made it unnecessary for most developed countries to borrow from the Fund, thereby denying it the requisite leverage for managing exchange rates. To quote from an address by IMF Managing Director, Michel Camdessus, at the Institute of International Economics, an influential Washington-based think tank: 'No major industrial country has borrowed from the Fund since the late 1970s partly, at least, on account of the increased availability of balance-of-payments financing from the world's greatly expanded private capital markets.' The IMF has therefore become irrelevant as a manager of exchange rates in the present chaotic world of floating rates.

Forced to turn its attention away from exchange rates in particular and the developed countries in general, in recent years the IMF has made its prime concern the medium-term adjustment of developing countries' balance-of-payment accounts. A series of 'shocks' – the oil crisis, the contractionary responses of the developed countries, high interest rates on debt, to name a few – have turned that concern into an ongoing agenda. In return for financing aimed at stabilizing the balance of payments of these countries in the short term, the IMF imposes, and therefore undertakes to finance, a program aimed at delivering medium-term adjustment. Taking on the task of medium-term adjustment in poor countries means that its consequences in the form of lower growth, rising unemployment and falling expenditures in social services must be addressed, and measures must be taken to mitigate them. Consequently, the IMF has been forced to involve itself with new considerations such as the provision of safety nets.

Faced with the prospect of such involvement, even the conservative establishment has declared 'enough'. Indeed, the independent Bretton Woods Commission itself, led by Paul Volcker, former Chair of the US Federal Reserve Board, argues that the Fund should withdraw from much of its work in both the developing and former centrally planned economies (CPEs), based on the view that the Fund should 'avoid duplicating functions' of the Bank.[1] Instead, it calls for a division of labor between the two, albeit not a very clear one, with the IMF giving up its independent programs in the poorest developing countries and restricting itself to offering macroeconomic inputs to programs run by the Bank.

The position of the Bretton Woods Commission makes it clear that it has been easier for the World Bank than for the

IMF to find itself an agenda in the post-reconstruction era. The Commission argues that there is still need for a development finance institution like the World Bank, even in the new global financial landscape characterized by substantial increases in the availability of private-sector equity and bond finance.[2] However, three caveats are applied: first, the Bank should concentrate its assistance in those countries where the need is greatest, using the criteria of income and access to financial markets to assess need. In other words, if a country is an acceptable client to international financial markets, then the Bank should not spoil the market by providing its own credit, either concessional or non-concessional. Second, as part of adapting to a world that has turned from public-sector dominance towards private enterprise and free markets, the Bank must operate on the principle that development assistance should be directed only at what the private sector cannot or will not do. Hence, the Bank must insist on a transfer of responsibility from public to private sectors, and it must be wary of financing state-owned enterprises. Third, the Bank must seek out ways of working with and for the private sector. It should enhance the role of its private-sector lending affiliate, the International Finance Corporation (IFC), and of the Multilateral Investment Guarantee Agency (MIGA), providing them with additional resources in terms of people and funds. It thereby serves as a 'co-financier' and facilitator of private sector investment.

The ideological thrust of this agenda is obvious. Having managed in the past to prise open markets and improve the climate for private transnational investment through conditional lending in the developing countries, the Bank should now increase the space available for the private sector by facilitating the retreat of the state wherever private enterprise is willing to play a role. The Bank should also have a hand in financing and facilitating that role. However, to the extent that there are countries which the private sector is unlikely to touch because markets are small, infrastructure poor, and skills undeveloped, the Bank may continue playing the role of development missionary.

Unfortunately, the restructuring of the Bank and the Fund has failed to ensure that the policies they are responsible for establishing in the developing countries actually work. The evidence is overwhelming that, while challenging the economic sovereignty of these countries, the policies do not guarantee balance-of-payments adjustment; they do not promote growth;

they contribute to environmental destruction; and they inevitably result in rising unemployment, increasing inequality and persistent poverty. This has led one commentator to argue:

> What the Bretton Woods institutions are now trying to do is to take these (economic) issues out of the realm of national political controversy and public choice by imposing conditions that imply that there are technical and non-controversial answers to these questions. [But] the capability of the Bank [or the Fund] to assume the full measure of its [their] responsibilities in the circumstances of the 1990s will depend not only on a massive increase in its [their] ... financing capabilities but also on a reconsideration of its [their] present philosophy.[3]

Assertions of this kind portray the current BWI policy paradigm as nothing more than an easily reconsidered belief system. However, what such assessments ignore is the close link between the prevailing development paradigm and the nature of the 1990s world economic order, whose defining characteristic is the visible dominance of finance capital. That dominance is in part the result of the recent increased fluidity of finance, which has led to a sharp increase in the volume of transborder financial flows, including flows to developing countries.[4] Capital today is not just fluid, it is drawn from across the globe to be invested in a few select areas deemed fit or creditworthy by a handful of transnational financial institutions.[5] Nations as well as corporations are now routinely rated for creditworthiness, based on a multitude of nebulous economic and political criteria. And even though multinational commercial or merchant banks do not exert exclusive control over financial flows, their lead is usually followed by a host of individual *rentiers*.

The opposite pole of this centralization of finance is the phenomenon of emerging developing-country financial markets. The recession in the industrial developed countries, where growth averaged just 1.5 per cent over the first three years of the 1990s, has substantially increased risk and reduced returns in their product and share markets. Many shares are seen to be overpriced relative to corporate performance. At the same time, growth in some of the more successful developing countries has amounted to a creditable 6 per cent, providing new investment opportunities and rendering their stock markets buoyant. The opposite movements in the stock markets of the developed and the developing countries provides the classic basis for hedging against risk through portfolio, as opposed to fixed, investment. These developments, matched by the deregulation of financial markets in developing countries strapped for foreign exchange, have had a noticeable effect on the nature of their external finance. The trend has been away from banks toward other source-country agents who, of course, are also dominant players in international financial markets.

Portfolio Investment Flows and External Vulnerability

On the surface, portfolio investment flows appear to be a promising alternative to banking system loans, which have become less available to the developing world since the 'debt crisis' of the 1980s. However, portfolio inflows have the disadvantage of increasing the external vulnerability of developing countries. To start with, these flows make it impossible to link foreign exchange access to foreign exchange earning capacity. This increases the chances that current expenditure of foreign exchange may exceed the country's future ability to earn foreign exchange. In addition, since a part of the inflow is not directly linked to imports, this mobilization of finance can lead to a build-up of reserves that strengthens domestic currency and under-mines export competitiveness, unless underlying economic growth raises the demand for imports, exhausting some of the reserves.

Thus portfolio inflows can present a no-win situation if other conditions remain constant. If they are used to finance imports directly, they are encouraging foreign exchange profligacy by delinking expenditure of foreign currency from the ability to earn it. On the other hand, if they are not used to finance imports, they result in an accumulation of reserves and ensuing appreci-ation of domestic currency, causing a decline in export competi-tiveness and a worsening of the current account of the balance of payments. Further, an increase in reserves, by leading to an increase in money supply, reduces the government's influence over monetary trends, causing it to lose macroeconomic control through monetary policy.

In fact, portfolio flows can increase financial vulnerability more than commercial borrowing. This happens because, although commercial inflows generate the need for further inflows in future, the 'herd instinct' of banks overexposing themselves in a few countries is far less irrational than that of atomistic investors influenced by brokerage firms interested only in making a killing in emerging markets. Typically, commissions earned by these firms on emerging market issues are more than 1 per cent, compared to 0.3 or 0.4 per cent for an American issue. This encourages them to push developing-country paper into the hands of uninformed investors. Developing-country profligacy combined with the irresponsibility of investors from developed countries can generate scenarios similar to the debt crisis. In that case, portfolio flows in the new liberalized financial environment can prove 'hotter' than short-term borrowing. If portfolios are embracing developing countries to hedge against risk, they would turn sharply against those countries at the first sign of overexposure. In short, portfolio flows in themselves increase external vulnerability rather than resolving it.

Accordingly, the 1990s can be seen as a period of not merely persisting, but accelerating external vulnerability, associated with the sharp increases in private financial flows to developing countries. It can be argued that the increase in vulnerability is in part the result of the market-friendly policies advocated by the Bretton Woods institutions.[6] What is more significant is that the capital flows further the process of liberalization because they render import substitution meaningless as a strategy for growth. The import-substitution approach was prompted in the first place by the external vulnerability that underdeveloped countries have faced ever since the Great Depression. In a world awash with easily accessed liquidity, external vulnerability hardly seems to be a problem, let alone a factor that should be the prime determinant of growth strategies.

Thus, there is a congruence between the 'Washington consensus'[7] – free markets and sound money – promoted by the Bretton Woods institutions and the fall-out of the rise to dominance of finance capital in the world economy. Not surprisingly, IMF-type adjustment precludes a direct assault on the liberalization that leads to external vulnerability. In its adjustment framework, a sustainable current account is defined to include a trade regime that is liberal or open: 'A viable balance of payments has two aspects. First, it implies that balance-of-payments problems will not be merely suppressed but eradicated, and second, that the improvement in the country's external position will be durable.'[8] This definition of viability forecloses a protectionist response to balance-of-payments difficulties. It is based on the presumption that the failure to transit to a non-interventionist and open policy regime only suppresses balance-of-payments problems, rendering even a comfortable balance-of-payments position unsustainable.

The Question of Feasibility

The success of the adjustment package depends on its ability to attract a persistent flow of financial capital from abroad, for two reasons. First, while the shift to an open economic regime tends to result in a sharp increase in imports because of pent-up demand, exports are slow to respond to both liberalization and devaluation. Consequently, the transition is normally accompanied by a widening of the current account deficit, which necessitates massive deflation if not properly financed. Second, since the package involves a retreat of the state, the revival of growth is dependent on buoyant private investment.

In the current open economic environment, which makes the world market the target for successful firms, a degree of foreign capital inflow to raise exports and growth is inevitable. Nevertheless, not all developing countries are beneficiaries of the needed capital inflows. It appears to be concentrated in a few middle-income countries considered creditworthy because they are perceived to offer an environment more conducive to private enterprise and macroeconomic stability. However, despite the advantages of access to that fully fungible asset called foreign exchange, the new fluidity of capital brings with it a whole host of problems for developing countries.

Foreign capital flows are of three kinds: direct investment aimed at productive capacity creation; portfolio investment which enters under conditions of easy repatriability and are therefore extremely unstable; and commercial credit from foreign institutions and non-residents. If the first of these flows is realized within a relatively open trade regime, the capacity created tends to be neutral between production for the domestic and external markets, and would therefore tend to enhance exports as well as imports.[9] On the other hand, flows of purely 'financial capital' tend to be speculative and have little impact on real output. They respond adversely to any instability, either of the real economy or of financial variables like the rate of inflation and the exchange rate:

> Capital flows exert a considerable influence on exchange rates and financial asset prices, and are themselves influenced by expectations regarding rates of return on financial assets denominated in different currencies. This means not only that domestic policies have a new channel of influence on exchange rates, trade, balance of payments and, hence, the

level of economic activity (namely, through their effects on capital flows), but also that these will all be influenced by financial policy abroad and by events at home and abroad that alter expectations.[10]

In such a world, the 'national space' available to the state as its area of control, within which it can act to promote development, is substantially eroded. The entire range of fiscal, monetary and external policies has to be adjusted to subordinate national requirements to the caprices of international capital, always keeping in mind the implicit conditions set by the fluidity of finance.

Dependence on fluid finance also means that in order to keep financial stocks in the country and maintain consistent flows over time, governments have to encourage relatively high interest rates by opting for a tight monetary policy. High interest rates are a prerequisite for the capital inflows that ensure balance-of-payments viability and exchange-rate stability. They also hold down inflation, dampening disincentives for financial asset holders. Needless to say, this generates a differential between domestic and international interest rates that discriminates against borrowers unable to access the lower interest international markets. High interest rates further discriminate against productive investment in favor of financial assets. Moreover, these costs are being suffered by developing nations to attract the inflows that, as was argued earlier, are in themselves volatile.

Thus, a dominant feature of Fund/Bank-type adjustment, is that rather than enabling developing countries to adjust in a manner that overcomes external vulnerability while spurring growth, it sets up a strong and direct relationship between growth and vulnerability. But that is not all. As has been reliably established, IMF-style adjustment tends to be extremely hostile to the aims of human development. According to the current paradigm, stabilization has to be ensured through means that do not suppress balance-of-payments problems. Therefore, starting from the concept that a current account deficit implies that a country is living beyond its means and requires a reduction in the domestic absorption of commodities, the Bretton Woods institutions advocate a specific way of ensuring that decrease: a reduction in the fiscal deficit of the government. The deficit reduction must occur through raising indirect taxes and administered prices (which erodes poor people's incomes), cutting subsidies (especially food subsidies), and decreasing welfare expenditures (such as health and education), not through higher direct taxes that impinge on the rich. These measures are combined with others that are aimed at 'getting prices right' by dismantling all regulation of the domestic and foreign private sector. Inevitably, the freeing of imports results in a fall of capacity utilization in domestic industry. And the reductions in government expenditure and investment aggravate the resulting recession. Thus IMF-type adjustment is intrinsically inequalizing. There are only two elements that can alleviate this tendency: an increase in exports that stimulates growth and finances foreign exchange expenditures, thereby assuring recovery; or access to foreign finance that allows a high degree of absorption even while liberalization is taking place. This inflow, however, only postpones the day of reckoning.

In any case, exports will not rise much in the short run, because the process of boosting exports, even if successful, always takes considerable time. And if exports do rise in the medium to long term, it would be for reasons that have little to do with the IMF package. In fact, the experience of successful exporters, particularly of manufactured goods, indicates that non-interventionist, market-based regimes are ill-suited to the expansion of manufactured exports. Export expansion requires decisive choices of the particular industrial sectors that are likely to succeed in world markets, and an interventionist industrial policy that encourages the growth of the chosen sectors along warranted lines. Put simply, markets alone do not deliver export growth: strategic intervention holds the key.[11] Experience with growth in the East Asian economies and, of course, with the successful Chinese program of reform, reinforce this perception.

Consequently, any reductions in current account deficits attributable to the Bretton Woods package come from a curtailment of either public investment for the poor or of imports that would be consumed by the poor. In practice, however, any such savings will be more than offset by the increases in imports that result from market liberalization. Therefore, the Bretton Woods package, although inequalizing and recessionary in character and consequence, is not particularly successful in correcting the disequilibrium on the current account. The effort at sustaining the balance of payments and spurring recovery can be successful only if acceptance of an IMF-type package generates an investor confidence that results in a large inflow of capital. In other words, the short-run success of the Bretton Woods package depends on the increase in vulnerability that results from portfolio flows.

ELEMENTS OF AN ALTERNATIVE

The Dichotomy of Production

What then is the alternative? It is indeed true that developing countries cannot return to a strategy of making optimum use of available foreign exchange earnings through import-substitution policies. Those policies attempted to control the rate of growth and diversification of consumption in the short run and reduce dependence on manufactured imports in the long run. They did this by utilizing scarce foreign exchange to create a capital-goods sector in general, and a machine-tools sector in particular. However, the problem with that strategy was threefold: first, it was really an option only to those developing countries that were above a critical minimum in the size of their domestic market and resource base. Second, even in those countries, the growth of manufactured goods production was determined by the scale and quality requirements of the domestic market. Therefore, an increase in the production of manufactured goods was not necessarily accompanied by an increase in the ability to keep pace with international innovations. This held back the export of manufactured goods and, in the long run, the rate of expansion of the system. Finally, given the inequalities within the system and the growing pressure from the wealthy to obtain access to products that defined the international lifestyles to which they were inevitably exposed, the ability of the state to restrict growth and diversification of consumption became increasingly undermined. Neither the savings rate nor the import-intensity of domestic production could adhere to the trajectory that the strategy had charted.

Given the parameters within which the strategy operated and the concept of development that it implicitly appropriated, import substitution was doomed to failure. Hence, the alternative must go beyond the *dirigisme* characteristic of old-style import substitution, even while retaining its principal objective, namely, that of reducing external vulnerability. This is all the more true because the very nature of external vulnerability has been recast in a world dominated by fluid finance capital.[12]

This brings us to the first aspect of the alternative adjustment package: it must transcend the dichotomy between production for the domestic market and production for export. In its archetypal form, that dichotomy is reflected in arguments that make a case for industrialization based on the home market because international inequality provides grounds for pessimism about the value of exports. In the debates that led up to the industrial revolution, one issue of contention was the relative roles of purely internal factors, in the form of structural change, as opposed to external factors such as the effects of commercialization and the growth of markets in determining the transition to capitalism. Whatever the merits of those contending arguments with regard to the principal determining role, one thing appears clear with hindsight: successful capitalist industrialization cannot occur in a context insulated from world markets. It requires consciously engaging those markets as part of the strategy for growth.

An Activist State

The term 'engaging' is used advisedly. World markets are not benign, autonomous forces that spur efficient Third World industrialization. On the contrary, they embody all the inequalities characteristic of the world system. Therefore, engaging world markets involves using all the weaponry available to a developing country, including the power of its government, the foundation that its home market provides, the ability of its scientific and technical personnel to override the technological control of a few transnational firms, and the advantages of the late entrant (varying from low wages to a less codified legal framework) to prise open those markets that would otherwise appear to be hermetically sealed.

This brings us to the second point: a successful growth strategy has to be based on an activist state. There is no relationship between the existence of an activist state and autarchy or, for that matter, insularity. One valid criticism of the import-substitution years in countries like India is that it neglected exports. While exports cannot constitute the basis for growth in a large developing country, in an interdependent world one cannot finance the imports that accompany the process of growth without an export thrust. For this reason all successful late industrializers, including the so-called newly industrialized countries (NICs), have pursued a mercantilist export policy that emphasizes pushing out exports at whatever cost.

A mercantilist export policy involves a continuous restructuring of the production base of the system in both quantitative and qualitative terms, and this requires both technology and investment. Investment becomes significant for two reasons: first, the larger the investment, the larger the share of it that can be devoted to modernization as opposed to expansion. Second, because higher investment implies higher growth, capacity expansion proceeds at a pace that allows the incorporation of new technology. For these and lesser reasons, the growth rate of an economy's manufacturing exports is dependent on the investment ratio. Not surprisingly, a preliminary investigation, using cross-section data for 17 underdeveloped countries from 1980 to 1989, found a significant and strong relationship between the rate of growth of gross domestic investment and the rate of growth of exports.[13]

State activism on the economic level should include two features as its corollary: first, an activist government pursuing a mercantilist growth strategy should be in a position to discipline its industrial class.[14] The need to be able to discipline the industrial class arises because the strategy elaborated above, although different from the detailed physical controls characteristic of the import-substitution years, requires substantial critical targeting and coordination by the state. Through incentives on one hand, and measures to enforce compliance on the other, the government must be capable of influencing investment decisions at a microeconomic level. The coordinating agency should be able to regulate the choice of product, technology, scale of production and price, based on the demands of the targeted segment of the world market. Second, activism requires mobilization by the state of adequate resources to sustain its strategy.

Land Reform

Needless to say, imposing such discipline requires the backing of other sections of society. Such support is most often won in a situation where land reforms have dismantled the structures that provide the base for a collusive elite. Accordingly, a program of land redistribution aimed at undermining land monopoly, followed by appropriate measures of cooperative cultivation, is the third element of an alternative strategy. The vital necessity of land reform is emphasized by the fact that the successful East Asian capitalist economies owe their success *inter alia* to their post-war land reforms.

But land reforms are not merely an instrument for mobilizing political support. A thrust towards land redistribution and greater social expenditures in rural areas, which is best undertaken under the aegis of directly elected decentralized governing bodies (such as the *panchayats* in India[15]) is also essential for an immediate widening of the home market. Land reforms thus stimulate a rapid increase in agricultural output (as has happened in West Bengal), and a corresponding expansion in the potential for direct and indirect employment. However, to reach that end, land reforms must be accompanied by investments in the agricultural sector – irrigation, water management and other kinds of rural infrastructure – that permit acceleration of growth. In order to be effective, this strategy requires the devolution of economic and political power and authority. Devolution would not only broaden a country's base of development but would also create the decision-making structures that are crucial for generating the strength and accountability needed to allow the state to function as a disciplining force.

Dealing with Macroeconomic Disequilibrium

This alternative growth strategy does involve economic reforms, though not those dictated by the Fund and the Bank. The objective of the reforms must be to widen the home market through appropriate structural change, in order to provide the broadest possible basis for development. But broadening the market base without providing for its satisfaction can be counterproductive, and a country faced with macroeconomic disequilibrium is hardly in a position to provide the needed stimulus for expansion. This means that macroeconomic disequilibrium, reflected in high budget deficits, has to be corrected through direct taxation and a reduction in unessential expenditure. Greater discipline in tax enforcement, and changes in tax laws that adjust rates for the top income brackets and remove certain exemptions should substantially increase the revenue from income taxation.

With greater recourse to direct taxation, the tendency towards garnering revenue from indirect taxes and administered price hikes should be reversed, an anti-inflationary measure in itself. Even so, it is necessary to protect the poor from the possible effects of such inflation. This requires an expansion of the public distribution system, extending it into the rural areas and widening its commodity coverage. To alleviate the strain on the exchequer of such an extension, the system should be targeted towards the poor.

The other component of macroeconomic disequilibrium that plagues developing countries is the deficit on the current account of the balance of payments. The growth of income and exports in the proposed strategy are not dependent on the pursuit of an open economic regime, but are a fall-out of state activism. This indicates that selective but stringent import controls combined with an export thrust can themselves provide the basis for a correction of balance-of-payments disequilibrium. Further, growth in a broad-based development strategy is not totally dependent on access to international finance, but uses the foothold offered by the home market. This means that the direct link between growth and vulnerability – the dependence on 'hot money' flows – is snapped, and the principal objective of the alternative transition is achieved.

Therefore, implementation of a package of the policies discussed above would not merely accelerate growth with some attention to equity, but would break the direct connection between an even minimal rate of growth and intensified dependence on foreign finance. Therefore, any external financing would essentially serve to enable a country to raise the rate of growth beyond the critical minimum. Consequently, that critical minimum would not be subject to the external vulnerability generated by dependence on international capital. In this way, the 'opportunity' offered by the dominance of finance capital can be used by a developing country to engage international markets. In the virtuous circle of this new environment, an effort by an activist state to engage international markets for goods and services provides it with the foundation needed to engage international capital markets and use them as a weapon to prise open unequal international markets.

The State and Markets

This brings us to the final, but not least significant, of the differentiating features of the alternative strategy: it must transcend the dichotomy between an interventionist regime that is corrupt, and a non-interventionist one in which the market becomes the cause of increased external vulnerability: in other words, it must change the dominant problematic itself.

Until recently, the crises in the erstwhile centrally planned economies (CPEs) were taken as adequate grounds to suspect any form of intervention by the state in the processes of development. It was argued that however inadequate free-market systems were, the essential lesson to be learned from Eastern Europe was that 'self-organizing systems' were the best available, in both allocative and innovative efficiency. However, the experience with transiting to market-friendly, if not market-dominated, regimes in the former CPEs has undermined the confidence in those arguments that rested on a simple dichotomy between interventionist and non-interventionist regimes. This means there must be more careful assessment of the possibilities of states where 'planning principles' work in tandem with markets as part of a growth strategy, because such regimes appear inevitable in the foreseeable future.

The real issue is not where the line should be drawn between markets with their arm's-length transactions, and interventionist structures that foreclose such transactions. If recent history is any guide, we can only agree with Maurice Dobb, who argued more than two decades ago that 'no clear-cut, logically defined frontier can be drawn between the province of centralized and decentralized decision', and that, 'concerning the expedient extent of one and of the other there remain many problems for experience still to decide. In the terminology of contemporary discussion ... the precise relation between plan and market remains undetermined.'16 The real issue is whether in letting experience determine the relative areas of centralized and decentralized market planning, we, in fact, need to be clear which aspect of this unity of opposites should dominate.17 There has been a tendency, both within and without the Bretton Woods institutions, to suggest that markets must essentially run systems. The notion of 'people-friendly markets' that is currently encouraged by the United Nations, ostensibly in opposition to the IMF and World Bank's undiluted defense of markets, provides one rather well-articulated presentation of this view.

A major feature of the United Nations Development Programme's (UNDP) *Human Development Report 1993* is the effort to work out a 'more pragmatic partnership between market efficiency and social compassion'. The fact that governments now face less opposition when transiting to a market-based framework, and are therefore willing to experiment with less *dirigiste* regimes, is considered a positive tendency for two reasons: 'free markets provide the most efficient mechanism yet devised for the exchange of goods and services'; and 'free enterprise provides a mechanism for unleashing human creativity and entrepreneurial ability'. Unfortunately, markets as we find them are not necessarily free, accessible to all, environmentally-friendly or, above all, equitable in distributing their benefits. The challenge therefore is to shape markets in a fashion that will not only maintain their dynamism, but will blend it with equity and sustainability. Markets, the *Human Development Report 1993* argues, should be rendered people-friendly:

Having markets serve people, rather than people serve markets requires concrete steps:

1. Preconditions

- Adequate investment in the education, health and skills of people to prepare them for the market

- An equitable distribution of assets, particularly land in poor agrarian societies

- Extension of credit to the poor

- Access to information, particularly about the range of market opportunities

- Adequate physical infrastructure, especially roads, electricity and telecommunications, and adequate support for R&D (research and development)

- A legal framework to protect property rights

- No barriers to entry, irrespective of race, religion, sex or ethnic origin

- A liberal trade regime, supported by the dismantling of international trade barriers.

2. Accompanying conditions

- A stable macroeconomic environment, especially ensuring steadiness in domestic prices and external currency values

- A comprehensive incentive system, with correct price signals, a fair tax regime and adequate rewards for work and enterprise

- Freedom from arbitrary government controls and regulations.

3. Corrective actions

- Protection of competition, through antimonopoly laws and safeguards against financial malpractices

- Protection of consumers, especially through drug regulations, safety and hygiene standards and honest advertising

- Protection of workers, through regulated working conditions and minimum wage standards

- Protection of special groups, particularly women, children and ethnic minorities

- Protection of the environment, particularly through incentive systems and by banning pollution or making polluters pay.

4. Social safety nets

- Adequate arrangements to look after the temporary victims of market forces to bring them back into the markets, primarily through human investment, worker retraining and access to credit opportunities – as well as more permanent support for groups such as the disabled and the aged.[18]

There are two levels at which these propositions need to be addressed: to what extent do they constitute a viable strategy of development; and how far have we progressed towards realizing them in the former CPEs and the less developed countries of the world. With regard to the first, the *Human Development Report 1993* understates the dangers involved in liberalization.

Apart from the inevitable skepticism about the efficiency of free markets, five issues of significance arise. First, egalitarian markets cannot be based on a relatively egalitarian redistribution of land alone. Assets come in more forms than just land. And, in the case of land, even if reforms ensure a relatively egalitarian structure, market functioning can lead to new differentiations that re-establish an inegalitarian setting. While it is true that doing away with medieval land relations is a first step forward in advancing the fight against absolute poverty, mass illiteracy and substandard health conditions, it does not guarantee equal market participation for all unless accompanied by a host of other conditions.

Second, markets essentially ensure effectiveness at the level of the individual worker through the disciplining intimidation that a combination of unemployment and the 'threat of the sack' involve. That is, the so-called efficiency of the market rests on incomplete participation of the labor force and the maintenance of a reserve army of workers.

Third, if markets that are people-friendly are predicated on a liberal trade regime, the role of the state in searching out and targeting export markets, shaping domestic investments in keeping with the requirements of those markets and making supportive investments (including those in research and development) must be substantial. International inequality, in a world without protection, necessitates strategic intervention that makes the participation of the state essential, as the experiences of many newly industrialized countries prove.

Fourth, if the purpose of liberalization is to internalize external markets, then successful countries are those that can maintain relatively high ratios of investment to income, because of the economies of scale determined by technology and research and development. But markets are quite inefficient in influencing atomistic decision makers to save enough to attain the critical savings ratios. Intervention by the state may be necessary to raise savings rates and channel them into the investment appropriate for penetrating and remaining competitive in world markets.

Finally, inasmuch as open trade regimes inevitably require relatively open capital markets, the state may find itself outmaneuvered by a feature of the international environment discussed in some detail earlier, namely, the centralization of finance. As a result, even if cross-border flows of goods and services were rendered 'free' across the globe, the factors that influence the direction of flow of capital are too numerous and too nebulous to permit a determinate theory of which investment location they will choose. In such a world, the national space available to the state, within which it acts to promote and control development, is substantially eroded. Therefore, the influence of international finance increases to the extent that liberalization tethers individual economies to the world economy.

These are, of course, mere logical arguments to suggest that the ambitious inventory of conditions listed by the *Human Development Report 1993* for realizing people-friendly markets is only a pragmatic minimum and includes elements that could prove hostile to human development. What is more disconcerting is that in much of the developing world even this pragmatic minimum is far from being realized. Most developing countries are characterized by a high concentration of land in the hands of few owners, insecure tenure systems, and a high proportion of under- and unemployed workers in the rural work force. Human development indicators suggest that developing countries have yet to invest adequately in human capital formation. Most of them lack adequate safety nets either for the unemployed or for special groups like women, the elderly, the disabled and children in poverty. That is, they are in need of most of the prerequisites for rendering markets people-friendly. Unfortunately, well before dealing with these immediate and pressing problems, most countries, because of both internal reasons and pressure from the BWIs, have already launched on liberalization programs that dismantle state regulation of markets without ensuring that those markets are actually free in terms of access and functioning.

In the former CPEs, the transition to market-friendly regimes has failed despite the presence of many of the enabling conditions specified by the *Human Development Report 1993*. This failure has been attributed to the absence of an entrepreneurial class that could successfully exploit free markets. As a result, an important component of the transition to market-based regimes in those economies has been the privatization of public enterprises. Of the nearly 7,000 state enterprises privatized between 1980 and 1991 across the world, 4,000 were in the erstwhile CPEs. But even privatization has failed to generate a viable strategy of growth, because the liberalization of trade and payments has completely eroded the national space available to these nascent entrepreneurs.

Put simply, even relatively people-friendly markets have proved a failure in ensuring growth, providing employment and foreclosing the immiserization that results in poverty. Whatever the proper pragmatic mix between state and markets needs to be, the new situation in developing countries must have a dominant component of state intervention that helps carve out the space for growth in an unequal international environment. This means that we need to distinguish between the command-economy structures that generated the crisis in the former CPEs during their intensive phase of growth and a situation in which an interventionist state leads the strategy of development as well as regulating markets. The latter scenario now appears to be a necessary component of any process of development that combines growth with the advancement of society's welfare.

CONCLUSION: HUMAN DEVELOPMENT AND INTERVENTION

Asia is characterized by an extremely skewed distribution in terms of the Human Development Index (HDI)[19] ranking, with four good performers (Japan, Hong Kong, Republic of Korea, Singapore) and a host of extremely poor performers, such as Bangladesh, Bhutan, Nepal and Afghanistan. One major factor accounting for this variation in performance is, of course, economic development narrowly defined. However, there are a number of instances where human development is so much better than that warranted by the income per capita which implies that countries had moved up from the 'low human development' category despite severe economic backwardness. The differentials between HDI and income per capita rankings were especially high in China, Sri Lanka and Vietnam.

The factors accounting for the rather sharp divergence between income per capita and human development performance in countries such as Sri Lanka, China and Vietnam raises some immediate questions. Analyses of the Sri Lankan experience have been quite convincing in establishing the link between government intervention in the provision of basic needs and human development performance.[20] Sri Lanka is one among a number of cases that point to the central role of public action, independent of the level of per capita income, in determining human development achievement. It barely needs emphasizing that the Chinese and Vietnamese experiences also support that conclusion, though recent years have seen a dilution in the emphasis on public action for human development in those countries. Similar experiences have been noted in individual states of other countries in the region, with the state of Kerala, in India, being the most striking and well-studied example. Kerala's human development record is vastly better than that of most other states in India,[21] despite the fact that the per capita net state domestic product converted at the official exchange rate stood at $215 in Kerala, compared with $276 in India as a whole.[22]

The role of public action in enhancing the quality of life at relatively low levels of development has been extremely important in Kerala. However, what determinants ensure constructive public action in some contexts and not in others is a question that needs answering. The effects of interventionist regimes with egalitarian objectives and policies are visible in China, Vietnam,

Cambodia and Laos, in both the positive influence intervention had in the past, and the present adverse effects of restructuring now under way in those countries. Elsewhere, while specific social and historical factors can be identified (in Kerala, for example, the matrilineal system in certain caste groups, the role of reform movements, and the influence of relatively strong and vibrant left-wing parties in setting the development agenda and its consequent progress on land reform), the direct and indirect role of popular pressure in furthering human development comes through in most cases.

It is not only the narrow economic goal of consistently raising per capita incomes, thereby doing away with absolute poverty, that warrants the proposed strategy involving an activist state. The evidence indicates that such activism and intervention is even more crucial when it comes to improving longevity and reducing morbidity, advancing literacy, and increasing the opportunities for participation in the economic, social and political processes that substantially enhance the quality of life.

In conclusion, evidence in many developing countries (including the recent Mexican crisis) has shown that structural adjustment does not provide equitable, sustainable and participatory development. An alternative adjustment strategy must

- transcend the dichotomy between production for the domestic market and production for export,

- be based on an activist state,

- include land reform and measures of cooperative cultivation,

- deal with macroeconomic disequilibria; and

- transcend the dichotomy between an interventionist regime that is corrupt, and a non-interventionist one that allows the market full sway despite increased external vulnerability.

Finally, development is more than the statistical increase in income per capita.

Notes

1. Bretton Woods Commission, *Bretton Woods: Looking to the Future* (Washington, DC: Bretton Woods Commission, 1994) pp. B–18 and B–19.
2. Bretton Woods Commission, *Bretton Woods: Looking to the Future*, p. A–7.
3. Sidney Dell, 'Reforming the World Bank for the Tasks of the 1990s' Exim Bank Commencement Day Lecture (Bombay: Exim Bank, 1990) p. 15.
4. Between 1989 and 1992, while global flows of foreign direct investment (FDI) declined from $234 billion to $150 billion, those to the developing countries rose from $29 billion to $40 billion, fueled by a $50 billion privatization drive in these countries. However, portfolio flows in the form of investments in bonds, equities, certificates of deposit and commercial paper rose from less than $10 billion in 1990 to $37 billion in 1992. All told, flows of this kind have risen from around $35 billion to more than $75 billion in the first three years of the 1990s.
5. Prabhat Patnaik, *Post-War Capitalism and the Problem of Transition to Socialism* (Shimla: Indian Institute of Advanced Study, 1993) mimeo.
6. The issues discussed here are elaborated in C.P. Chandrasekhar, 'The Macroeconomics of Imbalance and Adjustment' in Prabhat Patnaik (ed.), *Themes in Indian Economics: Macroeconomics* (New Delhi: Oxford University Press, forthcoming).
7. The term 'Washington consensus' was coined by John Williamson of the Washington-based Institute for International Economics. For a detailed description of the elements that comprise the 'Washington consensus', see John Williamson, 'What Washington Means by Policy Reform', in *Latin American Adjustment: How Much Has Happened?* (1990) pp. 7–38, as cited in Jo Marie Griesgraber, 'The International Monetary Fund and Latin America' in Lowell S. Gustafson (ed.), *Economic Development Under Democratic Regimes: Neoliberalism in Latin America* (Westport: Praeger, 1994) p. 205.

   For a critique of the rush by governments and markets to embrace the 'Washington consensus', see Stanford University economist Paul Krugman, 'Dutch Tulips and Emerging Markets' in *Foreign Affairs*, vol. 74, no. 4 (July/August 1995) pp. 28–44. Krugman sums up the 'Washington consensus' as:

   > By 'Washington' Williamson meant not only the US government, but all those institutions and networks of opinion leaders centered in the world's de facto capital – the International Monetary Fund, World Bank, think tanks, politically sophisticated investment bankers, and worldly finance ministers, all those who meet each other in Washington and collectively define the conventional wisdom of the moment.

Williamson's original definition of the Washington consensus involved ten different aspects of economic policy. One may, however, roughly summarize this consensus, at least as it influenced the beliefs of markets and governments, more simply. It is the belief that Victorian virtue in economic policy – free markets and sound money – is the key to economic development. Liberalize trade, privatize state enterprises, balance the budget, peg the exchange rate, and one will have laid the foundations for an economic takeoff; find a country that has done these things, and there one may confidently expect to realize high returns on investments. (pp. 28–9)

8. Mohsin S. Khan and Malcolm D. Knight, 'Fund-Supported Adjustment Programs and Economic Growth', *Occasional Paper no. 41* (Washington, DC: International Monetary Fund, 1985) p. 2.
9. The rise to dominance of finance capital has been accompanied by substantial changes in the nature of foreign investment, especially in its relation to trade. Foreign direct investment in colonial times was closely linked with the needs of colonial trade, and was primarily directed into areas such as plantations, extractive industries, shipping and insurance. Such investment strengthened the 'enforced bilateralism' in trade that colonialism implied. With the onset of decolonization and the adoption of protective, import-substituting strategies by independent post-colonial states aiming to industrialize rapidly, foreign investment often became a substitute for trade. With barriers, both tariff and non-tariff, foreclosing the developing country markets of leading international firms, the firms found the need to jump barriers by establishing production facilities that could service local markets. Not only have the recent revolutions in transport, communications and technology segmented production processes and expanded world trade and capital flows, but for the last two decades or so there has been a rapid dismantling of protective regimes and relaxation of regulations on foreign investors across the globe. This has affected the character of foreign investment because, after allowing for national peculiarities and variations in political structure, any production site worldwide is becoming a potential site for production for world markets. For transnational firms, which have become increasingly detached from dependence on home country resources, it offers the opportunity of locating in areas where they can overcome the disadvantages created by macroeconomic developments such as inflation, or microeconomic features like high wage levels, thereby substantially enhancing their international competitiveness. See Economic and Social Commission for Asia and the Pacific (ESCAP) *Economic and Social Survey of Asia and the Pacific, Part II: Expansion of Investment and Intraregional Trade as a Vehicle for Enhancing Regional Economic Cooperation and Development in Asia and the Pacific* (New York: United Nations, 1993).
10. Yilmaz Akyüz, 'On Financial Openness in Developing Countries' in

United Nations Conference on Trade and Development (UNCTAD) (ed.), *International Monetary and Financial Issues for the 1990s: Research Papers for the Group of Twenty-Four*, Volume II (New York: United Nations, 1993) pp. 110–24.

11. See Robert Wade, *Governing the Market: Economic Theory and the Role of Government in East Asian Industrialization* (Princeton: Princeton University Press, 1991) and Alice H. Amsden, *Asia's Next Giant: South Korea and Late Industrialization* (New York: Oxford University Press, 1989).

12. Prabhat Patnaik, 'Development Planning: The India Experience' (New Delhi: Centre for Economic Studies and Planning, Jawaharlal Nehru University, 1994) mimeo.

13. Using cross-section data for 17 underdeveloped countries and regressing the rate of growth of exports on the rate of growth of gross domestic investment gave the following results for 1980–9:

$$Y = -5.90 + 1.16 \ X \text{ with an R-squared of } 0.62.$$

See Prabhat Patnaik, 'International Capital and National Economic Policy: A Critique of India's Economic Reforms' in *Economic and Political Weekly*, vol. 29, no. 12 (March 19, 1994).

14. See Wade, *Governing the Market* and Amsden, *Asia's Next Giant*.

15. The *panchayat* is a sort of village council which still functions as mediator between persons or groups in many rural villages of India instead of a civil court. A *panchayat* may have three or more members, with the number of members depending in part on the size of the village. Traditionally comprised of the older, more experienced members of the community, *panchayats* today tend to include the wealthier villagers.

16. Maurice Dobb, *Welfare Economics and the Economics of Socialism: Towards a Commonsense Critique* (Cambridge: Cambridge University Press, 1969) p. 127.

17. The discussion that follows draws heavily from C.P. Chandrasekhar, 'An Asian Perspective on the Human Development Report 1993' prepared for the Human Development Report Office (New Delhi: UNDP, 1993) mimeo.

18. United Nations Development Programme *Human Development Report 1993* (New York: Oxford University Press, 1993) p. 31, Box 3.1.

19. The HDI is an unweighted average of the relative dimensions of longevity, education and resources. The proximate variables that measure these dimensions are life expectancy, literacy and mean years of schooling, and a modified measure of income per capita purporting to gauge the welfare generating capacity of income. As the appendix to the *Human Development Report 1993* (pp. 104–12) makes clear, the *concept* of human development is broader than the *measure* of human development.

20. See A.K. Sen, 'Public Action and the Quality of Life in Developing

Countries' in *Oxford Bulletin of Economics and Statistics* (Oxford: Oxford University Press, 1981) p. 43; J.C. Caldwell, 'Routes to Low Mortality in Poor Countries' in *Population and Development Review* (1986) p. 12; and Sudhir Anand and Ravi M. Kanbur, 'Public Policy and Basic Needs Provision: Intervention and Achievement in Sri Lanka' in Jean Dreze and Amartya Sen (eds), *The Political Economy of Hunger*, Volume 3 (Oxford: Oxford University Press, 1991) pp. 59–92.

21. In Kerala, life expectancy at birth for males and females was 67.5 and 73 years respectively in 1986–8, far above the overall Indian averages of 56 and 56.5 years, and better than the 1988 figures in China of 66 and 69 years respectively. Infant mortality rates of 17 per 1,000 in 1990 were substantially lower than the Indian average of 80 per 1,000 live births and the Sri Lankan record of 25 per 1,000. Male and female literacy rates were at 94.5 and 87 per cent in 1991, remarkable by any standards, and especially relative to the Indian averages of 52.1 and 39.4 per cent. With 106.4 hospitals and dispensaries per 100 square kilometer area and 254 beds per lakh [100,000] persons, access to health services was substantially better in Kerala than for the Indian population as a whole, which was serviced by 12 hospitals per 1,000 square kilometer area and 77 hospital beds per lakh [100,000] persons. Figures from V.K. Ramachandran, 'Notes on Kerala' (1993) mimeo.

22. Calculated by the Government of India, 1993.

3 The World Bank's Focus on Poverty

Barend A. de Vries

INTRODUCTION

Poverty must be a central concern of the World Bank. The essence of development is enabling people to be productive and to improve their levels of well-being. Whatever the Bank must do to enhance development should have the inevitable and ultimate effect of reducing poverty and strengthening the base for a higher standard of living.

After more than 50 years of operations, the Bank still faces a world where over 1 billion people live in deep poverty, with per capita incomes of less than a dollar per day. Many countries suffer poverty rates between 25 and 50 per cent of their populations. These conditions persist despite important improvements in critical social indicators such as life expectancy, infant mortality, access to safe water, primary school enrollment and immunization. It is urgent that the Bank steps up lending to improve basic conditions through lowering population growth and strengthening primary education, sanitation, health and nutrition.

POLICY CHANGES AT THE WORLD BANK

Poverty eradication has proven to be an extremely complex task. In recent years these complexities have been underscored by several non-governmental organizations (NGOs) which have moved into the center of the debate about the Bank's role in fighting poverty. NGOs have also been involved in a number of critical policy changes that the Bank introduced in the late 1980s, in particular:

- systematic attention to environmental issues in project and policy work, and the establishment of a Vice Presidency for Sustainable Development, including an Environment Department;

- greater attention to the role of women in development;

- greater attention to poverty issues that arose as a consequence of structural adjustment lending, especially in Sub-Saharan Africa (SSA), and the ensuing 'Poverty Reduction Program';

- greater participation in project preparation and implementation by people directly affected by these projects;

- establishment of the Inspection Panel to bring complaints about projects to the attention of Bank management and Executive Directors; and

- establishment of a public information center and increased availability of project and economic documents.

These and other changes have made the Bank an entirely different institution from what it was in 1985. Indeed, it is no exaggeration to say that the Bank has experienced an institutional revolution that is still in process. In each one of these changes, NGOs have pinpointed critical issues, persuaded the Bank to pay greater attention to them, and put pressure for appropriate policy change. Moreover, NGOs are working with Bank staff in preparing projects in the field. They also played a role in the formulation of programs to counteract the effects of structural adjustment lending on poverty, as in Bolivia. The extent of NGO involvement in Bank-financed projects has grown measurably since the late 1980s. David Beckmann found that '[o]f the projects the Bank approved in fiscal 1989 and 1990, 96 involved NGOs – up from an average of 14 projects a year for fiscal 1973–88'.[1]

World Bank management and staff meet regularly with NGO representatives[2] to explain Bank policy and to listen to comments to consider what action can be taken on them. However, NGOs, being more directly concerned with ethical issues and values and closely attuned to local culture and social conditions, often speak in a language different from that of the Bank. The Bank speaks the language of the professionals that contribute to investment projects and programs, such as economists, finance experts and engineers, not that of ethicists and social activists. (This does not deny that the Bank is directly concerned with human values and conditions, and that its policy conditions lay the foundation for a more civil society. Bank President Robert McNamara (1968–81) had a strong sense of moral commitment and, for example, spent much of his time learning about Africa and understanding its priorities.)

From Efficiency to Poverty Alleviation

The Bank started out with an almost overwhelming concern with efficiency and sound investment and business practices. Its primary interest was to ensure that projects were well-conceived, economically and financially viable, and operated on a business-like basis. In the early years, the Bank sought to establish itself as a financial institution recognized by the financial markets that had to absorb the Bank's bonds at a reasonable price.

But it is good to remember that the people who conceived of the Bank and wrote its initial charter were also concerned with the welfare of individuals, their development and full employment. Many of them were inspired by the liberal policies of US President Franklin D. Roosevelt's administration, which, with the British government, was the prime mover at the founding 1944 conference at Bretton Woods, New Hampshire. These founders included Harry Dexter White, John Maynard Keynes and Edward Bernstein, as well as many from the developing countries, such as Roberto Campos and O. Bulhoes (Brazil), Carlos Lleras Restrepo (Colombia), M. Desai (India), Rodrigo Gomes and Victor Urquidi (Mexico) and Felipe Pazos (Cuba).

The Bank sharpened its focus on poverty conditions under the leadership of George Woods (1963–68), who initiated lending for education and sanitation and began the long journey of professionalizing the Bank's economic work. This work continued during McNamara's management, especially after his 1973 Nairobi speech, signalling the start of the Bank's involvement in battling rural poverty by helping small-scale agriculture. Assistance for urban development followed, including housing, sewerage and sanitation, combined with more intensive attention to urban employment. In these 'new-style' projects, the Bank was prepared to take considerable risks. Subsequent evaluation has shown that these projects often had much smaller rates of return than more traditional projects, such as electricity and transport. During this time the Bank also began broadening its analysis of projects by paying attention to the social value of inputs and outputs, that is, the actual value of a project for a country. Under this method, the labor costs of projects designed to provide jobs and absorb abundant low-skilled labor would be set at zero, reflecting that the cost for this kind of labor is negligible for the country. The costs of a project employing low-skilled labor would therefore be lower than an alternative project designed to increase efficiency by substituting labor with machines. The low social cost of anti-poverty projects would make it easier for the Bank to justify its lending for anti-poverty purposes, thus allowing for poverty effects rather than efficiency alone. The broader conception of project justification is important not only for the operations of the World Bank, but also for other lending institutions and governments, since project evaluation is one area where the Bank has exercised considerable influence on economic thinking around the world.

Unfortunately, the World Bank's attention to poverty declined in the 1980s. The debt crisis which dominated the development scene in this past decade brought a setback in growth and social development and worsened poverty conditions, particularly in Latin America. At the same time, the Bank's economic work and operational stance assigned increasing weight to efficiency in resource allocation and outward orientation, and less to fighting poverty. In the late 1970s, the Bank began to increase non-project lending to assist countries in adjusting their economies to the changes in the world economy brought about by the second oil price increase and the consequences of adverse terms of trade, high interest rates and recession in the industrial countries. But in many countries, these structural adjustment loans were associated with an increase in poverty, which once again brought the issue to the foreground.

Structural Adjustment Lending

The Bank's charter permits non-project lending only in exceptional circumstances. The adverse impact of the second oil price increase in the late 1970s created unusually difficult conditions for many developing countries. Structural adjustment loans were designed to help countries overcome these adverse conditions by providing quickly disbursing aid that helped smooth cuts in consumption and imports, and at the same time made essential policy changes to adjust to worsening external conditions and overcome domestic inflation and fiscal imbalance. The more important elements of policies encouraged under adjustment loans were changes in real foreign exchange rates, introduction of more rational pricing and incentives for production, investment and labor-intensive manufacturing, and improved allocation of government resources, especially in public investment and state enterprises (by putting them on a self-financing footing so they would no longer be a drain on the government budget). These policies have increased export earnings, improved the internal terms of trade in favor of agriculture (where most labor is employed), freed financial resources for private investment by reducing the government budget deficit, and generally enhanced the growth and efficiency of the economy. In a broader sense, they help create an institutional framework that permits society to function in a more democratic fashion.[3]

In painstaking *ex post facto* analysis, the Bank's economists have shown that countries that received adjustment loans and implemented policies associated with these loans generally had better growth performance than other ('non-adjusting') countries.[4] Countries that had the best performance were the exporters of manufactures, such as Brazil, Korea, Morocco, the Philippines, Thailand, Uruguay and Yugoslavia.

In general, structural adjustment lending was most effective in countries that had an institutional framework for policy reform and a high degree of supply response. To allow for essential institutional changes, a much longer-term perspective was required in low-income countries, particularly in SSA, where growth declined, investment decreased in relation to gross output, and inflation worsened – regardless of whether or not the countries adopted adjustment policies. Social indicators (calorie intake, infant mortality, life expectancy, primary school enrollment, etc.) in SSA showed no improvement in the 1980s. (It is ironic that among the strongest early advocates of structural adjustment lending were economists who also had a strong interest in aid to Africa, where structural adjustment lending encountered the greatest obstacles.)[5]

It is important to realize that poverty eradication, or even alleviation, was not an initial objective of adjustment lending. In reality, the poor, especially in urban areas, suffered from the reductions in social expenditures and from the increase in prices of food and of imports as subsidies were removed and exchange rates adjusted. Reduced spending on primary education will have long-lasting negative effects. With contraction in the public sector, many civil servants were laid off and joined the ranks of the poor, as in Senegal. While some rural farmers benefited from higher agricultural incomes, especially if involved in export agriculture (for example, Ghana), most of Africa's small farmers and poor peasants are in fact outside the export economy and are effectively outside the organized economy to which structural adjustment lending was addressed. By the late 1980s, and especially with publication of the 1987 UNICEF report *Adjustment with a Human Face*,[6] it became clear that structural adjustment entailed a set-back for the poor.

Besides the adverse impact on the poor, structural adjustment lending was criticized for other reasons. In some cases the amount of lending was inadequate to cover minimal balance-of-payments change. Projections of economic effects were often overly optimistic. Design and conditionality were too inflexible in the face of different local and institutional circumstances. In other situations, especially in Africa, it became associated with an adversarial and tutorial approach to countries which were deemed not committed to essential policy reform.

Some NGOs opposed the World Bank's macroeconomic conditions. These NGOs would like to see the Bank give primary attention to microeconomic essentials such as human development, job creation, the environment and reduction in military spending. Thus, they would support macroeconomic conditions only to the extent that these conditions help the essential characteristics of development. Macroeconomic conditions can have undesirable side effects; for example, export development can reduce the supply of food for the poor and have unfavorable environmental effects.

In light of these criticisms, the World Bank has sought to redesign its structural adjustment lending. For example, subsidies can be reduced and producer prices raised in a more gradual manner. The consequences for budget expenditures may be compensated for by selective increases in taxation, especially of the wealthy. Social expenditures can be maintained, not cut, when they have a disproportional benefit for the poor, such as medical programs in Korea. Moreover, these expenditures can be targeted toward the poor where this is possible administratively, for example, in Chile. Finally, some countries have undertaken compensatory programs, like small public works in Ghana, Bolivia and Mexico, often with the help of external finance and NGOs. In Senegal, laid-off civil servants have been retrained and relocated.

From Structural Adjustment to Fighting Poverty

With structural adjustment lending underscoring, if not exacerbating, poverty in recipient countries, the Bank once again focused on poverty issues. The *World Development Report 1990* was entirely dedicated to a new poverty-reduction effort that became the center of operations. Bank staff started to undertake country-by-country poverty assessments that ascertain the who, where and why of poverty, and to lay the basis for policy discussions with governments. An increasing proportion of lending was dedicated to fighting poverty directly. At the same time, structural adjustment loans were redesigned to make sure they would not adversely affect the poor; some loans were made to improve the delivery of social services to the poorest population groups (for example, the 1994 loan to Zambia).

The Bank's poverty assessments assemble economic and social data that are essential to a dialogue on poverty issues confronting the countries concerned. These exercises encompass social impact assessments such as described by Jacklyn Cock and E.C. Webster in Chapter 4 of this volume. They identify, from the vantage point of the impact on the poor, shortcomings in policy, planning, sector priorities and investments and the delivery of social services. They consider the impact of long-term economic management on the ability of the poor to build up assets as well as the effects that short-term economic measures, inflation and cuts in public expenditures have on the poor.

The Bank's new poverty initiative was accompanied by greater attention to the role of women in development, under the guidance of President Barber Conable (1986–91). An abundance of facts have made it evident that women suffer the brunt of poverty, so development policies must explicitly address the need for improving the condition of women. The Bank has given greater attention to the education of women, a crucial element in reducing population growth, and to making a higher proportion of loans for human resource development that address women's issues.[7]

These lending operations were guided in part by a program of targeted interventions, loans with the *primary* objective of poverty reduction, especially for women and children, through basic education, productivity of small farmers, basic health conditions, sanitation and water supply, and basic infrastructure in regions of concentrated poverty. Loans in this category amounted to 12–15 per cent of total lending in 1991 and 1992. Moreover, the Bank's lending for human resource development – education, health, family planning and nutrition – has tripled since the early 1980s and is now 15 per cent of total lending.

While these activities mark a turnaround in the Bank's operational orientation, further policy changes are needed to broaden and widen this program. It is clear, moreover, that anti-poverty lending does not proceed in isolation from the Bank's advice on overall development policies. In his address to the Bank's 1994 Annual Conference on Development Economics, World Bank Vice President and Chief Economist for Development Economics Michael Bruno, tied together three critical elements in basic development policy:

- attainment of sustained average per capita growth is a necessary condition for sustained reduction in poverty;

- implementation of an adjustment package of policy reform is a necessary condition for sustained per capita growth; and

- fiscal and monetary restraint is a necessary condition for adjustment.[8]

But these necessary conditions are not sufficient. Economic growth must be combined with direct policies targeted at improving conditions for the poor. At the same time, anti-poverty policies require growing public resources for the financing of various measures. Anti-poverty measures are strongly correlated with the ups and downs of economic growth.

Poverty and the Environment

Environmental policies have opened a new window on anti-poverty action. The poor suffer most from environmental degradation, unclean water and indoor air pollution. Environmental degradation depresses the poor's income by diverting more time to routine tasks, such as collecting firewood, and lowering productivity of natural resources. The poor cannot afford to make investments in natural resources (for example, soil conservation) that produce long-term results. To the contrary, they will tend to overuse resources, as for example the overgrazing of lands in Africa. In Bangladesh, to survive, the poor have deforested the land which in turn has become more prone to flooding.

The Bank was late in helping improve environmental policies and integrating its operations with pro-environment activities, and still has a long way to go. Although many environmental economists and some more general economists (like Kenneth Boulding and Herman Daly) have been aware for decades of the shortcomings of conventional economics, until recently they had little impact on the economic analysis used in the World Bank and other lending institutions.

Once environmental considerations are given explicit recognition, no strand of conventional economic reasoning can remain untouched. For example, exports from Indonesia or Cote d'Ivoire of tropical hardwood logs that take centuries to grow must make allowance for depreciation of natural resources. The foreign exchange earned from such exports is not a net gain. More generally, the national accounts must be adjusted downward. They must allow for resource depletion and for the monetary cost of degradation; these two adjustments alone add up to 13 per cent of net domestic product in Mexico.[9] In addition to making explicit allowance for the causes and consequences of environmental degradation, environmental policies can be linked directly with anti-poverty measures: thus, distribution of food during periods of drought can help avoid the overuse of natural resources.

The Bank has recently begun to link its operations to the concept of sustainable development. Yet, few environmentalists will be fully satisfied with the work of an institution of the complexity, diversity and size of the World Bank. The Bank's environmental activities cut across many sectors, including agriculture and electric power generation and distribution. As a global institution, it is well suited to deal with many problems of a cross-border nature. It is administering the Global Environment Facility and is managing several environmental programs (for example, for the Mediterranean, Black and Baltic Seas and the Danube River Basin). In conjunction with officials in borrowing countries, the Bank is formulating environmental action plans for individual countries that lay the foundations for discussions on their environmental policies. In the year ending June 1993, it lent $2 billion for 24 projects with a primary environmental objective (that is, projects with over 50 per cent of project costs or benefits for environmental improvements).

THE BOTTOM LINE IS PEOPLE

The Bank's economic policy analyses and dialogues often appear far removed from a concern with individuals, although, of course, the recommended economic measures and engineering procedures are presumed to benefit individuals in the end. However, it is easy for a global institution with complex technical operations to overlook its impact on real people, especially the poor. To some extent this shortcoming is being corrected by the work of sociologists in the Bank.

For many years, the Bank has employed social anthropologists to help make individual projects and policy advice more compatible with the interests of people directly affected by the project, especially the poorest, including indigenous peoples. Sociologists point out that a people-based approach can produce results that are fundamentally different from the investment-based and economic policy-based approaches which have been customarily recommended by engineers and economists. They will draw attention to the characteristics of the recipient population, the social organization of people in the project area and the cultural acceptability of the project and its compatibility with the expressed needs and wants of the intended beneficiaries.[10] Following the advice of sociologists, since 1979 the Bank has initiated a policy governing the displacement of people by projects (usually big dams). This policy aims to relocate dislocated people at the same or higher standard of living and to assure that the project design reduces actual displacement as much as possible. (The Bank expects that 2 million people will need to be relocated by its projects *over a 10-year period*. The Bank's activity represents only a small fraction of what goes on in the world: *each year* work starts on some 300 big dams in developing countries that displace around 4 million people, of which the World Bank will fund no more than 3 per cent.) The Bank also seeks to ensure that indigenous people do not suffer adverse effects from new investments: projects must allow for their impact on indigenous people and make sure they are compatible with indigenous rights, customs and culture.

Sociologists have also urged the application of participatory investment planning at the local community level, as practiced in Mexico's huge rural development project, PIDER.[11] But in an institution dominated by the highly quantitative professions of economics and engineering, sociologists still have some way to go before they are fully integrated in the Bank's work. Michael Cernea has written on the institutional implications of the advice of sociologists and has succeeded in gaining explicit recognition of the sociological aspects of certain projects. But his publications do not identify measurable variables of special interest in poverty analysis (for example, the volatility of poverty characteristics depending on weather and growth conditions), nor has he applied sociological reasoning to the relation between military and civilians, a crucial relationship that reaches well beyond the economists' ratio of military expenditures to total government outlays.

However well-crafted the programs of the World Bank, to be effective they must be governed by local efforts. The people directly affected by these programs must be the prime movers in initiating and shaping them. Outsiders' advice can at best support and strengthen the efforts of the countries concerned. All essential facilitating measures – education, health and sanitation and social services – must have roots in home soil. Most of the finance for social and infrastructure programs must in any case come from domestic sources.

Moreover, without the personal motivation and commitment by the poor themselves to a program, no design can be fully effective against the many obstacles that must be overcome, most notably the sheer numbers of people seeking improved conditions, and the interests of those groups that want to maintain the *status quo*. In addition, those who work directly with the poor will understand well the importance of the poor's own motivation and commitment to a program. These people are in fact the critical agents that are able to strengthen the chances for a program's success.

The World Bank, for its part, can intensify its efforts against poverty and provide a broader, longer-term perspective and global leadership. To do so will require policy changes in at least three areas:

- the Bank must give its staff more opportunity to concentrate on situations in individual countries so it can be more in tune with the social and cultural diversity of these countries;

- the Bank must formulate a coherent overall *strategy for poverty eradication*; and

- the Bank will need to mobilize adequate resources for an expanded anti-poverty program which is bound to compete with claims from other important programs.

Dedicate Staff Resources to Fighting Poverty

To be effective in assisting individual countries in their fight against poverty, Bank staff must have intimate knowledge of these countries' culture, institutions, politics and social fabric, as well as the economic and technical ramifications of an anti-poverty program. Staff stationed in resident offices will need to be strengthened and work closely with NGO workers. Staff may have to spend considerable time, even years, working on individual countries or regions to attain an adequate level of knowledge and experience. (Bank personnel management now encourages staff to move to a new assignment after three years, that is, 'move on' in order to move up the corporate ladder. This movement may be seen as in the interest of managerial efficiency, but may run contrary to essential staff concentration on individual countries.)

If the Bank is to be serious about fighting poverty in many diverse country situations (or even diverse regions within individual countries), it must encourage interested staff to stay and to attain the familiarity that is needed for fighting poverty in ways suitable to the social and economic circumstances and conditions of individual countries. More generally, this kind of country-specific knowledge is also essential for obtaining *local participation* in project and program preparation and execution.

At present, the Bank's poverty assessments are technically competent reports, but they are highly standardized and make little allowance for countries' cultural and social characteristics. That must change if the Bank is to put flesh on its skeleton models and reach genuine undertakings with the countries concerned and assist them in making the social, political, economic and financial commitments necessary for effective action. The Bank has a strong professional basis for making these changes. As is evident from the Bank's research, economists in the Bank and elsewhere are adapting development economics to the realities of anti-poverty action.[12]

Towards an Anti-Poverty Strategy

Beginning with the *World Development Report 1990*, the Bank has done a competent and professional job in studying the dimensions of poverty, indicating basic measures to overcome it, mapping out different policy options, instructing staff how to proceed and laying the base for dialogue with member countries. But all this does not add up to a overall strategy; so far, the Bank has refrained from formulating such a strategy.

In this respect, the Bank's poverty reduction program is reminiscent of its lack of a strategy to deal with the debt crisis, which dominated the development scene in the 1980s. In the 1960s, Bank staff had already constructed a comprehensive theoretical and conceptual framework for dealing with debt in a development context.[13] It also had the data essential for tracking the debt build-up process, as well as in-depth knowledge of the economic situation of debtor countries, including medium-term projections of their balance-of-payments situation and external indebtedness. Its country analyses gave the Bank an undisputed insight into the nature and seriousness of the debt situation in the 1970s and early 1980s. But instead of laying out a strategy, first for avoiding, and then for overcoming the crisis once it burst upon the development scene, the Bank's management took a back seat. The Bank reacted only to the piecemeal initiatives of other players, mainly the main creditor countries, even though these initiatives did not begin to measure up to the dimensions of the problem as understood by World Bank economists.

In contrast to its approach to the debt crisis, the Bank has now set out to pursue poverty reduction as a central element of its operations. It has the tools to formulate an overall strategy which can give the world a new vision of what can and cannot be accomplished and can enable the Bank to provide badly needed leadership in this area. At a minimum, an overall strategy would:

- Set forth the objective of eradicating poverty in different types of developing countries and in the countries of Eastern Europe and the former Soviet Union.

- Specify the policies needed to reach the objective
  - by the countries themselves;
  - by the international community, including financial assistance for country programs and investments for overcoming poverty and associated operations in related areas such as environmental programs of particular interest to the poor; and
  - by the industrial countries, particularly in the area of trade.

- Clarify the time frame in which the Bank expects the recipient countries, the industrial countries and the international community to work.

- Indicate the resources and sacrifices required to reach the objective, on the part of the countries taking action, and in capital, financial and technical resources on the part of the World Bank, other lenders and bilateral donors.

- Present regular *performance progress reports* on what lenders, industrial countries and the international community are doing and on what progress is being achieved in poverty eradication. These reports would assess the performance under the Bank's and other programs. They would do for the poverty eradication program what the Wapenhans report[14] expects the Bank to do on the impact of projects that have been completed, and what the Bank is currently planning to do on performance under adjustment lending. Given the comprehensive nature of taking stock of performance in poverty eradication, the Bank, in exercising a catalytic function, may want to obtain cooperation from other institutions. However, it is important that it assumes essential leadership in this effort which so clearly falls in its domain.

In the framework of such a broader strategy, anti-poverty criteria should be applied to all the Bank's work, from the formulation of country assistance programs to the selection and design of projects, and be built into project conditions. In this way the Bank's poverty assessments would be carried out for all project undertakings.

Mobilizing Adequate Financial Resources

The Bank's poverty eradication program will have to compete for resources with other important programs such as the reconstruction and rehabilitation of states in transition from socialism, environmental and infrastructure lending, continued major programs in China, India, Latin America and the Middle East and special new programs in the former Israeli-occupied territories, South Africa and hopefully soon the republics of the former Yugoslavia and the salvation of the Amazonian rain forest. Moreover, poverty eradication will become more ambitious. For example, poverty eradication will have to extend to countries which still have regions with deep-seated poverty even though they have successfully followed policies of stabilization and adjustment. These countries have a greatly strengthened economic and financial base from which to attack poverty, and, moreover, attract substantial amounts of private capital. But private capital does not deal with Chiapas in Mexico and similar situations in Thailand and Venezuela, not to mention countries like Brazil which have lagged in adjustment. The Bank will have to extend its poverty lending to countries such as these if it is to lead a truly comprehensive effort against poverty. In this respect, the anti-poverty program should extend well beyond assistance to the poorest countries.[15]

It is not unreasonable to assume that the Bank will be able to mobilize the resources necessary to undertake a more ambitious anti-poverty program of this kind, and that it will get cooperation from other lenders, both multilateral and bilateral. Given the other claims on its resources, the International Bank for Reconstruction and Development (IBRD) may well have to seek an increase in its capital. Many countries that are creditworthy for IBRD loans are candidates for anti-poverty assistance, both technical and financial, and in countries where poverty rates are in the upper ranges, continued International Development Association (IDA) financing will be necessary. In the end, many parties will have to collaborate if the global community is to reach the goals of a realistic poverty eradication program.

CONCLUSION

Fighting poverty is and should be a primary objective of the World Bank, but it has sometimes been put on the backburner, as in the first half of the 1980s. This may happen again. Looking ahead, one can only hope that the Bank will persist in objectives of the early 1990s, and will broaden its programs as suggested. Strong and committed leadership will be essential if this is to happen.

Notes

1. David Beckmann, 'Recent Experience and Emerging Trends' in Samuel Paul and Arturo Israel (eds), *Nongovernmental Organizations and the World Bank* (Washington, DC: World Bank, 1991) p. 135.
2. Different World Bank staff meet with a variety of NGOs at different times, most formally at the annual meeting of the NGO-World Bank Committee, formed in 1982 and composed of senior Bank managers and 26 NGO representatives from around the world, three-fifths

from developing countries. See Beckmann, 'Recent Experience and Emerging Trends', p. 139.

3. For reviews of structural adjustment, see James H. Weaver, 'What is Structural Adjustment' in Daniel M. Schydlowsky (ed.), *Structural Adjustment: Retrospect and Prospect* (Westport: Praeger, 1995) pp. 3–17.

4. See World Bank, *Adjustment Lending Policies for Sustainable Growth*, Policy and Research Series No. 14 (Washington, DC: World Bank, 1990).

5. See, for example, Stanley Please, *The Hobbled Giant: Essays on the World Bank* (Boulder: Westview Press, 1984).

6. Giovanni A. Cornia, Richard Jolly and Frances Stewart (eds), *Adjustment With a Human Face – Protecting the Vulnerable and Promoting Growth*, A UNICEF Study (Oxford: Clarendon Press, 1987).

7. See, for example, World Bank, *The World Bank Annual Report 1993* (Washington, DC: World Bank, 1993) p. 44.

8. Michael Bruno, 'Development Issues in a Changing World: New Lessons, Old Debates, Open Question' from the World Bank Annual Conference on Development Economics, 1994.

9. Andrew Steer and Ernst Lutz, 'Measuring Environmentally Sustainable Development' in *Finance and Development*, vol. 30, no. 4, (1993) pp. 20–3.

10. Michael M. Cernea, 'The Sociologist's Approach to Sustainable Development' in *Finance and Development*, vol. 30, no. 4 (1993) pp. 11–13.

11. Michael M. Cernea, 'Using Knowledge from Social Science in Development Projects', *World Bank Discussion Paper no. 114* (Washington, DC: World Bank, 1991) p. 33.

12. See, for example, 'Proceedings of the January 1994 Meetings of the American Economic Association' in *The American Economic Review*, vol. 84, no. 2 (May 1994) pp. 211–65.

13. See Dragoslav Avramovic, *Economic Growth and External Debt* (Baltimore: Johns Hopkins University Press, 1964).

14. World Bank Portfolio Management Task Force, *Effective Implementation: Key to Development Impact* (Washington, DC: World Bank, 1992). This report is known as the Wapenhans Report after the director of the task force, Willi A. Wapenhans. A study of Bank projects, it found that an increasing portion were not performing according to the Bank's criteria for success, that is, earning a 10 per cent rate of return.

15. Barend A. de Vries, *Remaking the World Bank* (Washington, DC: The Seven Locks Press, 1987) Chapter 5.

4 Environmental and Social Impact Assessments

Jacklyn Cock and E.C. Webster

INTRODUCTION

Many development projects are flawed by two factors: first, a neglect of the social and political impacts of planned interventions, and second, inadequate levels of public participation. These problems can be addressed through threading social impact assessments (SIAs) through all planning, monitoring and evaluation stages of the development process. Social impact assessment (SIA) is a crucial means of ensuring that local communities can participate in decisions about developments which affect them. Since quantitative and technical forms of investigation often fail to reflect the cultural and social concerns of indigenous communities, SIA should utilize a mix of innovative research strategies. These research strategies must emphasize disaggregation and distributional impacts. Gender is a crucial aspect of this social disaggregation, as women are frequently excluded from formal decision-making structures. SIA therefore needs to implement a gender lens. After analyzing three case studies, this chapter reviews more theoretical aspects of SIAs and environmental impact assessments (EIAs) and concludes by arguing that there is a need for participants to come together to draw up a policy framework such as the newly adopted Reconstruction and Development Programme adopted by the Government of National Unity in South Africa.

THREE CASE STUDIES

The Thaba-Tseka Project in Lesotho

The consequence of the failure to take account of social, cultural and political factors may be illustrated with reference to the Thaba-Tseka Project in Lesotho. This project originated in 1975 as a livestock and 'range management' scheme and became a very expensive and complex 'integrated rural development' project.

It failed for two main reasons. First, the project ignored the most important fact about the history and present context of Lesotho, its dependence on its highly industrialized neighbor, South Africa. One result of this dependence is the extent to which its population subsists on wages remitted by labor migrants in that country rather than on local agriculture.

Second, the project ignored the pivotal cultural function of cattle. The Thaba-Tseka Project's aim to commercialize cattle-keeping collapsed in the face of the function of cattle as 'place-holders' for absent men engaged in mine labor in South Africa. Cattle represent a source of security for migrant laborers who invest portions of their earnings in them. At the same time, cattle provide a symbolic link between absent younger men and the older men who have retired from migrant labor and who dominate relations in the rural villages where the former must secure their futures.

The whole logic of the Thaba-Tseka project was to encourage the commercialization of cattle transactions. In his 1990 study,[1] James Ferguson argues that although male Basotho[2] sell cattle, they do so out of despair in conditions of poverty. In general, they continue to resist using cattle as means of cash accumulation. The ownership of cattle thus has involved a different, non-capitalist economic logic involved with community, security and prestige. This prestige is often resented by the owners' wives, who see the retention of too many beasts – especially those in poor conditions – as a source of misery for their families: '[n]on-commercial attitudes towards stock-keeping and an anti-market ethic where livestock are concerned are important parts of the local economic system, rooted in the network of local power relations generated in a labor reserve economy'.[3]

Overall, the planners of the Thaba-Tseka project failed to take account of two kinds of indigenous knowledge: the different world views, meanings and understandings of the local people, and the systematized knowledge of southern African researchers.

The incorporation of these forms of knowledge would have led to a very different outcome:

> Had the planners of the Thaba-Tseka project thought to incorporate the social, material and cultural significance of cattle to this migrant-labor dependent population, they might never have attempted to implement the programme they did. In the end, however, their efforts failed, effectively because they ignored the cultural structures of adaptation to such historical dependence which were so successful that the development project could not easily undermine them.[4]

In general, the question of development is a contentious one: 'Efforts to influence socioeconomic change are seldom neutral ... [and] the process is highly political and conditioned by constellations of power.'[5] Ferguson has provided a cogent critique of development which imposes a model on the local population without prior investigation of their real needs and wants. Because of unequal power relations, even well-intentioned interventions may produce 'unintended yet instrumental elements in a resultant constellation that has the effect of expanding the exercise of a particular sort of ... power while simultaneously exerting a powerful depoliticizing effect'.[6] Thus development without participation through all stages of a project has the potential to undermine those it is meant to benefit.

This is why Ferguson understands development as a form of statism, the domain of Popper's[7] holistic social planners committed to large-scale change from above, that is implemented by authoritarian, centralized systems.[8] Ferguson is highly skeptical of the development industry, but he does suggest two conditions for the involvement of the thoughtful social scientist in development. The first condition is that the social scientist should only become involved in development where it is possible to identify interests, organizations and groupings that clearly represent movements of empowerment.[9] The second condition is that demand exists on the side of those working for their own empowerment for the specific skills which the expert has.

Harmony Gold Mine

An attempt was made to meet these two conditions in a study of downsizing at Harmony Gold Mine in South Africa. This case study illustrates the importance of social factors, including the subjective perceptions of affected communities, as well as the need for extensive participation and close cooperation between social scientists and organized groupings from these communities.

The study focuses on the social impacts of down-scaling at Harmony Gold Mine in the Orange Free State region of South Africa. The Harmony policy is part of a general trend whereby South Africa's gold-mining companies are shifting to a smaller, more productive labor force. Until 1988, Harmony employed nearly 32,000 workers. By early 1993 it had cut its work force to about 14,586, less than half its previous strength.[10]

The study was designed with a three-pronged approach. First, unstructured interviews were held with members of the community – members of the white business community, town officials and mine management, and with officials of the local association of township residents (Medoling's Civil Association), shaft stewards from the National Union of Mineworkers, hostel residents and residents of the informal settlement which has grown up on the edge of the township since 1989. Because the study was particularly interested in exploring the relationship between changing labor policies and the rise of this informal settlement, the researchers surveyed a representative, random sample of 80 households using structured, open-ended questionnaires. Finally, ten retrenched Harmony workers were interviewed in Maseru, Lesotho about the impact of stabilization and down-scaling on their households.[11]

The study found that for communities that depend on the mining industry – from local businesses which served mine employees to households in Lesotho which survive on migrants' wages – the social impact has been devastating. The burden has fallen hardest on those with the least resources: black, less skilled miners and their families.

The study points towards the need for planned down-scaling which would allow the state, mining companies, trade unions, and political organizations jointly to plan some alternative economic strategy for the region, while allowing the region's population to survive the interim period. Thus, this study seems to support the argument of National Union of Mineworkers in South Africa that 'the scale and intensity of the suffering of people that has been brought on by the crisis in the mining industry calls out for state intervention'.[12]

The St Lucia Mining Controversy

The consequence of the failures to disaggregate the community, to apply a gender lens, or to secure extensive participation may be illustrated with reference to the largest environmental impact assessment ever undertaken in Southern Africa: an investigation of the impacts predicted for two possible land-use options for the St Lucia area of Natal, South Africa – mining or ecotourism.

Since 1989, a controversy has raged over Richards Bay Minerals' (RBM) proposal to mine a considerable amount of dune land on the Eastern Shores of St Lucia. RBM has a large mine and processing plant at the Richards Bay harbor, some 25 kilometers (16 miles) south of the St Lucia dunes. The company wants to expand its operations into the St Lucia dunes and strip-mine them for heavy metals. Company officials estimated that deposits of titanium and other heavy minerals that lie in the dune sands are worth some 5 billion Rand (US $1.5 billion),[13] and could provide 160 jobs. However, there are no promises that local people will benefit from these employment opportunities or whether they will be paid living wages. Richards Bay Minerals' record on this question, in other ventures, is not a strong one. Furthermore, these jobs are not sustainable, as the mining and rehabilitation will only last a maximum of 20 years. Most of the profits, taxes and royalties will flow out of the region. The R8 million ($2.4 million) per year which RBM offers to invest in social responsibility programs is simply derisory.

The Natal Parks Board maintains that mining will pose a significant threat to the great variety of plant and animal species that exist on the dunes and in the wetlands around St Lucia, and that St Lucia is a prime site for ecotourism which has the potential to provide more jobs than mining for a longer period of time without destroying the ecology of the dunes and the estuary. However, the record of the Natal Parks Board on community participation is not strong.

The St Lucia EIA is a landmark document in South Africa. But it is flawed by an inadequate treatment of social impacts and the exclusion of local people from full participation. Democratically elected representatives of the community were not included on any of the review and monitoring bodies established or recommended by the EIA. Local people and their representatives were not even included in the initial list of interested and affected parties. This omission becomes even more glaring when one notes that the US Embassy was identified as an interested and affected party.

Criticisms made by a number of commentators were that the views of only a small proportion of the South African public were presented in the environmental impact report, that the views of local people had not been adequately reflected, and that the attitudes of local communities needed to be canvassed and submitted to a review panel. To address these concerns, the 'Rural Liaison Programme' was subsequently established.

This program also failed to achieve any deep and extensive process of consultation since the methodology employed was extremely restrictive. The research was limited to employed workers, traditional tribal authority structures and one Inkatha[14] official and mainly took the form of community meetings convened by the chief. It was argued that these forums were the only option available.[15] It was clear that the local power relations severely constrained the discussions since it was acknowledged that 'it would not be possible for participants in these meetings to express views contrary to those of the traditional elite'.[16]

Important social groups such as youth and women were excluded from this research process since 'group meetings were dominated by men, thus suppressing the voices of women'.[17] No attempt was made to provide a voice for those women through in-depth interviews of key informants or through group discussions with the members of organizations such as church groups, savings clubs or burial societies. Nor was any attempt made to involve young people through their political, sporting or other voluntary associations. Since the limitations have been clear, other more qualitative and participatory approaches should have been considered, such as in-depth semi-structured interviews with key informants, oral histories, participant observation, focus groups, or participatory methods such as community report cards or mapping exercises. Nevertheless, the final report concludes:

> Participation by members of local communities, especially Zulu-speaking communities was limited. Nonetheless, the early interviews by Zingle of members of these communities and the Rural Liaison Programme initiated later at the request of the Review Panel did redress this imbalance to a significant degree.[18]

While it is important to acknowledge the pioneering nature of the St Lucia EIA and the research difficulties involved, these statements do not stand up to critical scrutiny. The lack of adequate consultation with the affected communities is serious. It also extends to the environmental lobby and is a potential source of alienation from the whole issue of environmental protection.[19] The majority of black workers at RBM's existing plant belong to the National Union of Mineworkers. They refuse to support the company's plans to expand production into the dunes but have also expressed reservations about the conservation lobby's failure to consult them during the controversy:

> We are sensitive to the growing environmental awareness in this country. But there is one question that our members at RBM are asking and that is: Why all of a sudden is there all this activity and protest to save animals when there was no reaction at the time when people faced removal? Is it because this time, there is a threat to the survival of a favorite holiday resort for whites? None of the environmental organizations have consulted us about the issue and some members are wondering if these groups think it is more important to save insects and animals while we have to sacrifice jobs and wages.[20]

The question at the core of the St Lucia controversy is: Who would benefit from mining or ecotourism? The answer depends on extensive community participation and a thorough investigation of social impacts.

Clearly, much wider participation and a deeper and more extensive involvement of social scientists in this research would have been desirable. However, it is not only social scientific research skills that are important to involve in the process of investigation; a sociological analysis of the social context within which this report was commissioned by the Department of Environmental Affairs and paid for by Richards Bay Minerals would be illuminating. The power relations operating in this context certainly privilege mining capital and exclude indigenous communities who lack vote and voice.

No one is disputing the need to develop the St Lucia region and increase the income and opportunities of the 850,000 inhabitants. Both the mining and the ecotourism options would contribute to the development of the region, but in dramatically different ways. To understand the significance of these differences, it is critical to thread community participation and a consideration of social impacts through all stages of the planning, monitoring and evaluation process involved in any development.

While the South African economy is heavily dependent on mining, tourism in South Africa is receiving increasing attention as a source of jobs and foreign exchange. 'Were it not for the violence ... tourism could equal the contribution of the mining sector to South Africa's GNP.'[21] About 1.7 million visitors come to South Africa each year. This earns some R2.5 billion ($750 million) in foreign exchange and provides some 300,000 people with jobs, about 1 out of every 14 actively employed people in South Africa.[22] A government White Paper on Tourism released in 1992 asserts that more than 89 per cent of foreign tourists (excluding those from Africa) come to South Africa in the first instance to enjoy the country's scenery, flora and fauna.

It is possible that ecotourism could become a major source of rural development in South Africa. SIA has a significant potential for mitigating the adverse impacts this could involve. The creation and maintenance of game parks, nature reserves or other types of protected areas have significant impacts on local communities. Adverse impacts may in the future (as in the past) include relocation where people are physically removed, restricted access to resources such as firewood or grazing land, the breakdown of traditional patterns of authority and reciprocity, and the disruption of traditional ways of life such as removal from ancestral burial grounds.

These 'adverse impacts can generate hostility on the part of the affected people which is dysfunctional to the protected area itself. Local resentment can easily be manifested in poaching and acts of vandalism such as the deliberate setting of fires'.[23] In these circumstances, SIA could play a major role, both in creating and monitoring solutions to traditional conflicts between local communities and protected areas and in assisting in the implementation of more cooperative community-based forms of management which benefit local people. The need for such an approach is dramatically evident in the St Lucia mining controversy.

ELEMENTS AND ASPECTS OF IMPACT ASSESSMENTS

The first case study, the Thaba-Tseka project, illustrated the dangers of planned interventions that do not take sufficient account of local cultural and economic conditions. It underlines the need for social researchers and planners to work closely with organizations that clearly represent movements of empowerment. The second case study illustrates an attempt to do this, and the third study demonstrates the need for planned interventions in partnership with local organizations. All of these problems can be addressed through threading environmental and social impact assessment through all planning, monitoring and evaluation stages of the development process.

Social Impact Assessment

Social impact assessment is something of a hybrid: a method of policy analysis, a planning tool and an investigation of the social impact of development plans, programmes and projects. It involves different research methods and techniques to investigate at least four major categories of impacts:

- demographic (for example, population changes, displacement and relocation problems);

- socioeconomic (for example, changes in employment patterns, systems of land tenure, income levels);

- institutional (for example, changed demands on local services); and

- community (for example, changes in social networks and levels of social cohesion).[24]

SIA can provide better information for decision making.[25] It offers great potential for integrating scientific policy analysis into a democratic political process and is a means of democratically integrating science and values. It can display the implications of a policy option in a form which generates focused rational, informed debate.[26]

Environmental Impact Assessment

The neglect of environmental impacts is a global problem. It is now widely recognized that achieving a balance between environmental protection and economic development means careful planning. A crucial part of such planning is the identification, analysis and evaluation of the anticipated outcomes of any particular development project. To achieve this end, a system of EIA has developed in the countries of the North.

But the system is imperfect: EIA has not always paid sufficient attention to the likely social, cultural, or economic effects on indigenous communities. Generally, the contribution of social science has been beneath its potential. Although environmental impact statements are required by law in the United States to make 'integrated use' of social science expertise, 'to date they have generally failed to do so ... Over 12,000 EIAs have now been prepared, but in most cases, the input of social sciences has not even been visible in the documents themselves.'[27.]

> Even though all major development projects are now required to follow a prescribed procedure to prepare an Environmental Impact Assessment, a closer examination of the content of a typical EIA suggests that the definition of 'environment' remains heavily biophysical and any assessment of impacts on traditions, life styles, interpersonal relations, institutions and living arrangements of residents in the impacted communities is conspicuously absent.[28]

SIA and EIA are necessarily interdisciplinary. This means establishing and maintaining effective working relationships between representatives of different disciplines working in research teams. These teams do not have 'the luxury of a common theory and methodology'.[29] Social scientists have often experienced difficulty in these interdisciplinary settings: 'Social scientists, as part of interdisciplinary research teams, often experience role ambiguity and conflict, which usually reduces the contribution they can make to program success.'[30] To be effective, the social scientist needs to have a clear sense of professional identity, an understanding of the relevance of social data in development programs, and the ability to communicate this to physical scientists, technicians and engineers.

Public Participation

SIA is an effective tool for informing the public, encouraging their participation in policy debate and reducing the disproportionate influence of special interests groups in the decision-making process. It can also provide a voice for indigenous communities who are most likely to be affected by a planned development but lack power and resources.[31]

Consequently, SIA is increasingly valued as a means of mobilizing public involvement and participation in the development process: 'The essentially political function of assessment is increasingly recognized as predominant over any limited technical orientation.'[32] In this participatory approach, the emphasis is on community development and the decision-making process; on bringing about social change by creating an active, informed public through a structured research process.

This participatory approach recognizes the value orientation of the social researcher and the necessarily ambiguous or subjective nature of studies of social phenomena. This is in contrast to the elitist or technocratic approach to EIA which emphasizes the product developed by a detached and objective social scientist. This technocratic approach centers on planners as decision makers assuming the role of experts with unchallenged authority bestowed upon them by their exclusive technical knowledge and detached scientific stance.

Much development planning in South Africa is elitist in this sense. In the past, EIAs have emphasized objective data, ignored social tensions and given only a token nod to public involvement in the process. EIAs have generally not been conducted around conservation projects, but rather around major capital investment projects. An emphasis on public participation is especially important given the history of exclusion of black South Africans from conservation. It is part of a wider process of democratization. Participation is a requisite of democracy. A society is democratic if and only if all members can participate in an informed way in discussions of political and policy issues. This condition is difficult to meet when technical analysis is the priority. As has been pointed out, two problems impacting democracy result. First, parts of the discussion become unintelligible to non-specialists. Second, because technical analysis is viewed as scientific, it carries great legitimacy, which is a source of power.[33] The outcome is a dependence on experts rather than full participation, a state of affairs which often serves the interests of those in power.

Public participation involves three aspects:

- education, or the dispersal of information to the public;

- the provision of opportunities for interaction between the informed public and the authorities; and

- the participation of these publics in decision making.

91

A criticism often levelled at participation exercises is that they are elitist in that only a small, interested and powerful segment of the population is involved. Overall, the issue of participation depends on an understanding of power relations. It is in this sense that SIA cannot be separated from the wider political context:

> SIA by its nature, is part of the planning process, a process that is embedded in the political system. Inevitably projects or programs favor one sector of the society, often at the expense of others. ... [I]f the project threatens the powerless but benefits those in power, it is highly probable that it will be enacted despite dire predictions by a social impact analysis. Efforts to develop appropriate methodologies without confronting the political issues can only legitimize the projects, and ultimately, the status quo.[34]

Participation without power is an empty notion:

> If a population has enough power, it can set the terms for its own participation, and it can influence the direction of or even stop a particular project that is generated from the outside. To create participation in the absence of such power is a key dilemma for SIA and for development projects. Many development projects are, in fact, undertaken to enhance the circumstances of the powerful, with little concern for the consequences for the powerless. In these circumstances, SIA is ineffective as a means for reform and can only serve to legitimize the status quo.[35]

The social scientist has a crucial role to play in the analysis of power relations. Public participation in SIA does not automatically provide an avenue for the empowerment of disadvantaged communities. Such empowerment depends on grass-roots mobilization. In their insightful discussion of the limits of SIA, Gagnon, Hirsch and Howitt[36] point out that local voices are rarely heard on environmental controversies. Often, effective opposition depends on a coalition of diverse interests which link pressure at local and international levels. Gagnon *et al.* argue that 'nominally unified and powerful actors' such as statutory authorities and transnational corporations often 'exhibit a range of internal tensions and divisions that created opportunities for locally empowering interventions ... Recognition of divided power is a source of empowerment in terms of viable and acceptable responses to affected groups.'[37] The identification of different social groups is necessary to understand that these social divisions inevitably involve conflict.

SIA is sometimes seen as a technocratic means to avoid conflict. In fact, conflict is inevitable and even positive. It can promote participation, and 'conflict at a certain level improves both the quantity and quality of information'.[38] It has been argued that SIA can promote a win-win approach to conflict:

> If a project proponent can be persuaded to realize that social dissatisfaction can affect long-term viability and security of investments, before decisions are made instead of retrospectively, it is possible for many proposals to be transformed into more locally acceptable forms, from which a wider range of impacted groups derive some direct and meaningful benefits (for example, acceptable compensation, training and employment guarantees, associated educational, infrastructural and other investments valued by the affected groups) ... While an SIA that adopts a participatory-emancipatory orientation to disputes does not avoid conflict, it facilitates win-win outcomes, through territorially based interventions.[39]

It is important to adopt an eclectic approach to research strategies: 'Wholesale adoption of one methodology over another should be avoided ... there is no right one – they depend on the particular development situation.'[40] There are a great many research techniques available, with some 85 different techniques listed as relevant to SIA, including surveys and questionnaires, scenario writing, social indicators, in-depth interviews with key informants, community report cards, focus groups, and mapping and modelling which allow for maximum participation.

Gender Lens

The emphasis on disaggregation and distributional impacts is pivotal. Gender is another crucial aspect of social disaggregation, as women are a social group who are frequently absent (for a range of reasons) from formal decision-making structures. Gender is a crucial aspect of social disaggregation as women are differently affected and often excluded from formal decision-making structures, as the St Lucia case study illustrates. Thus, there is a need for gender planning. This is based on a distinction between practical and strategic gender needs, as initially formulated by Caroline

Moser,[41] affirming both the necessity of addressing the hardships imposed on women by their gendered roles, as well as the necessity to transform gender relations. The importance of a gender analysis is also illustrated by the Thaba-Tseka Project. Women constitute the poorest section of the region but were automatically excluded from the project because of the exclusive male control over cattle.

Research is needed to explore the general nature of down-scaling. Most women in rural areas that send men to the mines depend on male remittances for cash income; many others have been abandoned, leading to high percentages of female-headed households throughout the region. Further research needs to focus on the way women from these 'sending areas' have experienced the decline in mining employment, the kind of survival strategies they have chosen and the way they understand the alternatives facing them in the future.

Technical, quantitative forms of investigation often fail to reflect the cultural and social concerns of indigenous communities, even when large-scale projects have been undertaken on their land and affect their lifestyles through, for example, depletion of fisheries, scarcity of game for hunting and so on. It could be argued that the qualitative approach may be more important when reporting SIAs on indigenous cultures. Quantitative methods such as questionnaires and surveys are very impersonal; they can fracture experience and distort people's understandings by forcing their responses into pre-set categories. Furthermore, they have the tendency of relating to individuals as atomized entities. The traditional quantitative approach often relies on formal leadership structures in data collection, which means that, because of the leadership's patriarchal nature, the voices of women are ignored.

Even in democratic political contexts, '[i]t is difficult for indigenous voices to be heard when there is a cultural gap between them and decision makers.'[42] Some forms of SIAs have used anthropological approaches to document indigenous attitudes, perceptions and aspirations, and to communicate them to decision makers.[43]

The Need for an Integrated Approach to Planning

The need for an integrated approach to environment and development at the policy, planning and management levels is articulated in Agenda 21, as adopted by the Plenary of the United Nations Conference on Environment and Development in Rio de Janeiro on June 14, 1992. To achieve this end, it proposed the following objectives:

- to conduct a national review of economic, sectoral and environmental policies, strategies and plans to ensure the progressive integration of environmental and developmental issues;

- to strengthen institutional structures to allow the full integration of environmental and developmental issues, at all levels of decision making;

- to develop or improve mechanisms to facilitate the involvement of concerned individuals, groups and organizations in decision making at all levels; and

- to establish domestically determined procedures to integrate environment and development issues in decision making.

CONCLUSION

This chapter argues that in all stages of the development process – planning, assessment and investigation, decision, implementation, and monitoring – social factors are crucial and require the involvement of social scientists. Social scientists should be included in the design of the EIA, especially at the scoping stage, which lays the foundation for the extent of public participation. Social scientists should utilize both analytical and research skills to produce reliable empirical data that is theoretically and historically informed. For example, the identification and analysis of different social groupings affected by a proposed policy, program or project is critical and requires social disaggregation. Without this, there is the danger of scientists assuming that communities are homogeneous entities which have monolithic, discernible goals which can be measured. It is important to avoid over-generalized concepts of the community and instead to disaggregate the impact assessment by location, income, gender, occupation and ethnicity, to identify the ways in which different social groupings will be differently affected by a proposed policy, program or project.

This chapter has demonstrated the need to anticipate the social implications of any policy intervention. The Harmony case study demonstrates the need for planning, especially for a planned down-scaling, rather than the kind of *ad hoc* process

currently underway. It also demonstrates the need for a democratic state to formulate a policy framework which prioritizes
social needs.

Such a framework has been developed by the African National
Congress, the dominant partner in the newly elected Government
of National Unity in South Africa, in its Reconstruction and
Development Programme (RDP). Five basic principles underlie
the economic and political philosophy of this program:

- the legacy of apartheid cannot be overcome in piecemeal fashion and requires coordinated policies;

- people's basic needs are the RDP's point of departure;

- the massive divisions in South African society require nation
  building, and therefore cannot be attacked piecemeal;

- growth and redistribution are interdependent; and

- these four principles are all dependent on the principle of
  democratization.

It is this last principle that points to a potentially different political culture from that of either statism or Popper's notion of
piecemeal social engineering.[44] The authors of the RDP call this
alternative approach 'participatory democracy'.

The first step in this direction was taken in drawing up the
document. It grew out of the forces struggling for the transformation of South African society and the demands of ordinary
members of the African National Congress (ANC) and its allies
in the trade unions, civic associations and other social movements
as well as many policy researchers linked to the ANC. It was
debated in many different conferences both inside the ANC and
amongst its allies. The sixth draft was made public, and a range
of actors outside the ANC alliance were consulted and invited to
comment on it. This open and transparent approach to policy
formulation is unique in South Africa's history.

However, the real test of the effectiveness of the program
will lie in its implementation. Democracy, the program argues,
is not confined to periodic elections: 'It is, rather, an active
process enabling everyone to contribute to reconstruction and
development.'[45]

To democratize and make the next government efficient is a

daunting task, especially as this new government will be crucially dependent – at least in the short to medium term – on public servants trained under the apartheid state. But the authors' intention is quite clearly not to rely on the state alone to deliver the new South Africa. The state will be the institution that supports and coordinates the formulation and implementation of social policy. The program envisages a partnership between the key actors involved in policy formulation and implementation: '[t]he democratic order we envisage must foster a wide range of institutions of participatory democracy in partnership with civil society on the basis of informed and empowered citizens.'[46]

This is what is different in the process of transition in South Africa from that of Latin America or Eastern Europe. Apartheid did not decline because of a change of heart among the rulers. Its demise was in large part a response to organized pressure from below.

The anti-apartheid struggle created powerful social movements and community-based organizations that the RDP conceives of as 'a major asset in the effort to democratize and develop our society'. The estimated 230 forums that grew up as institutions of transitional legitimacy during the early 1990s are mentioned as potential partners. Arguably, these forums are unique among those countries which are undergoing transition from authoritarianism. The program also envisages an important role for the estimated 15,000 non-profit, non-governmental organizations (NGOs). These organizations such as trade unions, NGOs and forums give concrete meaning to participation.

It was the struggles of anti-apartheid activists that led to the decline of the apartheid state. If statism is to be avoided in the new South Africa, then it needs to take seriously the RDP's aim of democratizing society, and not only the state. This will require giving all the organizations of civil society – the trade unions, the civic associations, women's organizations, youth and student organizations, the churches, the universities – a wider role in policy formulation and implementation.

This implies that SIA can only be an effective vehicle of participation in a society where the organs of civil society are strengthened. Whether this is achieved in South Africa depends on struggles over the implementation of the RDP over the next five years.

Notes

1. James Ferguson, *The Anti-Politics Machine: Development, Depoliticiza-tion and Bureaucratic Power in Lesotho* (Cambridge: Cambridge University Press, 1990).
2. Basotho are nationals of Lesotho.
3. Ferguson, *The Anti-Politics Machine*, p. 179.
4. A. Spiegel, 'The Anti-Politics Machine: Development, Depoliticiza-tion and Bureaucratic Power by James Ferguson' in *Social Dynamics*, vol. 18, no. 2 (1992) p. 102.
5. W. Derman and S. Whiteford (eds), *Social Impact Analysis and Development in the Third World* (Boulder: Westview Press, 1985) p. 3.
6. Ferguson, *The Anti-Politics Machine*, p. 21.
7. Karl Popper, *The Poverty of Historicism* (London: Routledge and Paul Kegan, 1957).
8. D. Bobrow and J. Dryzek, *Policy Analysis by Design* (Pittsburgh: University of Pittsburgh Press, 1987).
9. These notions of empowerment and participation must be subjected to critical scrutiny. M. Rahnema, 'Participation' in W. Sachs (ed.) *The Development Dictionary, A Guide to Knowledge as Power* (London: Zed Books, 1993) p. 126, warns that participation can become 'a deceptive myth or a dangerous tool for manipulation'. M. Murphree, 'Communities as Institutions for Resource Management', Paper presented at the National Conference on Environment and Development, Maputo, Mozambique, October 7–11, 1991, p. 5, warns that participation can mean 'the co-optation of local elites and leadership for exogenously derived programmes'.
10. G. Seidman, 'Shafted: The Social Impact of Down-Scaling on the Free State Goldfields' in *South African Sociological Review*, vol. 5, no. 2 (1993) pp. 14–34.
11. Seidman, 'Shafted: The Social Impact of Down-Scaling on the Free State Goldfields', p. 14.
12. National Union of Mineworkers (1992) p. 9, as cited in Seidman, 'Shafted: The Social Impact of Down-Scaling on the Free State Goldfields', p. 14.
13. One South African Rand (R) equals about 0.3 US dollars. Stated otherwise, there are about 3.3 Rand to the dollar.
14. The Inkatha Freedom Party is a political organization.
15. Council for Scientific and Industrial Research (CSIR), *Environmental Impact Assessment: Eastern Shores of Lake St Lucia*, vol. 3, Environmental Impact Report (Pretoria: CSIR Environmental Services, 1993) p. 6.
16. CSIR, *Environmental Impact Assessment*, vol. 3, p. 6.
17. CSIR, *Environmental Impact Assessment*, vol. 3, p. 2.
18. CSIR, *Environmental Impact Assessment*, vol. 4, p. 16.
19. In a discussion of the controversy over the northern Queensland

rainforest as a World Heritage site, R. Rickson points out that environmental organizations and large corporations, both characterized by centralized control, tend to this practice and ignore the needs and interests of local people. R. Rickson, 'Impacts of Rainforest Preservation on Rainforest People and their Communities' in *Impact Assessment Bulletin*, vol. 9 no. 4, concludes on page 53, that:

> central programs designed to save the world's tropical rainforest cannot be effective unless the social and economic costs of these programs to local people are considered. Unless this occurs, the movement to save the rainforests will flounder on the distrust and alienation of local people who are objecting to centralized control whether it is derived from environmental organizations, international industry or national governments.

20. Trade union organizer at Richards Bay, Mike Mabuyakhulu in *Weekly Mail*, November 17, 1993.
21. E. Koch, 'Real Development or Rhetoric? The Potential and Problems of Ecotourism as a Tool for Rural Reconstruction in South Africa', mimeo, 1993, p. 12.
22. Koch, 'Real Development or Rhetoric?' p.12.
23. P. West and S. Brechin (eds), *Resident People and National Parks: Social Dilemmas and Strategies in International Conservation* (Tucson: University of Arizona Press, 1993) p. 276.
24. M. Bulmer, *Social Science and Social Policy* (London: Allen and Unwin, 1986) p. 147.
25. E. Gramling and W. Freudenberg, 'Opportunity, Threat, Development and Adaption: Towards a Comprehensive Framework for Social Impact Assessment' in *Rural Sociology*, vol. 57 (1992) pp. 216–34.
26. T. Dietz, 'Theory and Method in Social Impact Assessment' in *Sociological Inquiry*, vol. 57, no. 1 (1987) pp. 54–69.
27. W. Freudenberg and K. Keating, 'Increasing the Impact of Sociology on Social Impact Assessment: Towards Ending the Inattention' in *American Sociologist*, vol. 17 (1985) p. 72.
28. D. Fu-Keung, 'Difficulties in Implementing Social Impact Assessment in China' in *Environmental Impact Assessment Review*, vol. 10, no. 1/2 (1990) p. 118.
29. R. Rickson and S. Rickson, 'Assessing Rural Development: The Role of the Social Scientist' in *Environmental Impact Assessment Review*, vol. 10, no. 1/2 (1990) p. 109.
30. Rickson and Rickson, 'Assessing Rural Development', p. 109.
31. H. Ross, 'Community Social Impact Assessment: A Framework for Indigenous Peoples' in *Environmental Impact Assessment Review*, vol. 10 (1990) pp. 185–93; and D. Craig, 'Social Impact Assessment: Politically Oriented Approaches and Applications' in *Environmental Impact Assessment Review*, vol. 10 (1990) pp. 37–54.
32. Bulmer, *Social Science and Social Policy*, p. 23.
33. Dietz, 'Theory and Method in Social Impact Assessment'.

34. Derman and Whiteford, *Social Impact Analysis and Development in the Third World*, p. 8.
35. Derman and Whiteford, *Social Impact Analysis and Development in the Third World*, p. 11.
36. C. Gagnon, P. Hirsch and R. Howitt, 'Can SIA Empower Communities?' in *Environmental Impact Assessment Review*, vol. 13, no. 4 (1993) pp. 229–53.
37. Gagnon *et al.*, 'Can SIA Empower Communities?', p. 244.
38. R. Rickson, J. Western and R. Burdge, 'Social Impact Assessment: Knowledge and Development' in *Environmental Impact Assessment Review*, vol. 10, no. 1/2 (1990) pp. 1–10.
39. Gagnon *et al.*, 'Can SIA Empower Communities?', pp. 245, 246.
40. R. Burdge, 'A Community Guide to Social Impact Assessment', Presentation at a Workshop organized by the Environmental Evaluation Unit, University of Cape Town, Johannesburg, South Africa, July 1992, p. 130.
41. C. Moser, 'Gender Planning in the Third World: Meeting Practical and Strategic Needs' in R. Grant and K. Newland (eds) *Gender and International Relations* (Bloomington: Indiana University Press, 1991) pp. 83–121.
42. Craig, 'Social Impact Assessment', p. 49.
43. A good example of this approach was the community SIA developed by Ross with an Aboriginal community at Turkey Creek in Australia. It was agreed that story-telling should be the principal method of research, and decided that 'the people's stories be recorded and compiled into a community social history showing how Aboriginal people have experienced major changes since white settlement of the area: that people's aspirations be presented as part of this continuing history; that the aim should be to "help kartiya (white man) understand", particularly those non-Aborigines in a position to assist or prevent the achievement of community aspirations, and to record the stories for the benefit of children and grandchildren'. (H. Ross (1989) p. 15, as cited by Craig, 'Social Impact Assessment', p. 51.) Story-telling 'was the medium with which the people felt most comfortable and through which they could most easily express their knowledge and views'. (Ross, 'Community Social Impact Assessment: A Framework for Indigenous Peoples' in *Environmental Impact Assessment Review*, vol. 10, no. 1/2 (1990) p. 188.) The outcome was 'a vivid and textured insight into Aboriginal perceptions'. (Craig, 'Social Impact Assessment', p. 52.) Furthermore, this story-telling approach gave Aboriginal people considerable power and control over the research process. Such empowerment is one of the objectives of participatory research.
44. In contrast to centralized, top-down planning according to a holistic blueprint; see Popper, *The Poverty of Historicism*.
45. African National Congress, *Reconstruction and Development Programme* (Johannesburg: Umanyano Publications, 1994) p. 7.
46. African National Congress, *Reconstruction and Development Programme*, p. 7.

5 Human Rights, Democracy and Good Governance: Stretching the World Bank's Policy Frontiers

David Gillies

INTRODUCTION

The international financial institutions (IFIs) have a profound impact on development in the South. During the 1980s, the World Bank Group and the regional development banks (RDBs) channelled $200 billion to developing countries. In 1992, International Bank for Reconstruction and Development (IBRD) and International Development Association (IDA) commitments amounted to $22 billion. In 1991 alone, the World Bank accounted for one-third of the $12 billion disbursed to Africa.

In response to this, a Zimbabwean political scientist, Jonathan Moyo, recently observed that everyone talks about economic structural adjustment but what Africa needs is political structural adjustment first. IFIs, including the World Bank, are increasingly aware that economic reforms may need to be accompanied by 'political adjustment' if they are to succeed.

On May 14, 1992, the World Bank announced on behalf of the Paris Consultative Group of Aid Donors for Malawi that it would not approve $74 million in new loans.[1] On November 26, 1991, the World Bank announced in Paris that a Consultative Group of Donors for Kenya would withhold new loans for at least six months. In 1990, the World Bank reduced its activities in Zaire to a minimal core program, following Belgium's decision to sharply cut bilateral aid to its former colony. On July 15,

1989, the Group of Seven (G–7) served notice at their Paris Summit that the World Bank would freeze new lending to China in the wake of economic uncertainties following the Tiananmen Square massacre.[2]

Issues of governance and human rights played a part in each of these decisions. The denial or postponement of development aid is sometimes described as political conditionality. Political considerations, such as human rights and democracy, have traditionally been regarded as beyond the purview of the World Bank's lending policies. But issues of governance and human rights are likely to figure more prominently in World Bank deliberations in the 1990s. This may be in response to reductions of bilateral aid or because of pressure from lender governments at the Bank. The key challenge is to further human rights without impairing the effectiveness of multilateral development institutions, such as the World Bank.

There are at least four aspects of World Bank activity that have human rights implications:

- the social dimensions of structural adjustment (social safety nets for the poorest);

- the human and ecological implications of Bank-sponsored mega-projects;

- popular participation in the design and implementation of Bank projects; and

- civil and political rights as a component of 'good governance'.[3]

The Bank has made some progress in responding to calls for 'adjustment with a human face', greater transparency and participation in project design, and in safeguarding against adverse human and ecological impacts of major development projects.

This chapter focuses on civil and political rights because the defense and promotion of this set of rights pose problems for an institution with formal prohibitions against political interference, and whose traditional area of competence is, on a generous reading, social and economic rights.[4] Institutional issues which can enhance the Bank's accountability to its most important stakeholders are also considered.

What is Political Conditionality?

Political conditionality is the legitimate intervention by aid donors in the domestic affairs of borrowing countries to alter the political environment in ways that sustain economic and human development. It may take three main forms: support through technical assistance to promote human rights and democratic development, persuasion through policy dialogue, or political pressure.[5] Specific actions include imposing a timetable of reforms, rewarding countries that undertake political liberalization, or using (or threatening to use) economic sanctions by withholding aid to regimes that violate human rights.

Because persuasion and support are not generally controversial, this chapter will focus on the tactic of pressure, as it may apply to the mandate and activity of the components of the World Bank Group, specifically the International Bank for Reconstruction and Development and the International Development Association.[6]

The International and Institutional Context

A convergence of international, institutional and intellectual factors form the policy environment of political conditionality at the World Bank. This constellation of influences includes:

- the normative global appeal of human rights and democracy, prompted in part by the collapse of authoritarian regimes in Eastern Europe and parts of the South;

- an erosion of the principle of state sovereignty;

- recasting the development agenda around the concepts of sustainability and participation, with civil and political rights as key ingredients of 'good governance';

- new funding pressure (from eastern and central Europe) on scarce donor resources, and hence a preoccupation with questions of rate of returns and efficiency;

- the Bank's shift to more policy-based lending and with it the discovery that 'good governance' may be crucial to the success of economic reforms;

- the onset of multiple donor conditionality in the economic, environmental and military arenas;[7]

- potential spill-over effects from the policies of bilateral donors to link human rights and foreign aid disbursements; and

- the Cold War's demise, which has reduced the need for ideologically motivated manipulation of the Bank, and improved the prospects for consensus and coordinated action by its most powerful members.

Of these influences, three are key to the argument that civil and political rights should be considered in World Bank lending policies: rethinking sovereignty, rethinking development, and the spill-over effect of bilateral donors and other multilateral institutions linking human rights and development aid. But before addressing these, it is worth considering the arguments against linking human rights and World Bank lending.

THE CASE AGAINST LINKAGE

At least five arguments can be mustered against linking human rights criteria to IFI policies. Some of these are serious, while others are not compelling.

The Bank's expertise is in economic development and the alleviation of poverty. Its comparative advantage is in the promotion of social and economic rights, not democracy or civil and political rights. In a comment as apposite for the Bank as for the Fund, Sir Joseph Gold observed that:

> The swimmer who goes out too far may seem to be waving but is drowning. The Fund that swims out too far, even in a moral cause, will risk drowning. It will have lost the full confidence of its members. It will be less able to promote universal prosperity. That task is the Fund's moral cause.[8]

But non-governmental organizations (NGOs) and many citizens of the South would take issue with the view that the Bank promotes universal prosperity, the recent conversion to 'adjustment with a human face' notwithstanding.[9] Moreover, pressure to respect civil and political rights may be less costly for governments than the structural adjustment is to the social and economic rights of the poorest.

Another objection is that the addition of human rights concerns would undermine the Bank's credibility by 'politicizing' an otherwise professional and impartial institution. But the Bank's political neutrality is a myth. It is hard to think of anything more political than deciding how money is spent. Moreover, power and influence is concentrated among the most powerful lender countries, particularly the United States. Indeed, many development NGOs ask how an unequal and undemocratic organization can credibly foster democratic governance abroad. Finally, the governance agenda, and now human rights, are simply extensions of the shift to more policy-based lending.

A stronger argument is the concern that multiple conditionality (economic, environmental, military, political) is an unethical intrusion on state sovereignty, with the IFIs as the new colonialists. Moreover, it may be impossible for borrowing countries to progress on all fronts simultaneously. Finally, the new conditionalities impose institutional burdens on Bank staff expected to operationalize these new values. The expertise argument cannot be dodged:

> There is a limit to [the] 'institutional elasticity' [by] which institutions created ... for other purposes can be 'stretched' in order to get them to perform human rights functions, especially when those functions are accomplished at the expense of their manifest functions.[10]

Official donors also say that withholding loans will doubly penalize the poorest. Why should they pay for the sins of their rulers? This tired argument is well off-base in regard to the Bank. The political conditionality envisaged here consists of short-term suspension of new fast-disbursing structural adjustment loans or loans for major infrastructure projects. These modalities do not generally have immediate benefits for large numbers of poor people. Bank projects that demonstrably promote basic human needs should never be suspended.

Finally, some skeptics say human rights and other political phenomena pose problems of measurement. Indicators are 'soft' in comparison with 'hard' economic data. Judgements based on them are thus unreliable or not objective. In fact, there has been a rapid increase in the volume of human rights data collected by governments and NGOs.[11] Moreover, it is possible to identify with some precision a range of circumstances that might trigger political conditionality.

THE CASE FOR LINKAGE

Rethinking Sovereignty

State sovereignty has been eroding for some time. It is under challenge from within by ethnic groups seeking greater autonomy or complete secession, and from without by growing economic and political interdependence.

In countries where external aid makes up a significant proportion of total government budgets, sovereignty is almost a fiction. The globalization of trade and money markets involves both reciprocal gains and mutual vulnerability, and hence evidences the interdependence of all states. Finally, a host of transnational issues call for collective resolution by the international community. In addition to global poverty and human rights, these include the environment, drug trafficking and terrorism. And while powerful nations retain considerable autonomy, sovereign self-determination has diminished in all states.

State sovereignty and the related principle of non-intervention in domestic affairs are two of the organizing principles of international relations. States, not persons, have traditionally been viewed as the main subjects of international law. Historically, what a state did to its own citizens was its own affair and beyond the reach of international action. Without falling hostage to any fiction about a new world order, there are signs, both rhetorical and substantive, that sovereignty is being rethought.

The issue of humanitarian intervention to protect groups during civil wars is germane to the debate on political conditionality. In one of his last speeches as UN Secretary General, Javier Pérez de Cuéllar was convinced that:

> We are clearly witnessing what is probably an irresistible shift in public attitudes towards the belief that the defense of the oppressed in the name of morality should prevail over frontiers and legal documents.[12]

Fitful signs of this 'shift' are evident in the UN provision of a safe haven for Iraqi Kurds at the close of the Gulf War. In effect, the Security Council considered human rights abuses as a threat to international peace and security. Similar humanitarian actions have been undertaken by the Economic Community of West African States (ECOWAS) in Liberia, by the European Community (EC) and the United Nations in the former Yugoslavia, and by the Organization of American States (OAS) in Haiti.

On what moorings should a new structure of international law and humanitarian practice rest? And what are the implications for international financial institutions, such as the World Bank? There are five principles:

- State sovereignty is not sacrosanct. True sovereignty resides in the will of the people. As the Universal Declaration of Human Rights puts it: 'The will of the people shall be the basis of the authority of government.'

- Respect for fundamental human rights is a *sine qua non* of legitimate governance.

- State sovereignty is abused and loses its legitimacy when it seeks to shield gross violations of human rights or grievous and deliberate human suffering.

- The principle of non-intervention cannot be used to prohibit legitimate international action to protect human rights.

- The international community has a duty to act for the relief of human suffering and to end the gross violation of human rights.

Just as it is no longer acceptable for society, the police or the courts in a growing number of countries to turn a blind eye to family violence, so it is unacceptable for international organizations that represent the family of nations to ignore violence and repression within national borders.

In sum, sovereignty must not be used to excuse the 'inept or malevolent practices of governments'.[13] Human rights is one of the three pillars of the UN Charter, 'one of the keystones in the arch of peace'.[14] State sovereignty must not only bow to these higher principles, it is also most secure when it respects them. The central development message in rethinking state sovereignty is that the concerns of citizens, not states, should be the primary focus of all development aid.

Rethinking Development

The World Bank would be failing in its task as the leading global development agency if it failed to take account of prevailing intellectual currents in development thinking. Yet, as will be explained below, this seems to be precisely what a narrow interpretation of good governance by the Bank staff amounts to, one which argues that the abuses of civil and political rights have no implications for the Bank's development work or country lending policies.[15]

The development agenda of the 1990s is being built on the concept of sustainable development. Durable development requires a political environment that sustains economic growth and empowers people. That means respect for human rights, because, as the UN Development Programme (UNDP) puts it: 'People are the real wealth of a nation.'[16] This enabling environment is now known as 'good governance' although, as explained below, the Bank has formally adopted a narrow reading of the parameters of good governance.

The conventional wisdom that civil and political rights are a distant aspiration to be postponed while states attend to the business of growth is now under scrutiny. A growing body of opinion holds that respect for civil and political rights must accompany, not lag behind, economic development. The UNDP 'indexes' on human development and human freedom show a remarkable correlation between high levels of human development and high levels of human freedom.[17] Similarly, the Development Assistance Committee of the Organization for Economic Cooperation and Development (OECD) sees 'a vital connection ... between open, democratic and accountable political systems, individual rights and the effective and equitable operation of economic systems'.[18]

This nexus was affirmed by more than 180 nation-states at the 1993 Vienna World Conference on Human Rights, which declared that 'democracy, development and respect for human rights are mutually interdependent and reinforcing' (Article 1, paragraph 8).

There is growing consensus that the real purpose of development is the enhancement of human capacity and choice. Ensuring that the individual is at the center of the development stage is the thrust of the UNDP's *Human Development Report*. This emphasis is echoed by the 1986 UN Declaration on the Right to Development,[19] which states that 'The human person is the central subject of development and should be the active participant and beneficiary of the right to development.'

The Right to Development was vigorously promoted by the South and explicitly adds human rights to the objectives of development. NGO coalitions from the South have also made the empowerment of individuals and groups a centerpiece of their development visions.[20]

In contrast to international human rights law, which underlines the interdependence and indivisibility of all human rights, the World Bank functionally separates rights into different generations. On this view, civil and political rights can be postponed until basic human needs are met. This attitude, of course, is precisely that adopted by 'development dictatorships' in many parts of the South.[21]

Contrary to narrower World Bank arguments that political questions are beyond the institution's purview, attention to civil and political rights is an indispensable component of sound development strategies. Civil rights, such as freedom of expression and association, empower citizens in their material struggles, and help civil society criticize unjust or inefficient state policies. Moreover, regimes that systematically suppress civil and political rights risk economic costs.[22]

Information, a commodity in short supply in repressive regimes, is essential to manage an economy. Such regimes may be economically inefficient because they foster apathy and corruption and politically unstable because they foster disaffection. Regimes without legitimacy require coercion which may drain scarce resources towards security and away from sustainable development. States that restrict political space may force the opposition underground and towards armed conflict, with potentially adverse effects on creditworthiness. An unequal distribution of national development resources is another issue where politics and economics are intertwined. Discriminatory economic and public policies are a potent recipe for ethnic conflict and long-term economic decay.

Access to information and a free press can help uncover the developmental 'inefficiencies' of corruption and malevolent governance. A free press is essential as an early warning device against impending famine by ensuring a public debate and prompt state action. Conversely, several famines, notably in China (1958–61) and in Sudan and Ethiopia (1984), have occurred under authoritarian regimes with little free expression and public debate of state policies.[23]

In summary, there is a growing appreciation that fostering democratic processes in government and society contributes to economic development by releasing creative energies, enhancing accountability and deepening participation. Development agencies, including the World Bank, must therefore go beyond poverty alleviation (often equated with social and economic rights) to embrace issues of empowerment and participation – the essence of civil and political rights. In an expanded definition, only development with participation is sustainable.

Bilateral Donors and the European Bank: Linking Rights and Aid

Most of the action on political conditionality has thus far come from bilateral aid donors. This may build pressure on the Bank to follow suit. The spill-over effect has happened indirectly through the impact of the Donor Consultative Groups, which the World Bank hosts, and more directly through the leverage of G–7 and other OECD Executive Directors at the World Bank to withhold loans to China.

Several aid donors have begun to add human rights to aid funding decisions. Others have begun programs for good governance or grass-roots participation. In 1991, Canadian Prime Minister Brian Mulroney informed the Commonwealth Heads of Government Meeting in Harare and the leaders of *La Francophonie* at Chaillot that Canada intended to condition its bilateral aid on the human rights performance of recipient countries, rewarding countries set on a more democratic path and reducing aid to countries that abused human rights. Canada has subsequently reduced, suspended, reviewed or redirected its aid to Zaire, Haiti, Indonesia and Kenya.

Similar links between human rights, good governance and aid disbursements have been made by the United Kingdom, the Netherlands, Nordic countries, the United States, France and Japan.[24] The European Community has added a human rights clause to its Lomé IV Convention, which formalizes trade and aid relations with the African, Caribbean and Pacific (ACP) countries.

Finally, a new IFI, the European Bank for Reconstruction and Development (EBRD), explicitly acknowledges the intertwining of political and economic reform. The Bank must foster the transition towards open market-oriented economies in the Central and Eastern European countries committed to and applying the principles of multiparty democracy, pluralism, and market economics. EBRD is thus bound by its charter to pay attention to the human rights and governance dimensions of its lending policies and operations.

EBRD has established a political unit with a mandate to review the human rights situation of borrowing countries. The accent is very much on civil and political rights, such as the right to property, free speech, free association, rule of law and so on.

The European Bank's General Counsel has indicated that the

Board of Governors 'may postpone, restrict or suspend operations' if a borrowing country is 'implementing policies that are inconsistent with the Bank's purpose'.[25] Ratification of the European Convention on Human Rights and acceptance into, and continued good standing in, the Council of Europe are 'positive indicators' of a borrowing country's commitment to the EBRD's political principles.

In sum, the trend among bilateral donors to link human rights and aid, and by the European Bank to link economic reform to human rights and democracy, are potential analogies and incentives for Northern Executive Directors to nurture an expansion of the World Bank's purview to include civil and political rights.[26]

DEFENDING HUMAN RIGHTS:
WHEN AND HOW TO CONDITION AID?

If political pressure is an option, when and how should it be applied? The basic standard for such pressure and aid conditionality should be a pattern of systematic, persistent and flagrant violations of fundamental human rights. The key abuses here are those which attack the physical integrity of the person: extrajudicial killings, systematic torture and deliberate withholding of food as a political weapon. Another marker might be widespread arbitrary arrests and prolonged detention without trial. The Bank could consider withholding loans where there is unequivocal evidence of state complicity in the perpetration of human rights abuses. Genocide as a systematic state policy should also trigger conditionality.

Human rights law has weak compliance mechanisms. Regimes can legitimately restrict many civil and political freedoms in times of bona fide emergency (so-called 'states of exception'). Despite these qualifications, the legal and normative weight of several human rights are unassailable. Extrajudicial killing and torture are two 'non-derogable' rights that must be respected even during states of emergency. The illegality of abusing these fundamental rights, together with systematic arbitrary arrests and prolonged detention without trial, is now virtually beyond discussion. Respecting such rights is part of customary international law and thus binding on all states, irrespective of their political character.[27] The Bank's freezing of new loans to China after the Tiananmen Square incident is one example where the severe violations of fundamental rights appropriately prompted political conditionality.

A more difficult judgement is using Bank leverage when other civil and political rights are restricted. While the contribution of such rights as free association, free speech and the rule of law to economic growth is now being appreciated, many civil and political rights may not only be legitimately restricted by emergency regulations, but their democratic flavor may imply Bank interference in the 'political character' of the regime. Action to defend these rights may hence be viewed as illegitimate. This conundrum is taken up in the discussion on Kenya below.

The case can be made that conditionality triggered by reference to human rights norms is easier to justify than leverage to encourage or defend electoral democracy. The Bank may legitimately cite human rights norms to which all UN members are nominally bound. By contrast, promoting democracy is a much broader, complex and diffuse policy agenda.[28] Moreover, the precise meaning and desirability of multiparty democracy is still a subject of intense debate, the collapse of socialism notwithstanding.[29] Clearly anti-democratic actions – a military coup, a violent or fraudulent election, or a crackdown on civil society and political parties – can all be responded to by invoking human rights norms rather than by lofty pronouncements on making the world safe for democracy. Moreover, as the case study on Kenya underlines, political pressure that insists on multi-party elections may be both naive and politically explosive. It is difficult to predict whether the outcome of elections will lead to durable democracy or unleash previously latent ethnic conflict or an anti-democratic backlash. An unscrupulous autocrat intent on staying in power may foment ethnic conflict to discredit the democratic process as a pretext for further repression in the name of law, order and national unity.

Finally, what can be called 'electoral conditionality' identifies with the narrow agenda of the political opposition, rather than with the call for human rights and political openness by civil society at large. By contrast, human rights conditionality – to permit press freedom, to relax restriction on NGOs, or strengthen the rule of law – may be a slower but surer way to encourage the emergence of a durable democratic civil culture.

These 'proactive' reforms, coupled with the resources (technical and financial) to implement them, should certainly be considered in the normal 'policy dialogue' between the Bank and a borrowing country where appropriate. Persuasion and agreement are obviously better than coercion and evasion.

There is in any case no substitute for a case-by-case judgement on political conditionality. A thorough appreciation of the historical, social and cultural traditions of each country should underpin the Bank's responses to such problems. As Joan Nelson cautions, some coups may occur 'because civilian politics has reached a total impasse'. In such circumstances, a military takeover (Algeria) or constitutional coup (Peru) may 'at least permit improved governance and economic growth, while sacrificing an empty shell of democratic process'.[30]

Aid withholding is also a dubious instrument in countries experiencing civil war, in part because human rights violations are likely to be committed by all sides in the conflict, in part because embattled governments may not be able to respond. In extreme cases, such as Somalia or Liberia, anarchy may prevail and there may be no rule of law or effective central government in control. Suspending projects or loans in such circumstances is a pragmatic recognition that serious development work is impossible in zones of conflict rather than a commentary on human rights.[31]

If political conditionality is to be effective, how should it be applied? There are several options:

- placing ceilings on new funding;

- postponing fast-disbursing loans, or projects in the pipeline;

- dissuading applications for new loans by threatening to vote against such applications;

- voting against new loan applications;[32]

- curtailing industrial loans and public-sector finance, but continuing private-sector loans;

- curtailing central government-directed projects, but continuing local public-sector loans and technical assistance projects;

- reshaping Bank activity towards pro-poor and participatory development projects, where the 'absorptive capacity' permits; and

- adding human rights education programs to Bank education-sector projects, including human rights training of the military and police forces where possible.

A timetable of reforms could be agreed upon as preconditions for the restoration of frozen loans and a return to business as usual. Depending on the individual country's circumstances, international donors could insist on the release of political prisoners, the establishment of national and independent human rights commissions, access by international human rights monitors, action to stem corruption and improve government accountability and transparency, and the relaxation or dismantling of legislation circumscribing the role of NGOs, freedom of the press and of association.

Building on the key human rights principle of non-discrimination, bilateral donors and the World Bank could explore ways in which additional resources could be directed to ethnic minorities that may have been disadvantaged in the allocation of central government resources. Such initiatives, however, are better communicated by the bilateral donors, through the Consultative Groups, in order to preserve the Bank's political neutrality.

Joan Nelson has argued that 'semi-authoritarian' single-party regimes, where the political elites include some progressive elements, may be especially ripe for the judicious application of political conditionality.[33] The degree to which civil society is organized and autonomous is also a key influence on the sustainability of Bank or donor-imposed human rights reforms.

In summary, political conditionality may be an appropriate lever to defend human rights in a limited range of circumstances, but less so to promote Western-style multi-party democracy. It is primarily a lever of last resort in extreme cases of unequivocal state culpability in the perpetration of deliberate, systematic or persistent human rights violations. UN Security Council actions which treat human rights as a threat to international peace and security may legally trigger mandatory sanctions by UN specialized agencies or their affiliates, such as the World Bank. Bank-imposed political conditionality may play a modest role in nurturing respect for civil and political rights and the rights of minorities. An aid bonus should be made available to regimes that are taking visible steps to safeguard human rights. In the current climate of donor fiscal restraint, this seems unlikely, however.

Political conditionality is most likely to be successful if applied through sustained donor coordination in aid-dependent economies. This fact, coupled with the need for a case-by-case approach, and the commercial and foreign policy interests of the most powerful Northern countries, will make for the inconsistent and episodic application of political leverage to defend human rights. Consistent, pristine behavior is, however, as rare in international life as it is in personal action. Half a loaf, even a quarter, is better than none. Inconsistency is endemic in all arenas of human rights diplomacy – at the United Nations and in bilateral aid and trade – and is not simply a Bank problem. Human rights NGOs should see the inconsistency argument as a challenge to develop a Bank policy on civil and political rights.

WHAT ARE THE BOUNDARIES OF 'GOOD GOVERNANCE'?

'The question is,' said Alice, 'whether you can make words mean so many things.' 'The question is,' said Humpty Dumpty, 'which is to be master – that's all.'

Lewis Caroll[34]

Allow me to be blunt: the political uncertainty and arbitrariness evident in so many parts of Sub-Saharan Africa are major constraints on the region's development ... *I am not advocating a political stance here*, but I am advocating increased transparency and accountability in government, respect for human rights and adherence to the rule of law.

Barber B. Conable[35]

The Bank is not a monolithic institution. On the contrary, its size, diverse country membership, and manifold activities make it ripe for internal dissension and debate. Such is the case with political conditionality. At the risk of oversimplifying a complex and diffuse term, there appear to be at least two readings on 'governance' at the World Bank. The 'narrow' version, which is emerging as *de facto* Bank policy, focuses on technical criteria connected to efficiency and excludes consideration of most civil and political rights.

There are signs, however, of a broader interpretation of human rights among some Bank staff, which concedes that sovereignty is not sacrosanct and acknowledges that the core characteristics of governance 'in large measure derive from or are related to, the Universal Declaration of Human Rights'.[36] On this view, the relationship between rulers and the ruled (legitimacy) is as central to good governance as questions of administrative efficiency. And that means respect for such fundamental human rights as the safety and security of the person (Articles 3 and 5) and for the rule of law –

not simply commercial law, but law to defend citizens against the abuse of state power (Articles 7–11, and 28), and to guarantee freedom of association and expression (Articles 19 and 20).[37]

The Bank's current preoccupation with good governance emerged alongside a shift, in the 1980s, to more policy-based lending in 'structural adjustment programs'. The SAP reforms were in turn a response to the balance-of-payments crises experienced by the developing countries during the late 1970s and early 1980s.[38]

While the good governance agenda makes no presumption about the political form of government, there is an assumption that the success or failure in achieving sustainable economic development is contingent on the quality of governance.

It is no accident that the good governance agenda emerged most powerfully in connection with Bank activity in Sub-Saharan Africa. While there is a self-serving element in the North's tendency to focus blame for Africa's development woes largely on internal variables,[39] the governance dimension does tap genuine currents of economic malaise. As the influential World Bank blueprint on Sub-Saharan Africa puts it:

> Underlying the litany of Africa's development problems is a crisis of governance. By governance is meant the exercise of political power to manage a nation's affairs. Because countervailing power has been lacking, state officials in many countries have served their [own] interests without fear of being called into account ... [and] patronage becomes essential to maintain power. The leadership assumes broad discretionary authority and loses its legitimacy. Information is controlled and voluntary associations are co-opted or disbanded. This environment cannot support a dynamic economy. At worst the state becomes coercive and arbitrary. These trends, however, can be resisted ... [by building] a pluralistic institutional structure, [respecting] the rule of law, and vigorous protection of the freedom of the press and human rights.[40]

The political conditionality implied by 'good governance' stems from staff and lender country frustrations with the inadequate rate of returns of many Bank projects and programs. It is primarily aimed at reforming and enhancing state administrative capacities for 'sound development management' and in nurturing an 'enabling environment' for a dynamic market-oriented economy with a flourishing private sector.

The Bank's structural adjustment agenda began a process of limited intervention in so-called 'public-sector management' reforms of the civil service, para-statal enterprises and public expenditure processes. Loans were made conditional on borrowers agreeing to reduce the number of civil servants, restructure ministries, liquidate or privatize public enterprises.[41]

The governance agenda has simply widened the range of conditionalities that may be potentially applied by the World Bank. It now includes three new items: accountability, the legal framework for development and information and transparency.[42] At issue are such concerns as probity, procurement practices, rent seeking, property rights and user financing of welfare services.

The accountability of state officials can be enhanced by sound audit systems and has led to an insistence on strict enforcement and penalties, such as conditioning new loans on compliance with previous loan requirements, or suspending disbursements. Accountability is also an issue in the decentralization of decision-making and public participation in local government, and future Bank activity could support mechanisms for public recourse against local government agencies.

The World Bank's interest in the *rule of law* is carefully circumscribed: 'The rule of law is not an end in itself' but important only to the extent that it contributes to economic development.[43] A predictable set of rules is essential to reduce business risks, enforce contracts, lower transaction costs and prevent arbitrary government decisions. Hence, in a narrow governance agenda it is commercial law that is privileged, not the defense of civil rights. It has been suggested that enhancing the predictability of commercial law can have spill-over benefits for other aspects of the legal system.[44] This may be optimistic. Legal reforms may enhance the predictability of commerce in authoritarian regimes, but have little impact on other aspects of the legal culture, such as courts too weak to tackle human rights cases (Chile under Pinochet), or constitutional laws used in the defense of the state, and not of its citizens (China currently).

On the boundaries of the narrow governance agenda is growing Bank attention to what might be called the 'political economy of adjustment' – to issues of the timing, design, and the political viability of reform.[45]

INSTITUTIONAL ISSUES:
GOVERNANCE *WITHIN* THE BANK

The Bank's governance agenda stems in part from concern about the poor rates of return of many projects and programs. Good governance should also apply to the Bank itself. Yet the Bank is virtually immune from any form of accountability to the intended beneficiaries of its activities: the citizenry of developing countries and project-affected populations. In recent years the Bank has been the target of vocal criticism by groups protesting projects that uproot and resettle communities and destroy fragile environments. The Sardar Sarovar dam project in India is only the tip of an iceberg of grievances.[46]

An absence of transparency, accountability, and popular participation in Bank decision making calls into question its legitimacy to function as a governance institution.[47] Poor governance has also contributed to the weak performance of many projects.[48]

This situation could be substantially remedied if there were an independent monitoring of the design, appraisal and implementation phases of the project cycle. From a rights perspective, the World Bank has an obligation to put its projects under a rule of law which will protect all project-affected populations. Just as the environmental impacts of development activities are now being scrutinized, so too must the human rights implications of Bank projects and policies be assessed and standards to secure rights established.[49]

The Bank has made real progress in responding to concerns regarding transparency, accountability and participation.[50] The Bank's willingness to establish an independent expert group to assess the human and environmental impact of the Sardar Sarovar project demonstrates a commitment to greater transparency.

These first steps are now being institutionalized. The Inspection Panel could go a long way to improve the Bank's credibility with its stakeholders, and with the wider international community.[51] This complaints and overseeing mechanism would also contribute to better quality control of Bank activity and safeguard against projects that abuse or retard the social and economic rights of project-affected populations. It is now incumbent on human rights NGOs and project-affected populations to test the independence and effectiveness of the Panel by bringing to its attention cases of projects that have seriously abused the rights of local communities.[52]

EVOLUTION OF THE 'POLITICAL' AT THE WORLD BANK

In broad sweep, there are four eras of Bank history on the 'political' aspects of its mandate. In the longest phase, from 1946 to the mid-1970s, the Bank maintained a strict dichotomy between economics and politics. This attitude stemmed from a legitimate concern to establish the Bank's credibility as a multilateral institution based on the equal treatment of sovereign states. In the context of the Cold War, the political prohibition was a sensible defense against US efforts to stymie loans to its ideological enemies. But the political prohibition also applied when the UN General Assembly called on the Bank not to lend to South Africa on human rights considerations.

During the US Carter administration, Congress passed legislation to condition IFI lending on respect for human rights.[53] This legislation, which is still in force, did not apply when loans were directly beneficial to 'needy people'. As in other arenas, the Carter administration's human rights activism at the Bank was undermined by the inconsistent application of the legislation. It was also rendered ineffective because few other Western countries added their voice or vote to the US position.[54]

During the Reagan era of the 1980s, the US played the human rights card at the Bank for geopolitical and ideological, not principled, reasons. The United States tried to prevent loans to socialist regimes, particularly Nicaragua, using human rights as a camouflage for *realpolitik*.[55]

By the late 1980s, however, there was growing consensus among the lender countries at the Bank on the legitimate use of political conditionality. We are now in an era of its fitful application under the rubric of 'good governance'. The debate today focuses on how far the governance agenda should be widened (to include civil and political rights or focus solely on social and economic rights?), on the dividing line between political phenomena that have an economic impact and those that do not, and on the appropriate triggering circumstances for political conditionality. Bank approaches to some of these questions are still evolving.

Hear No Politics, See No Politics

The Articles of Agreement of the IBRD and IDA contain provisions to insulate these institutions from political considerations of three kinds: the political 'character' of borrowing countries; the political interests of lender states, and the political manipulation of Bank staff.

Hence in the IBRD Articles of Agreement, loans are to be made 'with due consideration to considerations of economy and efficiency and without regard to political or other non-economic influences or considerations' (Article III, Section 5b). Similarly, 'the President, officers and staff of the Bank, in the discharge of their offices, owe their duty entirely to the Bank and to no other authority' (Article IV, Section 10). There is, finally, this oft-cited injunction:

> The Bank and its officers shall not interfere in the political affairs of any member; nor shall they be influenced by the political character of the member or members concerned. Only economic considerations shall be relevant to their decisions, and these shall be weighed impartially ... (Article IV, Section 10).

The Bank's political prohibition was insisted upon by the intellectual architects of the Bretton Woods system, John Maynard Keynes and Harry White. It made eminent sense at the time: a world war had been fought on the basis of ideology and nationalism; Cold War rivalries had already surfaced. As Keynes put it:

> If these new institutions are to win the confidence of the suspicious world, it must not only be, but appear, that their approach to every problem is absolutely objective and ecumenical, without prejudice or favour.[56]

We have seen that even the narrow-gauge governance agenda is widening the scope of what constitutes 'efficiency'. What must now be challenged is the notion that concern for civil and political rights constitute 'non-economic' criteria, unwarranted judgements on the 'political character' of a borrowing country, or 'interference' in the 'political affairs' of a member state.

'Stretching' the Articles of Agreement

The World Bank's General Counsel, Ibrahim F.I. Shihata, has set the Bank's current position regarding the political aspects of its mandate. Shihata has creatively 'stretched' the Bank's mandate to include some attention to human rights and popular participation, without distorting the original Articles of Agreement. As he puts it: '[w]hile the *purposes* of the Bank are exhaustively stated, the *functions* which allow the Bank to serve such purposes may be expanded as deemed necessary or desirable'.[57]

Systematic abuses of civil and political rights are not appropriate triggers of Bank conditionality except in rare circumstances. At present there appear to be four such circumstances:

- when the Bank must respect binding decisions of the UN Security Council not to lend to a particular country for reasons of international peace and security;

- when international sanctions affect the economic prospects of a potential borrowing country;

- when an escalation of armed conflict affects the viability of Bank projects and the safety of its personnel; and

- where it can be unequivocally demonstrated that political phenomena have demonstrably adverse economic consequences.

With the exception of Security Council decisions, the Bank must thus respond not to human rights *per se*, but to the operational and efficiency consequences of abuses, or to the actions of other players. The Bank's General Counsel has judged that the

> violation of political rights may ... reach such proportions as to become a Bank concern either due to significant direct economic effects or if it results in international obligations relevant to the Bank such as those mandated by binding decisions of the UN Security Council.[58]

In effect, the Bank should not allow 'political factors or events ... to influence its decisions *unless* ... it is established that they have direct and obvious economic effects relevant to its work. For these to be taken into account, such economic effects have to be preponderant.'[59]

The General Counsel has also outlined aspects of governance beyond the Bank's mandate. These include:

- the 'political character' of member states;

- interference in the domestic affairs of member states, particularly in the sphere of multi-party or domestic politics; and

- acting on behalf of bilateral donors in 'influencing the recipient country's political orientation or behavior'.[60]

The political prohibition remains a sensible defense against the vested interests of powerful member states. Moreover, economic growth has taken place in a variety of political systems. That said, however, does it follow that: 'Political choices, along with their underlying values and trade-offs, are for each country to make; the Bank's concern is for the economic effects and result-ant degree of efficiency in the allocation of resources'[?][61]

This perspective comes perilously close to saying that 'devel-opment dictatorships' which close down civil and political rights for reasons of 'growth' are immune from the Bank's concern because such 'values and trade-offs' are either culturally specific or 'efficient'.

Moreover, despite injunctions that Bank staff have no author-ity to act as 'political messengers' or to be swayed by the 'politi-cal preferences or ideals of bilateral donors', the Bank is being increasingly drawn into the political conditionality debate by the actions of bilateral donors.[62]

Significant reductions in or suspension of bilateral aid on human rights or governance considerations may threaten the ability of the Bank to carry out its long-range structural reforms. This usually occurs in the Consultative Groups, which the Bank chairs.[63] If the bilateral donors pull out, the Bank may have to act as lender of last resort, something it will not normally do. Because it is the Bank's task within the Consultative Group to put together an overall financing plan for a borrowing country, reductions of bilateral official development assistance (ODA), particularly of funds earmarked for balance of payments support, necessarily prompt the Bank to reconsider its commitments.

As the case of Kenya underlines, the Bank may find it difficult to draw a 'clear line'[64] between its coordinating role and questions of political influence or pressure when the bilateral donors choose to act in concert.

Popular Participation: A 'Sensitive' Case

The issue of popular participation is a 'sensitive' case on the boundaries of the Bank's governance agenda. On this view, it is within the Bank's mandate to consult with domestic and inter-national NGOs on matters pertaining to the design, implementa-tion and management of Bank-funded projects, or to the resettlement of affected populations. The Bank is slowly responding to calls by environment and development NGOs for improved access to information and participation in the design of major infrastructure projects.[65]

However, some NGOs in the South are calling on the Bank to condition its lending by requiring states to ensure that there are adequate structures for popular participation.[66] The Bank currently views this broader goal as 'off-limits' because it may be construed as offering political prescriptions to borrowing countries. This interpretation is perhaps overly restrictive.[67] The popular participation agenda addresses the information gap in public policy. The Bank appears to appreciate the growing role of NGOs as deliverers of services in many developing countries, but seems unwilling to address, in its dialogue with a recipient country, such pertinent issues as laws which circumscribe NGO activity, or the need to preserve the autonomy of universities as repositories of intellectual innovation and policy debate.[68]

CASE STUDIES

Imposing Democracy in Kenya?

Once viewed as an African exemplar of a stable capitalist state, Kenya has been under growing international scrutiny in the 1990s as domestic pressures for political pluralism mount and evidence accumulates of a corrupt, repressive, and inefficient government.[69]

Kenya's drift towards a repressive autocracy began in 1982 when an abortive coup-attempt prompted President Moi to amend the constitution. This transformed Kenya from a *de facto* to a *de jure* one-party state. Moi also ended life tenure for justices, thereby stripping the judiciary of its autonomy. Since then, economic recession, mounting foreign debt servicing, rising unemployment and shrinking welfare services have fed open dissent (by journalists, the churches, intellectuals and lawyers) and armed underground opposition.

Since 1987, in particular, there have been increases in incommunicado detention, disappearances and deaths in police custody. Among the most infamous unexplained deaths were those of former Foreign Minister, Robert Ouko, in February 1990 and Anglican Bishop Alexander Muge. Ouko was undertaking an investigation into official corruption at the time of his death.

123

The crackdown that followed demonstrations protesting the alleged political murder of Ouko led to restrictions on press freedom, free speech and free assembly. While other African governments, from Benin to Zambia, were prepared to permit peaceful change through the ballot box, President Moi promised only to 'hunt down like rats' the 'subversive' elements pushing for political reform.

Kenya has long been dependent on international largesse. It has also been of some strategic importance in recent years – providing refueling bases for the US Navy patrolling the Arabian Sea, for example. This and Kenya's capitalist credentials contributed to the relative silence of the donor community to evidence of Kenya's gradual political decay through the 1980s. In 1989, Western countries gave Kenya nearly $1 billion in development aid, about one-third of it from the World Bank. However, with the demise of the Cold War, Kenya has lost its strategic significance.[70]

By the November 1990 Paris meeting of the Consultative Group for Kenya, the World Bank's communique reflected a carefully modulated shift in donor attitudes towards Kenya.[71] The press release noted that 'general agreement [among the donors] that economic development and political stability and consensus are intertwined'. In particular, 'delegates noted the importance of good governance, participation, accountability and transparency for sustained economic development'.[72]

These concerns did not, however, prevent the Consultative Group from maintaining their aid, pledging $1 billion for 1991, of which $400 million was to be for balance-of-payments support. The delegates of the Consultative Group for Kenya were evidently encouraged by the decision to appoint Vice-President Saitoti to a Review Commission examining the nomination, election and disciplinary rules of the Kenya African National Union (KANU), at the time Kenya's only legal party. In December 1991, the constitution was changed to allow other political parties. This was taken as evidence of a commitment to good governance.[73]

Several bilateral donors, including the United States, Norway and Denmark then became more active on human rights and governance issues in Kenya. Kenya severed diplomatic relations with Norway when Oslo protested the detention of a Kenyan dissident. Denmark and the United Kingdom reduced their government to government aid as a response to corruption. The United States reduced its aid from $80 million in 1989 to $40 million in 1991 and suspended military assistance.

In November 1991, just ten days before the Consultative Group for Kenya met in Paris, President Moi tempted fate by suppressing a peaceful demonstration calling for more political openness. The Consultative Group[74] suspended for six months any release of new aid to Kenya and in stronger terms than the previous year set out the reasons for their decisions. First, delegates 'emphasized that there was growing competition for increasingly scarce donor resources, and that aid programs were being re-examined with a view to ensuring the most effective use of these resources'. Moreover, 'Delegates underlined that good governance ... would ... be a major factor influencing aid allocations [and] stressed the need for early implementation of political reform to reinforce the benefits of economic structural change.' Some delegates also expressed concern over the 'misuse of public funds'.[75]

While the World Bank was not in theory bound by the decision of the 'bilaterals' to pledge new aid, it was obliged to follow suit because of the financing gap. Moreover, the Bank ended up, despite the General Counsel's injunctions, as the political messenger of the bilateral donors. Since Vice President Saitoti was unwilling to deliver the bad news to President Moi, the World Bank resident representative was obliged to inform the President of the Consultative Group's decision.[76]

At first blush, the Consultative Group's political leverage appeared to have paid off. Just one week after the funding freeze, President Moi announced that he would re-establish a multi-party political system and he discarded the constitutional amendment (Section 2A) used to create a *de jure* one-party state.

But it would be foolhardy to predict whether conditionality can engender Western-style democracy in Kenya. President Moi appears to be prepared to foment the latent 'tribal' tensions in Kenyan society. And the opposition, which will be challenged to mobilize effectively and quickly for elections, subsequently splintered worryingly along ethnic lines.[77]

The Kenyan case is remarkable in at least two senses. First, Kenya's human rights performance, while deteriorating throughout the late 1980s and early 1990s, was not markedly worse than several of its African neighbors. The political issue, in effect, is democracy, not human rights narrowly defined.

Second, the Bank was able to deflect the allegation of unwarranted political conditionality by justifying a $150 million loan freeze on the basis of economic criteria – corruption at the top, and the Kenyan government's inability to meet the Bank's timetable of economic reforms.

It is possible, however, to imagine a country that had performed well on economic criteria – a strong adjuster – but then embarked on a pattern of egregious and systematic human rights violations. China after Tiananmen Square is just such a case.

China Spring: Using Economics to Mask Politics

Last June there occurred in Beijing [Peking] a rebellion which was supported by hostile forces abroad and constituted an attempt to overthrow the legitimate Government of the People's Republic of China. The Chinese Government took resolute measures to quell the rebellion in the interests of the overwhelming majority of the Chinese people. This is entirely China's internal affair and is a matter different in nature from the question of human rights.[78]

The death of Hu Yao Bang, former Communist Party General on April 15, 1989 sparked demonstrations by about 3,000 students who presented a 7-point petition of grievances to the National People's Congress, China's Parliament.[79] On April 24, students at 30 of Beijing's 70 colleges began a strike to press for reforms of the political structure. On May 4, the seventieth anniversary of China's first modern political campaign, as many as one million people occupied Tiananmen Square and its environs. The students were joined by civil servants, lawyers, doctors, nurses and miners.

It is not necessary to recount the horrifying denouement of that Chinese Spring. Some features of the Tiananmen 'incident' are, however, worth recalling. First, the demonstrations were almost entirely peaceful. Second, conventional methods for the dispersal of crowds were not attempted, and troops opened fire at random or shot deliberately into the crowds. Their actions thus constituted gross and systematic extrajudicial killings. Third, intense international media coverage prompted global calls for principled action by the international community. Fourth, in the aftermath of Tiananmen Square, the Beijing leadership embarked on a massive campaign of repression, reprisal and propaganda.

One surprising aspect of the Western response to Tiananmen Square was a decision by two IFIs, the World Bank and the Asian Development Bank, to 'put on hold' several loans already in the pipeline, and to freeze the consideration of new loans to China.

Establishing and maintaining a united front among the OECD lending countries was key to maintaining pressure on China. An *ad hoc* OECD group met regularly after 1989 to coordinate IFI policy towards China. The G–7 took the lead, announcing at their Paris Summit that '[i]n view of the current economic uncertainties, the examination of new loans by the World Bank will be postponed'. In unmistakably political language, the G–7 further called on 'the Chinese authorities to create conditions which will avoid their isolation and provide for a return to cooperation based upon a resumption of movement towards political and economic reform, and openness'.[80]

Interviews with senior Bank staff and officials from several of the member-country Executive Directors (EDs) supplied this account of the World Bank's response to Tiananmen Square:

- the G–7 EDs bluntly informed Barber Conable, the President of the World Bank that there would be no new lending to China and that if staff presented any new loans for consideration by the Board, the G–7 EDs would vote against them.[81] On a strict reading, this intervention contravened the Bank's articles of agreement;

- economic arguments were used to convey a political message;

- avoiding a vote avoided humiliating China or openly politicizing the situation;

- Bank staff sought an early return to normal lending practices with China and doubted that Tiananmen Square had created lasting adverse economic consequences; and

- China and the other Southern EDs put pressure on senior Bank staff to introduce new loans. EDs from India, East Asia, Saudi Arabia and the Middle East (Part II countries) strongly opposed the freeze on new loans out of concern that the China freeze might be precedent-setting and that any one of them might be next.[82]

Consensus among the G–7 did not last long. It was weakened in a series of steps. First, Barber Conable introduced one unobjectionable humanitarian loan application to 'test the waters'. However, when the ante was upped by introducing a loan for infrastructure assistance for a railway, Canada's Executive Director, Frank Potter, used a procedural device to call for a postponement.

Such procedural deferments normally last for a maximum of

two days so that EDs or Bank staff can clarify technical matters. But there is no time limit to the postponement, and it is up to the Bank president to reschedule the loan application. Conable clearly saw which way the wind was blowing and chose to defer the application indefinitely, despite protestations from the Chinese Executive Director.[83]

Discussion at the Bank seems then to have evolved to permitting new loans for basic human needs projects. A sign of growing pressure to return to normal lending was the EDs' consensus decision that Bank staff undertake a comprehensive assessment of economic conditions in China. The subsequent 'Country Economic Memorandum' was debated on May 29, 1990. Several OECD countries remained skeptical about the Memorandum. A Canadian official described it as 'a crowd pleaser'.[84]

The OECD consensus began to unravel when the United States decided to renew China's Most Favored Nation status. Japan and the EC were reportedly keen to resume lending. At the G–7 meeting in Houston in July 1990, Japan reactivated its $5.6 billion loan package to China, undermining what slim consensus remained. The decisive event was China's agreement to support the Security Council's call for an embargo against Iraq, a *quid pro quo* that paved the way for a return to normal Bank and export credit lending. Ironically, this thaw in Western policy towards China coincided with an Amnesty International report claiming that more than 500 people had been executed in China in 1990.[85]

What lessons can be drawn from all this? First, economic arguments were used to mask the blunt application of political conditionality. The arguments were tenuous at best. Aside from a temporary drop in its credit rating, China's economy continued to grow and the economic reform program remained substantially on track.[86] Second, the Chinese have made extraordinary gains in the alleviation of poverty and the provision of basic social and economic rights. Should their leadership have been penalized for a solitary political misdeed? Third, the Bank's China program is now undergoing a modest shift towards more poverty-oriented projects with greater popular participation in their design, implementation and maintenance.[87]

Fourth, the Bank's response on China was a rare example of consensus and political coordination among the major Northern shareholders. That it was undertaken against one of the most powerful Southern borrowers suggests that political conditionality need not always be confined to weak, aid-dependent countries. The key question is: 'Was the OECD consensus precedent-setting or a unique event never to be repeated?'

DIRECTIONS FOR REFORM

There are several practical steps that could be taken to ensure that human rights considerations are added to the World Bank's projects and policies:

- Lender countries should ensure that human rights and good governance are added to the criteria determining IDA replenishments.

- The Bank should begin to develop a comprehensive human rights policy. Such a policy would be have at least four components:

  - promoting social, economic, civil and political rights where these visibly enhance economic efficiency;
  - guidelines for temporary freezes on new policy lending where gross human rights violations have demonstrably adverse efficiency consequences;
  - human rights impact assessments of Bank-funded project proposals; and
  - adding human rights standards to project loan agreements between the Bank and borrower governments.

- The World Bank's new Inspection Panel should be accorded sufficient resources and functional autonomy to investigate complaints about the operations and policies of the Bank, publicize its findings and advise the Board on actions to improve the Bank's performance. The Panel should provide officials with a non-partisan, independent review of Bank activity, provide a vehicle for public participation or input in Bank policies, and help redress injustices or human rights abuses that stem from Bank projects or maladministration. Explicit use could be made of human rights principles in a public annual report that can be made available to relevant UN bodies and Bank stakeholders.

- The Bank should examine the efficiency consequences and the development dividends to be gained by promoting civil and political freedoms. The Bank should broaden its conception of good governance, particularly the legal framework for development, and examine how it may promote security of the person, freedom of opinion and freedom of association in ways consistent with its development mandate.

- As a UN affiliate institution, the Bank should deepen its dialogue with other UN development agencies and with UN human rights bodies on mutually important issues of governance, human rights and democratic development. The final report of the 1993 World Human Rights Conference called on 'prominent international and regional finance and development institutions to ... assess the impact of their policies and programmes on the enjoyment of human rights'. Improved dialogue among IFIs, specialized agencies and UN human rights bodies could be achieved through regular round-table meetings.

- Promoting human rights: dialogue, persuasion and promotion are ultimately more effective than confrontation. Donors should encourage borrowers to develop a sense of ownership over proposed political reforms. The Bank's comparative advantage is in promoting social and economic rights. However, even within a 'narrow-gauge' reading of governance, one that confines itself to the efficiency dimensions of development, the World Bank has considerable scope to nurture a thriving civil society. For example:

  - Debt for Democratic Development: The Bank could join with bilateral donors at the Paris Club to formulate 'Debt for Democratic Development' packages. Debt overhangs are a significant brake on the prospects for sustainable democratic development. Debt also contributes to policies which threaten the social and economic rights of the poorest. Consultative Group meetings could be used to formulate plans that would permit IFI and other official debt to be paid in local funds.
    The debt crisis continues to fester in Africa. At the Tunis Regional Meeting of the World Human Rights Conference, African governments undertook to 'formulate a national programme to support democracy, with a view to promoting human rights and development, with the financial and logistical support of the international community'. The Tunis

meeting also proposed that sustainable development strategies be partly financed by the conversion of public debt into
a national fund to promote human rights and civil society
institutions.[88]

- Women and property rights: The Bank could deepen its
interest in property rights (a principle embedded in the
Universal Declaration of Human Rights) by examining ways
in which traditional and legal barriers to women's empowerment can be removed to ease their access to credit, land and
other forms of property. The inability of many women to
access credit, or own and use land represents a significant
opportunity cost, an economic dividend that is lost to
national development.
- Access to land: The Bank could extend its policies and
programs to increase access to land.[89] Policies that redistribute land, expand tenancy or provide clear title often create
opportunities for the rural poor. Greater effort in this field
can be justified by emphasis on 'efficiency' – clear title gives
farmers an incentive to invest in the land and use better
technologies – and by drawing on the language of social and
economic rights to property and food.
- Civil society and economic policy: The Bank could also support the creation or institutional development of chambers
of commerce, professional associations or economic policy
institutes to ensure that there is informed public debate on
national economic development.

Through its aid dialogue with governments, the Bank could
encourage borrower governments to ratify without reservations
the major human rights conventions, such as the Covenant on
Civil and Political Rights and the Convention on the Elimination
of All Forms of Discrimination Against Women.

Consistent with the Bank's growing work with NGOs in
service delivery and in the 'social dimensions of adjustment', the
Bank could encourage policies that facilitate the building of a
dynamic voluntary sector with fewer restrictions on registration,
access to funds and participation in public policy.

Finally, the Bank could promote and defend the principle of
academic freedom as a corollary to its practical support for the
capacity building of economic think tanks and professional
associations.[90]

CONCLUSION

The World Bank is the leading international development agency, with significant influence on the political and economic fate of developing countries. The Bank is *de jure* part of the family of UN institutions. In practice, it has had substantial autonomy to pursue its development objectives substantially unhindered by political considerations. There are signs that the Bank's strict separation of economics and politics is weakening.

A key challenge is to get the World Bank and other international financial institutions to sign on to the human rights principles of the UN Charter and the International Bill of Human Rights without impairing the effectiveness of these multilateral development agencies.

The World Bank should not be immune from momentous upheavals in the global political and intellectual landscape. These include:

- the normative global appeal of human rights and democratic governance;

- an erosion of the principles of sovereignty and non-intervention;

- the demonstration effect of bilateral donors linking human rights and foreign aid;

- the addition of human rights and democracy to the charter of the European Bank for Reconstruction and Development;

- the normative conviction that development must enhance human capacity and be sustainable; and

- the conviction that human rights are a *sine qua non* of legitimate governance.

This post-Cold War environment gives NGOs some momentum to challenge the World Bank to rethink its lending policies towards governments culpable of gross, systematic and persistent violations of human rights.

The World Bank is now addressing issues of popular participation in the design and implementation of its projects, providing social safety nets for the poorest communities adversely affected by structural adjustment programs, and strengthening the efficiency and accountability of state officials and state structures. However, the Bank will not add concern for civil and political rights to its development mandate, except in rare circumstances where these have profound and unequivocal economic effects. Civil and political rights are 'off-limits' because their consideration allegedly constitutes political interference. This decision of non-interference is itself a *de facto* political decision.

However, human rights are universal values to be defended and promoted, not a judgement on a particular political system. Human rights are a pillar of the UN Charter to which all states are bound. International human rights conventions oblige states parties to respect human freedoms and invite scrutiny of domestic human rights performance. Concern for human rights thus does not constitute political interference.

As a UN specialized agency, the Bank has an obligation to ensure that its activity does not contribute to human rights deprivations. Crafting a sound human rights policy to defend and promote all rights – civil, political and cultural, as well as social and economic – would further, not undermine, the Bank's development mandate.

The purpose of development is to enhance human capacity and choice. 'People are the real wealth of a nation.' Human development is indispensable to economic advancement. Regimes which systematically suppress civil and political rights stunt human development and dampen the ability of civil society to participate in public policy and hold governments accountable for inefficient or corrupt governance.

The World Bank's adoption of policy-based, structural adjustment lending has led to a growing appreciation that economic reforms may not succeed without attention to the political climate in which they are undertaken. However, the Bank's current conception of 'good governance' is unduly restrictive. It is an extension of public-sector management in structural adjustment programs. Enhancing the accountability of government officials and structures is a necessary, but not sufficient, component of political reform. Donor agencies, including the World Bank, must also help strengthen civil society's capacity to hold governments accountable.

Civil and political rights equip citizens to empower themselves, struggle for social justice and material well-being, and hold governments accountable. They are indispensable for economic development. Social and economic rights, which the Bank sees as its comparative advantage, will not be realized in their absence.

Political conditionality is legitimate intervention by aid donors to alter the political environment of recipient countries in ways that sustain economic and human development. It has promotional as well as coercive dimensions. Proactive reforms, which should be adopted through dialogue and persuasion, might include: selective land reform; improving women's access to land and other forms of property; enhancing citizen participation in local government through, *inter alia*, support for professional associations, chambers of commerce or economic policy institutes, and the human rights training of security forces in Bank support for demobilization. Coercive actions include legitimately freezing loans to states culpable of persistent, flagrant and systematic abuses of such fundamental rights as freedom from extrajudicial killing, torture and arbitrary and prolonged detention. Political conditions in Bank lending may also be invoked to counter blatantly anti-democratic actions, such as a military coup, a violent or fraudulent election, or a crackdown on civil society and political parties.

However, conditionality triggered by reference to human rights norms is easier to justify than pressure to encourage or defend electoral democracy. There is, moreover, no substitute for a case-by-case approach to the tactic of political pressure; one based on the historical, social and cultural conditions of each country.

Political pressure will be applied unevenly because leverage is greatest in aid-dependent countries and because powerful lender states may have conflicting commercial, ideological or geopolitical interests. Inconsistency is not, however, peculiar to the World Bank; it bedevils human rights action in all arenas of international life. Inconsistency is a challenge to be confronted, not a pretext for silence. Moral complexity is no excuse for inaction.

Case studies of Bank responses to human rights abuses in China and Kenya show that the Bank is being drawn into political conditionality, either through pressure from Northern member states, or by default through coordinated aid reductions by bilateral donors. The absence of a policy on human rights contributes to inconsistency and undermines the Bank's credibility by confirming Southern complaints of double standards and political interference.

Intense public criticism of the harmful human impact of Bank project's can be moderated by the establishment of an ombudsperson or independent inspection panel reporting directly to the

Executive Directors of the Bank and systematically examining the human impact of all Bank projects and policies. The establishment of such an office would be a positive contribution to the Bank's need for enhanced internal democratic governance.

Notes

1. The World Bank May 13, 1992 press statement on behalf of the Consultative Group expressed

   > deep disappointment at the [Malawian] Government's lack of responsiveness to [governance] concerns and what they perceive as its continued poor record in ensuring basic respect for human rights, release or trial of detainees, better conditions in the prisons, respect for the rule of law, and independent judiciary, public sector accountability and transparency, freedom of speech, and open public participation and debate on policy options and freedom of association.

2. *Declaration on China*, Summit of the Arch, Paris, July 15, 1989.
3. Good governance describes 'the use of political authority and exercise of control over a society and the management of its resources for development'. See Dunstan M. Wai, 'Governance, Economic Development and the Role of External Actors', paper delivered at the Conference on Governance and Economic Development in Sub-Saharan Africa, Oxford University, May 1991.
4. For a survey of World Bank activity in the fields of health, nutrition, education and women's rights, see Ibrahim F.I. Shihata, *The World Bank in a Changing World: Selected Essays* (Dordrecht and Boston: Martinus Nijhoff Publishers, 1991) pp. 97–134.
5. Joan Nelson, *Encouraging Democracy: What Role for Conditioned Aid?* (Washington, DC: Overseas Development Council, 1992).
6. The World Bank Group comprises: the International Bank for Reconstruction and Development (IBRD, a hard-loan facility); the International Development Association (IDA, the soft-loan facility); the International Finance Corporation (IFC, which promotes the private sector); and the Multilateral Investment Guarantee Agency (MIGA, which covers risk and guarantees loans). This chapter considers only the IBRD (commonly referred to as the World Bank) and IDA.
7. On military spending, the Bank favors a proactive approach to assist with demobilization and the conversion of military industries. Mozambique, Angola and Ethiopia have asked the Bank for assistance with demobilization.
8. Sir Joseph Gold, 'Political Considerations Are Prohibited by Articles of Agreement when the Fund Considers Requests for Use of Resources' in *IMF Survey*, May 23, 1983, p. 148.

9. For a cautionary evocation of the risks of a BWI reform agenda based on human rights and democratic pluralism, see Lisa Jordan and Peter van Tuijl, *Democratizing Global Power Relations* (The Hague: Institute of Social Studies, 1993).

10. W. Michael Reisman, 'Through or Despite Governments: Differentiated Responsibilities in Human Rights Programs' in *Iowa Law Review*, vol. 72, no. 2 (1987) pp. 391.

11. For a statistician's positive view on human rights data, see David Bank, 'Measuring Human Rights' in I. Brecher (ed.), *Human Rights, Development and Foreign Policy: Canadian Perspectives* (Halifax: Institute for Research on Public Policy, 1989).

12. United Nations, Secretary General's Address at the University of Bordeaux (New York: United Nations, 1991).

13. See Wai, 'Governance, Economic Development and the Role of External Actors'.

14. Javier Peréz de Cuéllar, Address to the University of Florence, November 22, 1991.

15. This argument against the relevance of rights abuses for the Bank's work is made even as the Bank has acknowledged that development encompasses such things as 'more equality of opportunity, greater individual freedom and a richer cultural life'. See World Bank, *World Development Report 1991* (Washington, DC: World Bank, 1991) p. 4.

16. United Nations Development Programme (UNDP), *Human Development Report 1992* (New York and Oxford: Oxford University Press, 1992).

17. See UNDP's Human Development Report 1991. This is not to deny formidable methodological hurdles in 'measuring' freedom.

18. Organization for Economic Cooperation and Development (OECD) *Development Co-operation in the 1990s: Policy Statement by DAC Aid Ministers and Heads of Agencies* (Paris: OECD, 1989).

19. For details, see R.K. Kiwanuka, 'Developing Rights: The UN Declaration on the Right to Development' in *Netherlands International Law Review*, vol. 35, no. 3 (1988) pp. 257–72.

20. Compare, for example, the Arusha Charter on Popular Participation by African NGOs, the Manila Declaration on People's Participation in Sustainable Development, the Covenant on Philippines Development, and *Put Our World to Rights*, by a group of largely Southern-based Commonwealth NGOs.

21. See Rhoda Howard, 'The "Full Belly" Thesis: Should Economic Rights Take Priority Over Civil and Political Rights? Evidence From Sub-Saharan Africa' in *Human Rights Quarterly*, vol. 5, no. 4 (1983) pp. 467–90.

22. See Robert E. Goodin, 'The Development Rights Trade-Off: Some Unwarranted Economic and Political Assumptions' in *Universal Human Rights*, vol. 1, April–June 1979, pp. 31–42.

23. See Human Rights Watch, *Indivisible Human Rights: The Relationship of Political and Civil Rights to Survival, Subsistence and Poverty* (New York: Human Rights Watch, 1992).

24. For example, see Lynda Chalker, 'Good Governance and the Aid Programme', Speech given at the Overseas Development Institute Conference, Chatham House, England, 1990; and Chalker, *Governance Working Paper: Africa Bureau Democracy and Governance Program* (Washington, DC: US Agency for International Development, 1992).

25. Andre Newberg, 'Economic Development and Human Rights: The Role of the European Bank for Reconstruction and Development', Address to the Association of the Bar of the City of New York, November 1, 1991.

26. In this respect, I disagree with Shihata that EBRD's human rights responsibilities represent a response to a unique and 'peculiar' set of circumstances. See Shihata, *The World Bank in a Changing World*, p. 58.

27. For a development of this argument, see David W. Gillies, 'Evaluating National Human Rights Performance' in *Bulletin of Peace Proposals*, vol. 21, no. 1 (1990) pp. 15–27.

28. Nelson, *Encouraging Democracy*, pp. 62–3.

29. See Gerald J. Schmitz and David W. Gillies, *The Challenge of Democratic Development* (Ottawa: North-South Institute, 1992).

30. Schmitz and Gillies, *The Challenge of Democratic Development*, p. 64.

31. For example, the World Bank was forced to suspend its involvement in the Mahaweli dam and irrigation project as a result of the intensification of the Sri Lankan ethnic conflict in the early 1990s.

32. Option C is more likely since consensus is the *modus operandi* of the Bank's loan deliberations. It is rare that votes are cast on any particular loan, and voting is usually a sign of serious conflict among the Executive Directors of the Bank.

33. Schmitz and Gillies, *The Challenge of Democratic Development*, p. 90. In *Encouraging Democracy*, Nelson includes many African development dictatorships, and one-party-dominant states, such as Mexico and Tunisia.

34. Lewis Carroll, *Through the Looking-Glass, And What Alice Found There*, Chapter IV: 'Humpty Dumpty' (London: Macmillan, 1871) as reprinted in Lewis Carroll, *The Annotated Alice*, (New York: Clarkson N. Potter, 1960) p. 269.

35. Barber B. Conable, Address to a meeting with African Governors of the World Bank, September 1990, as cited in Wai, 'Governance, Economic Development and the Role of External Actors', p. 13.

36. Pierre Landell-Mills and Ismail Serageldin, 'Governance and the External Factor', paper presented at the World Bank Annual Conference on Development Economics, Washington, DC, April 1991, p. 6. See also Wai, 'Governance, Economic Development and the Role of External Actors' and Mark C. Blackden, 'Human Rights, Governance, and Development', Inter-Divisional Thematic Team on Governance, Sub-Group on Human Rights (Washington, DC: World Bank, October 1991).

37. Landell-Mills and Serageldin, 'Governance and the External Factor', p. 7.
38. This shift toward policy-based lending should not be overstated. Policy-based lending remains about 25 per cent of Bank funding, and there is a commitment in the 1990s to shift to social sectors.
39. For a critique of this Northern donor fixation, see Richard Sandbrook, 'Taming Africa's Leviathan' in *World Policy Journal* (Winter 1990) pp. 673-701; and Thandika Mkandawire, 'North-South Links and Democratization in Africa' in *Development*, vol. 3, no. 4 (1991) pp. 39–41.
40. World Bank, *Sub-Saharan Africa: From Crisis to Sustainable Growth; A Long-Term Perspective Study* (Washington, DC: World Bank, 1989) pp. 60–1.
41. Shihata, *Issues of 'Governance' in Borrowing Members: The Extent of Their Relevance Under the Bank's Articles of Agreement* (Washington, DC: World Bank, 1990) p. 9.
42. Barber Conable, *Managing Development: The Governance Dimension* (Washington, DC: World Bank, 1991). While Conable, the former President of the World Bank, took care to call this a 'discussion paper' not a 'policy paper', it appears to have the imprimatur of the senior staff and many country Executive Directors. It is thus a *de facto* policy statement on the institutional parameters of governance.
43. Conable, *Managing Development: The Governance Dimension*, Annex 1, p. 38.
44. Interviews with staff of the Canadian Executive Director to the World Bank.
45. World Bank, *Report on Adjustment Lending II: Policies for the Recovery of Growth* (Washington, DC: World Bank, 1990) at paragraph 4.64; and Nelson (ed.), *Economic Crisis and Policy Choice: The Politics of Adjustment in the Third World* (Princeton: Princeton University Press, 1990).
46. Sardar Sarovar is a dam construction project in India's Narmada Valley. For over ten years, the project has been opposed by the more than 30,000 valley residents because of insufficient resettlement plans and negative side-effects on the environment. The project has been partly financed by the World Bank.
47. Jonathan Cahn, 'Challenging the New Imperial Authority: The World Bank and the Democratization of Development' in *Harvard Human Rights Law Journal*, vol. 6 (1993) pp. 159–94.
48. An internal review, known as the Wapenhans Report, found significant problems with the Bank's loan portfolio. World-wide, 39 per cent of borrowing countries are experiencing problems with more than 25 per cent of their Bank-funded projects. See World Bank, Portfolio Management Task Force, *Effective Implementation: Key to Development Impact* (Washington, DC: World Bank, 1992).
49. For example, see the Draft Charter 'To Secure Human Rights in Development Processes and to Set Out the Human Rights Obliga-

tions of Development Agencies' proposed by Clarence Dias and James Paul, International Center for Law in Development, New York, 1994.

50. For details, see Shihata, 'The World Bank and Non-Governmental Organizations' in *Cornell International Law Journal*, vol. 25 (1992) pp. 623–41. The Bank has also established a 'Participation Learning Group' which recently articulated a series of principles towards best practice in fostering participation and accountability in project design.

51. Drawn from the statement of Professor Daniel Bradlow of Washington College of Law, American University, to the House of Commons Subcommittee on International Financial Institutions, Ottawa, February 18, 1993.

52. Some participants at the Rethinking Bretton Woods conference, skeptical of the degree to which the Inspection Panel will be insulated from internal conflicts of interest, called instead for an external watchdog 'Bank Watch' along the lines of the human rights 'watch committees' to undertake independent evaluations of Bank projects. Also see Cahn, 'Challenging the New Imperial Authority', p. 190.

53. Section 701 (a) of Public Law 95–118, October 3, 1977. For an account of its application under President Carter, see Lars Schoultz, *Human Rights and United States Foreign Policy Toward Latin America* (Princeton: Princeton University Press, 1981).

54. Notable exceptions were the Netherlands and the Nordic countries, who opposed loans to Chile during much of the Pinochet era.

55. See Center for International Policy, *Enforcing Human Rights: Congress and the Multilateral Banks* (Washington, DC: Center for International Policy, 1985).

56. Speech of Lord Keynes before the Inaugural Meeting of the Board of Governors of the Fund and the Bank, 1946.

57. Shihata, *Issues of 'Governance' in Borrowing Members*, p. 13.

58. Shihata, *The World Bank in a Changing World*, p. 79.

59. Cited in Shihata, 'The World Bank and Non-Governmental Organizations' in *Cornell International Law Journal*, vol. 25 (1992) pp. 623–41.

60. Shihata, *The World Bank in a Changing World*, pp. 81–4.

61. Shihata, *The World Bank in a Changing World*, p. 82.

62. Shihata, *The World Bank in a Changing World*, p. 83.

63. The Consultative Groups are forums to coordinate development assistance to the following countries: Bangladesh, Bolivia, Cameroon, Caribbean, Ghana, Honduras, India, Kenya, Malawi, Mali, Mozambique, Nepal, Nicaragua, Nigeria, Pakistan, Uganda, Tanzania, Zambia and Zimbabwe.

64. Shihata, *The World Bank in a Changing World*, p. 83.

65. The World Bank/NGO Committee has been a special focus for conveying these concerns to Bank staff.

66. Shihata, *The World Bank in a Changing World*, pp. 92–3.

67. One official from a Southern borrowing country argued that popular participation as an agency-wide principle could be misused by ethnic or 'ideological' NGOs. Development NGOs are, moreover, only one constituency among many and may not be representative of wider civil society. Interview in Washington, April 13, 1992. Also see Alan Fowler, 'The Role of NGOs in Changing State-Society Relations: Perspectives From Eastern and Southern Africa' in *Development Policy Review*, vol. 9 (1991) pp. 53–84.

68. With assistance from SIDA, the Swedish development agency, the Bank is now undertaking a major research program on popular participation.

69. Africa Watch, *Kenya: Taking Liberties* (New York: Africa Watch, 1991).

70. A temporary exception was during the Gulf War, when Mombasa was a refuelling haven for US 'ordinance'.

71. The bilateral donors of the Consultative Group for Kenya include Canada, Denmark, Finland, France, Germany, Italy, Japan, the Netherlands, Sweden, Switzerland, the United Kingdom, and the United States.

72. World Bank press release, Paris, November 20, 1990.

73. Interview with a World Bank official, Washington DC, April 13, 1992.

74. According to a World Bank official present at the Paris meeting of the Consultative Group for Kenya, only the United Kingdom formally addressed the difficulties raised by introducing political conditionality in an economic forum. The UK delegate was also concerned that the Consultative Group's message could be misunderstood by the Kenyan authorities, namely, that just by calling for elections and permitting multi-party elections, the government had done all that was necessary to restore aid. Interview in Washington, April 13, 1992.

75. World Bank press release, Meeting of the Consultative Group for Kenya, Paris, November 26, 1991.

76. Interview with a senior World Bank official, Washington, DC April 15, 1992.

77. National Democratic Institute for International Affairs, 'NDI Mission to Kenya', February 3–7, 1992, p. 5.

78. Speech by the Permanent Representative of the People's Republic of China at the United Nations, New York, December 1, 1989.

79. These original grievances were centered on issues of corruption and civil liberties. The phrase 'pro-democracy movement' thus seems overstated.

80. *Declaration on China*, Summit of the Arch, Paris, July 15, 1989.

81. Interview with Ibrahim F.I. Shihata, World Bank Vice President and General Counsel, in Washington, DC, April 13, 1992.

82. Interviews reveal that some staff in Part II countries understood the strong line taken by the Part I lenders. An Indian official noted that

Indian 'thought processes are close to those of the Part I EDs', but leverage must be opposed because it was the thin end of the wedge. Interview in Washington, DC, April 13, 1992.

83. Shihata interview, April 13, 1992.

84. Interview with Mr Ferry de Kerchove, Ottawa, June 6, 1990.

85. Charlotte Montgomery, 'Amnesty Decries China Executions', *The Globe and Mail*, September 13, 1990.

86. For details, see World Bank, *China: Between Plan and Market* (Washington, DC: World Bank, 1990); and Kathleen Hartford, 'Reform or Retrofitting? The Chinese Economy Since Tiananmen' in *World Policy Journal*, vol. 9, no. 1 (1991) pp. 36–66.

87. Interviews with officials from the office of the Canadian Executive Director, Washington, DC, April 12, 1992.

88. See UN General Assembly A/CONF.157/AFRM/L.2.

89. See World Bank, *World Development Report 1990* (Washington, DC: World Bank, 1990) pp. 64–7.

90. In Africa, the Council for the Development of Economic and Social Research (CODESRIA) established the Kampala Declaration on the Right to Academic Freedom. Also see the Declaration on Academic Freedom at the UNESCO Conference on Human Rights and Democracy, Montreal, March 1993.

6 Foreign Assistance: Catalyst for Domestic Coalition Building

Daniel C. Milder

INTRODUCTION

The heyday of neoliberals at the World Bank lasted from about 1982 until around 1987, by which time the shortcomings of their strategy for structural adjustment were apparent. Neither the economic policies neoliberals prescribed, the domestic political approach they promoted, nor the high-pressure tactics they practiced, worked out as planned. Most African, Middle Eastern and Latin American economies remain in dire straits more than a decade after structural adjustment lending was launched. Those few countries that have resumed growth and access to credit have done so only after a decade; few of these have regained full economic health. These exceptions, as well as the Asian economies which have done very well, have done so in part by avoiding the full force of neoliberals' influence.

The Bank has learned many lessons from this experience, and has done much reformulation. However, political assumptions embodied in the original neoliberal approach continue to undergird the thinking of many Bank strategists. Revisions to the neoliberal approach have fallen short of challenging these assumptions. As a result, the Bank today is caught between following the old approach and crystallizing a new approach.

Like most institutions facing new challenges, the Bank has adapted its ongoing program, rather than developing a new one. The challenge is to integrate its realization that economic reform depends on political change. The Bank has responded by adding new strategies on top of the old, rather than by replacing them, producing contradictory effects. It has added strategies to promote positive political changes, while continuing economic policies aggravating political conflict.

For many at the Bank, countries' problems with structural adjustment result primarily from incapable, uncommitted governments. Conditionality, that is, the Bank's threat to cut off lending to governments that do not comply with its policy reforms, has proven insufficient to force leaders to carry out reforms with the necessary vigor, when leaders are not convinced reforms serve their interests. Leaders who are convinced and committed to reforms cannot carry them out when their bureaucracies lack the capacity or accountability. To the extent governments do carry out reforms, their extreme dependence on the support of privileged elites leads them to avoid reforms that challenge those elites, and so the main burdens of reform fall on weaker groups, take longer, and cost more than necessary, all of which cause unrest and deter investors.

In response to this analysis of the political obstacles to reform, the Bank has made three main revisions in its approach. First, in place of conditionality, it emphasizes 'dialogue' to convince leaders to assume 'ownership' of reforms, that is, to become more committed to reforms. Second, to increase the capacity and accountability of the bureaucracy, it promotes 'institutional reforms' to improve 'governance'. Finally, to address the unequal impact of reforms on weaker groups, the Bank supports 'Social Investment Funds', and participation by the poor in grass-roots organizations (GROs) that decide how to use these funds and take responsibility for doing so.

These new strategies have aimed primarily at winning leaders' faith in reform and making bureaucracies more capable, obedient tools of leaders. They have not aimed at making reforms more popular or at offering compromises to turn opponents of reform into supporters. It remains the dominant assumption among Bank analysts that reforms cannot be made more popular without undermining their economic effectiveness, which depends on carrying them out in a bold, comprehensive and necessarily unpopular way that cuts down opponents first and produces supporters later.

The Bank has rightly recognized that the success of economic reforms depends on solving political problems. But the Bank takes a simplistic view of political problems and resists altering its economic designs in any way to help solve them. The problem is more than weak or selfish leaders and bureaucracies. It is divided societies. Improving governance depends on the formation of societal compromise. To nurture compromise, the state must take an activist economic role in building cross-class coalitions. But the Bank pushes an economic prescription that works against state activism and coalition building. The importance of social compromise in more successful efforts at adjustment has been largely overlooked. If the Bank supported coalition building as a central guideline in its reforms, its aid could catalyze the mobilization and redistribution of domestic resources, worth many times the value of Bank loans.

This chapter is divided into five sections. First, the importance of structural adjustment is discussed, and its broader meaning is distinguished from the neoliberals' narrow definition. The section describes: the impact of neoliberals on the Bank's design of structural adjustment in terms of particular economic prescriptions; the domestic political approach neoliberals assumed would be necessary for carrying out structural adjustment; and how neoliberals hoped to pressure developing countries to adopt their approach.

Second, I consider how well these neoliberal strategies worked in practice, and how they compared with the strategies followed by relatively successful reformers. It is argued that activist economic policies are central for political as well as economic reasons. It is explained how activist policies have helped to reduce the costs of reform, to distribute the burdens of reform more fairly, to share the benefits of reform and to initiate positive economic responses to new incentives. The reasons why structural reform depends on broad support are elaborated.

Third, I examine the Bank's revisions of its original approach of promoting policy reforms. New efforts to promote ownership, governance and participation are shown to operate on the same flawed assumptions that caused the original neoliberal approach to fail and that hurt efforts at democratization.

Fourth, it is explained how the common non-governmental organization (NGO) critique of the Bank's structural adjustment programs fails to identify these flaws, and how NGOs' alternative strategy of empowerment falls short of providing a basis for coalition building.

Fifth, I propose further changes the World Bank should make to promote positive political change in developing countries. Because activist economic policies can make reform politically easier, and because coalition building can make activist states more accountable and effective, the Bank needs to make coalition building an explicit priority.

STRUCTURAL ADJUSTMENT AS MORE THAN MARKET REFORMS

The term structural adjustment was originally used by Latin American structuralist economists to distinguish between short-term stabilization as practiced by the International Monetary Fund (IMF) and the structural changes they considered necessary to keep countries from having to return again and again to the IMF. In their view, the IMF approach only treated symptoms, rather than attacking the roots of balance-of-payments problems. In their usage, structural adjustment meant changes in the structure of the economy that would make stability more sustainable. Such changes would require more time and more finance than IMF programs provided.

When the World Bank first launched structural adjustment lending in 1979, the term 'structural adjustment' was used in the following sense. With many developing countries facing mounting debts and being forced to turn to the IMF, the Bank became concerned that countries would have to adjust too much by cutting demand and imports. Structural adjustment was a way for the Bank to offer large-scale balance-of-payments loans to counter the deflationary impact of IMF stabilization programs, and to enable countries to adjust more by raising supply and exports. In particular, structural adjustment lending was seen as necessary for the success of the Bank's efforts to promote redistribution with growth.[1]

At the same time, the IMF began experimenting with a more structuralist approach to adjustment which addressed many concerns of developing country critics. The Indian loan of 1979 was a radical change from IMF orthodoxy in several respects. It was larger, longer-term and less strict, and so encouraged India to address imbalances well before they produced a crisis. It emphasized macroeconomics rather than market reforms, allowing the public sector to stimulate export supply and import substitution, rather than requiring a devaluation to cut import demand.[2]

Around 1982, however, the meaning of structural adjustment lending changed. Rather than seeing adjustment as a shift in the structure of the economy, Bank publications began treating economic liberalization as the main goal of adjustment. Since neoliberals at the World Bank began to use structural adjustment lending as a vehicle for promoting market reforms, the term structural adjustment has become a synonym for economic liberalization. The more neutral meaning of structural adjustment has been lost. As a result, critics of the neoliberal approach to adjustment have attacked structural adjustment *per se*, and lost sight of its importance.

In more neutral terms, structural adjustment means shifting what a country produces and consumes in order to make the economy more stable, flexible, competitive and efficient. These are not controversial priorities that constitute the vital signs of good economic health which are necessary for development, however development is defined. In that sense, countries have no more choice about making adjustment a priority than people who are sick have about making getting well a priority.

There are many choices, however, about what selection, timing and sequencing of shifts in economic structure are most necessary for improving an economy's health. Adjustment can be market-led or state-led, with or without growth; with easy finance to keep up imports or with capital outflows forcing austerity; during economic crisis, or before or after economic crisis; inequitable or with all groups sharing costs and benefits. It can target one or several structural imbalances that make developing countries vulnerable to crises and constrain them from making the best use of their resources.

Most developing countries suffer from a number of such imbalances. For example, poor countries tend to rely on imports for a large share of production inputs, while also depending heavily on a few primary exports to earn the foreign exchange to buy those inputs. They tend to have low agricultural productivity outside the export sector, with a large share of the work force made up of subsistence farmers and landless peasants who cannot produce enough food to satisfy urban demand nor provide much domestic demand for industrial wage goods. They tend to develop modern sector enclaves that use capital-intensive processes to produce durable goods for up-scale consumers, while small to medium-sized firms and farms in the informal sector are starved of capital that could boost their productivity. They tend to have weak entrepreneurial classes who face severe disadvantages in international competition and suffer from their government's weak capacity to provide public goods such as human, physical and financial infrastructures. Governments face huge demand for public goods, but lack the capacity to raise much revenue, due to the threat of capital flight and the tradition of relying on trade taxes and foreign bonds for revenue.[3]

Development economists in the early post-war period focused largely on identifying such imbalances, which in their view made developing economies structurally different from developed ones, and so required different solutions from those that worked in developed economies. Most development economists held the structuralist view that such imbalances were historical inheritances that could be overcome only by government interventions. Free-market policies that worked for more developed countries would not resolve structural problems. Development would help to create conditions in which markets could function more effectively. More recently, neoliberals have challenged this view and argued that most imbalances have been produced by bad government policies that stifled price mechanisms.

In the current mainstream view, these imbalances result from both market and government failures, with the relative importance of each depending on the particular case. Structural adjustment therefore requires some combination of market reforms and government interventions. What makes a reform structural is its focus on changing' fundamental structures, whether by economic liberalization or by state activism or by some combination of the two. Neoliberals and structuralists often agree in their identification of which structures need adjustment. Though they disagree on the best means of adjustment, they share a common understanding of the distinction between structural adjustment as concrete changes in the economy and economic liberalization as one means to affect such changes.

Neoliberals and structuralists also agree that imbalances are structural because many forces are working to keep them in place. A major obstacle to change has been those groups who have benefited from such imbalances. Any kind of structural adjustment involves a reallocation of resources, which implies a redistribution of power. For this reason, structural adjustment is directly relevant to poverty reduction. Not only does adjustment improve the economy's capacity to attack poverty, it also forces better-off groups to give up some claims to resources, which then may be directed toward investment in the poor.

Neoliberal Economic Prescriptions

According to the neoliberal diagnosis, most of the economic miseries of developing countries resulted from government interventions and a public sector which had expanded to the point where it crowded out market forces. Neoliberals argued that the success of private-sector firms had grown so dependent on government decisions that developing economies differed little from socialist economies. With government distorting relative prices, resources were channeled into inefficient activities and many workers remained underemployed or idle.

For many countries, there was much truth in this critique, and since the early 1960s all kinds of economists had given increasing attention to it. The Bank first became concerned in the 1970s, when it found that distorted prices were undermining the effectiveness of some Bank-funded projects. More importantly, the Bank became convinced that excessive state interventionism was doing damage on a scale that far overshadowed any good done by projects. 'Getting prices right' was a solution just waiting for a problem to come along to bring it to the top of the agenda, when the debt crisis hit. So the rise of this solution was not simply the result of the rise of neoliberals to top positions at the Bank. But the form this solution took owed a great deal to the rising influence of neoliberals at the Bank.[4]

The contribution of neoliberals was not so much that they emphasized the problem of excessive interventionism. Rather it was their analysis of the sources of the problem that shaped the Bank's solution. They blamed the problem almost entirely on self-interested governments using economic policies for political purposes. At its core, they saw the problem as political, a matter of vested interests, not the result of poor policy choices, or of difficult economic dilemmas without easy answers. Therefore, persuasion and material aid could do little to solve it. Governments would continue to adopt economically irrational policies, because this served the interests of those in power.[5]

The powerful included politicians, bureaucrats, businesspeople and labor elites who together dominated the state and used it to enrich and protect themselves. The only way to break the stranglehold of these privileged interests over Third World states would be to force governments to reduce radically their economic role, and thereby destroy the sources of these predators' power. Hence, what was needed was not just a redressing of the imbalance between states and markets, but rather state minimalism. Only a radical reduction of government's economic role could stop government from harming the economy.

This profoundly cynical view of the state explains in part why neoliberal policy prescriptions went beyond what mainstream neoclassical economists would recommend. For example, where mainstream economists might argue that interest rates need to be raised, or the exchange rate needs to be devalued, or public enterprises need to be reformed, neoliberals called for freeing interest rates, floating exchange rates and privatizing whatever could be peddled. Neoliberals tend to treat the maximum determination of prices by the market as the optimum. The more radical the reduction of the state's role in the economy the better. It is not so much that they believe that market forces alone suffice to solve all serious economic problems. Rather, they feel certain that governments cannot be trusted with correcting for market failures. The neoliberal credo has been summarized as the belief that 'imperfect markets are better than imperfect states'.[6]

Neoliberal Political Theory

In addition to particular policy positions, the Bank's overall design of policy reform packages reflected neoliberal political assumptions and aims. The rapid, comprehensive approach to policy reform was explicitly based on political as well as economic considerations. To be sure, various economic reasons justified this approach. For example, bold action was deemed necessary for establishing credibility with the markets and comprehensive liberalization necessary for interdependent markets to produce the right prices. When distortions are reduced in some markets but not in others, it is not certain that the resulting relative prices will be more 'correct' than before. Without comprehensive liberalization, markets cannot work their magic.

But there were also good economic arguments for why a more gradual, incremental approach might be more credible and effective, arguments which neoliberals accepted in theory. Governments might take easier steps first in order to build support for more difficult ones, and with support increase their credibility. Governments might take responsibility for setting some prices that are difficult to liberalize at an early stage of reform. Governments might promote the expansion of market competition in some sectors such as agriculture and small business, before taking on restructuring of others, like public enterprises, so that laid-off workers might have somewhere to look for new opportunities.[7] Governments might take many actions to manage the timing, scope and distribution of the costs of reform in order to make the process of reform less traumatic, to build trust and to facilitate the private sector response to reforms. Neoliberals along with mainstream economists recognized that, in economic theory, more gradual and managed reforms could be less costly.[8]

In practice, however, neoliberals were convinced that few developing countries had governments strong enough and public-interested enough to succeed at such a strategy. Once a weak state tries to make bargains to balance the interests of different groups, it quickly ends up captured. Better not to try a compromise approach. Besides, neoliberals saw most governments as already captured by opponents of reform. The first political aim of reform had to be to defeat this opposition, not to build support. While a gradual approach might broaden support, it also gave opponents time to regroup and counterattack.[9]

This priority of defeating the opposition followed from neoliberals' public-choice theory of who would oppose and support reforms and who mattered. Since the essence of reform was seen as the radical reduction of state spending and controls, with which governments by definition rewarded society's most powerful groups for their support, it followed that the main losers and opponents of reform would be the politically powerful. All the weaker groups in society, at whose expense government had been serving privileged groups, would benefit from reforms reducing the flow of favors to the powerful.[10]

Reformers could not count on such weak groups to give them enough backing to overcome the opposition. Aside from the political weakness of such groups, the logic of reform required, in the neoliberal view, that such groups also pay some of the short-term costs of reform, which would make them unlikely supporters of reform. Building support in the short term required the public to understand that without painful reforms things would worsen, while with reform their lives would improve. In the neoliberal view, non-economic efforts to build broad support such as persuasion, appeals to nationalism, displays of fairness and political liberalization were unlikely to impress groups that faced immediate costs, especially when powerful opponents of reform would be working hard to convince them that reforms will not help them. So in the short term, there would be little chance of building support, and thus little to be lost by taking a more rapid, higher-cost approach to reform.

On the contrary, the more rapid the reforms, the faster benefits and support would arrive. The more reformers moderated initial reforms to soften opposition, the less likely reforms were to work.[11] This deductive vision of the reform process posed a daunting dilemma. How could a system so valued by the status quo powers ever be changed, and by whom? How could reformers succeed against opposition from the main groups that government depended on for support, when it would take some time for government to build new bases of support, that was sure to be weaker than the opposition? How could governments survive and sustain painful reforms in the face of opposition from major groups within government itself, with a large share of bureaucrats and politicians likely to lose from reform? How could the state be expected to cut back its own size, powers and support?

The answer for many neoliberals was a 'revolution from above'. Many neoliberals encouraged the concentration of policy-making power in a small cadre of dedicated technocrats, backed by the head of state, funded and coached by the Bank, and 'insulated' from the demands of other politicians, bureaucrats and private interests.[12] If this cadre could shut down government interventionism, it could cut off privileged groups' sources of power and force them to face market discipline. Rather than trying to reform the state and make it more responsive to the needs of the majority, a task which could take decades, the cadre strategy offered a short-cut around politics: *the economy could be fixed without fixing the state*. The cadre could cut back the state to an absolute minimum and the economy could live just fine without it. But to do this, the cadre had to act boldly, to achieve a *fait accompli*. Before the opposition knew what happened, the cadre could strip away its protection, its patronage and its power to resist.

This account of the neoliberal political strategy sounds like a tale of attempted revolution, because many neoliberals themselves have seen their mission as turning developing societies upside-down. Like neo-Marxists, they have seen the state as little more than the executive committee of the ruling classes. They have believed that the *ancien regime* would resist any compromise, and must be destroyed, before a truly new system could be built. They have welcomed the 'heightening of contradictions', that is, the collapse of developing countries' economies, as the revolutionary crisis necessary for making a sharp break from the status quo.

Obviously, a movement with revolutionary aims is not supportive of class compromise and cross-class coalition building. Instead, neoliberals have portrayed the situation in Manichaean terms. They have labelled all groups who benefited from government policies 'privileged' and any groups hurt by those policies 'exploited'. The former deserve any rough justice that market liberalization deals them, while the latter are bound to gain from the demise of government interventionism. The cadre of technocrats would be the intellectual vanguard leading the exploited majority to see their own interest in a new economic system.

Neoliberals have also promoted a dichotomous view of the available choices: radical reform or the status quo. Countries can either undertake 'real reforms' leading to a vibrant, free economy, or they can pursue 'piecemeal, partial reforms' miring them in stagnant, statist ways.[13] Governments can either get out of the way and let the private sector take over, or they can continue to take an activist economic role that stifles entrepreneurism. By defining the essence of reform as 'reducing political constraints on economic policymaking', neoliberals imply that policymakers can design policy to serve economic purposes or political purposes, but not both.[14] By speaking of reform as a transition from one kind of system to an entirely different kind, neoliberals imply that there is no middle ground.[15] By portraying reform as a revolution, they imply that high transitional costs are inevitable. By promising miraculous benefits from change, they imply that change is worth any price.

Neoliberals' Strategy of International Influence

Neoliberal theories of the domestic politics of developing countries also influenced the Bank's strategies to persuade Third World policymakers. The Bank assumed that most developing country governments would not undertake reforms that posed such great political risks to them, and that the Bank would have to use financial pressure to make the risks of avoiding reforms greater than the risks of attempting them. The Bank did so by making the continued dispersal of structural adjustment loans (SALs) conditional on whether countries implemented the reform package. It was a way to pressure government leaders to break free from the grip of powerful interest groups. If the Bank itself did not get tough on governments, in the neoliberal view, governments would never take on the powerful.

Neoliberal ideas were also reflected in the Bank's use of the debt crisis to promote radical reform. The Bank knew that international factors were the overwhelming proximate cause of the debt crisis.[16] And it could have advocated a response to the crisis that made recovery, or preservation of growth the first priority. Whatever the deeper structural problems that lay beneath countries' balance-of-payments crises, structural reforms to address those problems could be undertaken after recovery, in a context of growth and access to finance and imports. Neoliberals were not the only ones who identified excessive statism as an important underlying cause of debt problems, but it was consistent with their philosophy to push for market reforms at a time when countries were weakest. It fitted their view that countries would only adopt market reforms in a time of crisis when people were more open to radical changes and more ready to pay difficult costs. The debt crisis was the opportunity to push for fundamental change, even if that meant incurring the increased costs of stabilizing and restructuring at the same time. In fact, reformers were less worried about costs than they were about the possibility that economic recovery would come before radical reforms were 'irreversible'.

Had the Bank been concerned with borrowing countries' ability to build support for reforms, it might have been more concerned with keeping the costs of reform low, and with ensuring adequate finance flows to reforming countries. But instead, the Bank endorsed a response to the debt crisis by donors which produced net capital outflows from many adjusting countries for most of the 1980s. The Bank was much less worried that too little finance would make reforms too difficult, than it was that too much financing might be available too easily, enabling opponents of reform to hold out against change. This attitude was consistent with the neoliberal theory that destroying the opposition came before building new bases of support. Bankrupting the state was not a bad way, from the neoliberal view, of destroying the old regime.

NEOLIBERAL THEORIES IN PRACTICE

While some observers question the effectiveness of conditionality in pressuring developing countries to reform, there is no question that the World Bank's activities and influence expanded tremendously in the 1980s as a result of adjustment lending. Due in part to the Bank, neoliberalism gained a strong foothold in countries of every region in the world.

After more than ten years of structural adjustment, the economic results are largely unsatisfactory. The main economic lesson has been that the economy cannot be fixed without fixing the state. Markets only work well in conjunction with a strong state. Economic liberalization is not a politically easier economic approach than state activism. Comprehensive liberalization does more harm than good.

The main political lesson has been that power and wealth cannot be redistributed simply by a cadre of technocrats pulling economic levers and minimizing the role of the state. Market reforms have not automatically punished retrograde *rentiers* or rewarded competitive entrepreneurs. Rather than benefitting weaker groups, reforms have concentrated wealth further and made poor much of the middle class. Weaker groups can and do take actions that set back reforms, when governments do little to ensure that burdens are shared. The cadre strategy has been effective at imposing costs, but not at inducing positive responses so critical to reform. Where reforms have produced the best results, countries have practiced a very different kind of politics. They have built up broad support during the process of reform, not just as a result of reform.

Strategies of International Influence in Practice

After some eight years of structural adjustment lending, Bank critics and sympathizers alike concluded that the results of structural adjustment had been disappointing in most countries. The Bank blamed shortcomings on inadequate implementation of reforms, and suggested that with patience and further implementation, reforms would yet yield rapid, sustainable growth. Critics either claimed that critical reforms had been implemented and had not worked, or that failure of countries to implement reforms more fully indicated that reforms were politically unrealistic.

A conclusive verdict in the debate over how much reform has been implemented remains to be reached, and depends on theoretical arguments about which are the most critical reforms. The Bank argues both that it has succeeded in pressuring borrowers to comply with conditions and that failures are due to insufficient compliance. Both arguments are no doubt true to some degree, depending on the case.

The Bank has given most attention to insufficient compliance, and to explaining why the threat of withdrawing loans to punish non-compliance has not been effective. The most obvious answer to the latter has been that the Bank cancelled few loans. The Bank was assigned the task of moving money so debtors could pay back industrialized countries' private banks. Thus, it could not easily cancel loans. It was also under pressure to produce successes, which made it reluctant to give up on countries that were trying to comply. Some countries with no intention of adopting reforms found they could keep the funds flowing just by pretending to reform.

Still, the threat of withdrawing loans probably had some impact, especially in weaker, more desperate, less geopolitically vital countries. The threat surely raised perceived risks of non-compliance. And while few loans were terminated, many were interrupted. For politicians concerned about the short term, even the temporary interruption of loans represented a serious threat. This was especially true of countries desperate for foreign exchange, or countries concerned about gaining or maintaining access to private lenders, who used compliance with Bank conditions as a criterion for judging countries' creditworthiness.

The most popular explanation for lack of compliance has been the lack of ownership of reforms by borrower governments. Because reform has required a long, sustained effort, only governments genuinely convinced that reforms will work and serve their interests, have been willing to sustain the commitment necessary for carrying out reforms. Persuasion may matter more than pressure. Assuming that only selfish interests could explain reluctance to reform, neoliberals dismissed governments' genuine doubts about reform, and emphasized financial pressure above persuasion, often weakening their local allies, and probably hurting their chances of being persuasive.

Two other explanations for lack of compliance have been less noted. First, for the threat of cutting off loans to have much impact, adequate financial rewards for compliance would be necessary to raise hopes that reforms could work. Instead, good behavior was not rewarded with increased net inflows of capital or debt relief for most countries until the 1990s. Compliant countries were rewarded with only enough finance to allow them to remain current on their debt payments, a situation which could not help governments make reforms popular.[17] Peasants and workers understood better than many international economists that austerity was keeping industrialized countries' banks out of crisis. Second, the difficulty of gaining compliance obviously depended on the question, 'compliance with what?' A less radical and antistatist version of reforms might have accomplished more.

The Bank's own studies of compliance indicate that most countries have either complied rather fully or hardly at all. Although it is clear that much reform has taken place in many countries, it remains unclear whether this was due to the financial pressure tactics of conditionality, to the persuasive influence the Bank exerts as an intellectually powerful institution, or to the transnational technocratic networks the Bank has built up around the world.

Where compliance has resulted entirely from pressure, and government has a weak commitment to reform, the sustainability of reforms, and the utility of pressure remains in doubt. Pulling macroeconomic levers has proven much easier than reforming institutions and changing attitudes. The most difficult stage of reforms lies ahead for most countries. In addition, it has turned out that governments have found ways to comply with economic conditionality without undermining privileged interests. Conditionality has succeeded at getting governments to implement very painful reforms that hurt the general public, more than it has succeeded at pushing reforms that challenge the privileged, but hurt the public less. Pressure has not achieved its political aims.

Perhaps the most important effect of Bank influence has been the concentration of power in cadres of neoliberal technocrats in developing-country governments. Policy conditionality strengthened the hand of the Bank's allies in countries' finance ministries which led local pro-reform factions. Their power in policy debates was enhanced by Bank funds provided if policy advice were heeded. Often, politicians appointed finance ministers preferred by the Bank in order to smooth access to funds. Many high-ranking policy positions, including those of chief executives, have been filled by economists who had trained in the United States or had worked for the Bank.

Critics of the neoliberal approach, located in other government departments such as planning and commerce, were cut out of debates. Cadre members often followed the neoliberal dictum to insulate themselves from interest groups, and to regard such groups as enemies of the public interest. Whether governments followed a cadre strategy of reform depended most on domestic factors. But the encouragement from Bank neoliberals added to their belief that it was a legitimate strategy. It is difficult to gauge the Bank's power as a vehicle for the diffusion of both economic and political ideas. But it is surely underestimated by measuring the Bank's influence only by the size of its loans relative to borrowers' GDP.

Limitations of Economic Liberalization

Neoliberals' determination to push radical market reforms in the midst of a debt crisis accounts in part for the high costs and slow progress of reforms. Their promotion of comprehensive liberalization, their opposition to any economic role for the state and their emphasis on cutting public spending, rather than raising revenues, has undermined efforts at stabilization and hurt the private sector. Relying on major devaluations in the context of a debt overhang contributed to translating external imbalances into high domestic inflations, as Bank economists now admit.[18] The Bank has also re-evaluated its opposition to price controls, admitting the need for heterodox policies to address inertial sources of inflation.[19]

Combining stabilization and liberalization also hurt the trade balance. Attempting import liberalization when trying to fight inflation with an anchored exchange rate raises the external debt and domestic interest rates.[20] Financial liberalization on top of this combination only makes export promotion more difficult.[21] In recent years the Bank has retreated from promotion of comprehensive across-the-board privatization and liberalization of prices, foreign exchange and finances.

Besides complicating stabilization efforts, liberalization alone proved insufficient to bring recovery. The most common and critical failing of structural adjustment has been the lack of a strong investment response, without which restructuring cannot proceed. Many states have drastically cut protection and public spending, but are still awaiting growth. Austerity alone has not raised investment, deregulation of exchange and interest rates have not raised savings, and import liberalization has not raised exports.

Relying on comparative advantage to raise exports does not work so well in a world where the products developing countries produce most efficiently face high trade barriers and low income elasticities of demand in the industrialized countries. Sharp reduction of trade barriers does not attract multinational corporations looking to invest in protected markets. Good debtor behavior has not necessarily brought much direct foreign investment or access to long-term private international finance. In general, prohibitions against government using any selective incentives to stimulate investment or exports have left investors waiting for a sign. Getting the prices right does not automatically release repressed entrepreneurial forces, but withdrawal of the state from providing subsidized credit and managing interest rates may bankrupt large numbers of firms. Rather than countering urban bias and improving agricultural productivity, price reforms accompanied by reduced government inputs to agriculture can worsen the plight of peasants.

Bank economists have found strong evidence that public investment tends to crowd in private-sector investment, rather than crowding it out as neoliberals said it did.[22] Both investment and savings depend on growth. Neoliberals called consistently for cutting spending, rather than raising revenue to balance government budgets. But there may be structural limits to the amount of sustainable cuts that can be made in public spending. After a certain point, cutting spending and wages can cripple the supply response, and hurt chances of boosting exports, leading to further devaluation and spending cuts. A compelling case can be made for making a central aim of adjustment the resurrection and reform of bankrupt states, for which increasing the tax base is a necessity, not just an optional means of cutting deficits.[23]

Insulation Before Accountability: Putting Reform Before Politics

Lack of state activism has hurt not only the economic effectiveness of reforms, but also their political viability. The two have been inextricably intertwined. Without the state taking an active role in ensuring that the burdens of reform are tolerable and the benefits of reform are shared, the privileged have not been 'disciplined', the weak have not been rewarded, and the capacity and motivation of the state to play an active role have not been reinforced. Neoliberals were naive to think they could carry out a revolution without either using force against opponents, or mobilizing the masses to give them the power to defeat opponents. There are structural limits to how much peaceful redistribution of wealth and power a society can carry out. Opponents are not easily stripped of their resources, and weak groups expected to benefit have the power to block reforms if they have to wait too long for benefits or have to pay harsh up-front costs. Groups whose fate under reforms is uncertain, have been lost to the opposition by states unwilling to adapt economic policies to political needs.

Neoliberals have been right to argue that accelerating growth requires taking on privileged interests. However, they underestimated the resourcefulness of the privileged. Reforming national macroeconomic policies has not cut off *rentiers'* control over government resources, especially not at the local level. And forcing protected producers to face the discipline of market forces has not helped where states have not played an active role in ensuring that markets are competitive. Liberalization does not automatically produce competition. Deregulating the financial system does not necessarily make more credit available to more deserving entrepreneurs. Creation of cartels, price-setting and rent-seeking go on in the private as well as the public sector.

On the other hand, when technocratic cadres have tried rapid, comprehensive liberalization to force protected businesses to face the full force of international competition all at once, they have often destroyed viable firms, or driven them into investments that contribute less to the domestic economy. Many efficient, competitive firms have been liquidated by getting caught in the crossfire of interest and exchange rates that explode when governments abandon responsibility for their management.[24] By relying on the market to discipline protected producers indiscriminately, rather than bargaining with the business sector over the process of reform, neoliberals have alienated potential supporters and developed an adversarial relationship with the business sector. Technocrats in many countries have adopted the neoliberal attitude that interest groups are the enemy, and that policymakers' duty is to ignore them.[25] Business groups' lack of access feeds their fear that policymakers could take arbitrary, unpredictable actions that could undermine their investments.

Instead of bringing more rapid recovery and the growth of support, the radical liberal approach unnecessarily hurt potential supporters and failed to restore investors' confidence. Neoliberals have blamed weak investment response on inadequate implementation of reforms. But both of these problems can be traced to neglect of the need to build support in the short term. When the weak have been neglected, they have proven powerful enough to intimidate governments and markets, if not to gain much power of their own. Also, lack of broad support has made leaders less brave about taking on predatory groups. Rather than reforms producing support, reforms did not work well without support.

Advocates of a revolution from above argue that governments can and may have to survive for quite some time without support.[26] But even most dictatorships cannot survive for very long without some minimum of broad support or acquiescence. Even where freedoms are restricted and political activity is punished, people still strike out when they get angry enough, and dictators still worry about how people will react. When the poor have protested or rioted in reaction to rapid, bold reforms that produce severe trauma, other more politically powerful groups, including militaries, have lost confidence in governments and tried to replace them. If governments have managed to survive, they still have tended to retreat on reforms when faced with popular protest, causing the reform process to lose momentum and credibility.[27] As long as leaders worry, and take economic policy actions to try to prevent strong opposition, the fact that groups have no access does not mean they have no influence. It is what leaders are thinking that measures how autonomously they are acting.

Where popular turmoil in reaction to a high-cost approach to reform has not undermined governments, or their determination to forge ahead with reforms, it has still weakened investment. Political instability in the form of people taking to the streets or peasants taking to the hills have deterred investors in many cases. Chiapas is only the latest example. Even lack of broad support for government has been enough at times to hurt investment. When investors doubt that governments feel secure enough in their support to stick to reforms, they just wait, rather than respond to price changes.

Neoliberal political assumptions have also led reformers to view many groups as inevitable opponents, when some moderation of the approach to reform might have made them supporters. It was simplistic to assume that all groups had clear material interests in opposing or supporting reform, that groups could not be persuaded about what was in their interest, or that groups' attitudes towards reform depended entirely on perceptions of economic self-interest. It was also an oversimplification to see only the conflicting interests between groups and not their mutual interests, which could provide a basis for compromises. Neoliberals were not looking for compromise.

Coalition Building by Successful Reformers

Countries that have achieved the most success with structural reforms[28] did so by building support among the poor, the middle class and the wealthy. Contrary to neoliberal doctrine, the most successful reformers have not been those who most radically reduced the state and most resolutely imposed the harsh, necessary costs of adjustment. The most successful did cut back on excessive or arbitrary statism and did impose some painful costs, but they also maintained an active state role in moderating the costs, making all classes share the costs, avoiding deep, lengthy recessions, and facilitating positive responses to economic changes.

Most importantly, successful reformers also induced positive responses, both political and economic. To provide adequate confidence and capacity for groups to respond, states must both restrain their coercive powers and choose economic policies that balance economic and political needs.

Historical and International Context.   Due to good fortune and healthy skepticism, the most successful economies have avoided the pressure and proselytizing of Bank neoliberals and forged their own paths to reform. Most of these economies also managed to escape the debt crisis without major trauma. Some had historical experiences that had made them highly averse to inflation. Some had economic structures which enabled them to adjust more easily to trade shocks. Some benefited from good timing or good location. But almost all have been able to pursue adjustment with growth, a much easier political task than adjustment without growth.

The limitation and diffusion of costs depended on pragmatic policies. Successful reformers largely avoided the self-inflicted wounds suffered by those economies that got carried away with neoliberal ideology. Policymakers in more successful countries had ample confidence in their own capacities, and their policy debates included nationalists, industrialists and structuralists as well as neoliberals. They often had historical reasons to be concerned about the distributional impact of reforms. Some had gone through major peasant uprisings. Some faced external threats that made them worry about national solidarity. Some had ethnic divisions they had to take into account. Some had political systems that forced them to seek a broad base. While most were not responding to empowerment of the poor, they were responding to fears of what the poor might do if neglected. The lesson for other countries, where historical factors do not lead leaders to feel concerned about the poor, is that empowerment may be more necessary than it was in many of these countries.

Pragmatic Policies.   Successful adjustment does not involve destroying the predators who controlled the old statist regime and replacing them with new entrepreneurs. Rather, the state changes the rules so that it becomes more difficult for those with wealth to keep it unless they invest it in a way that helps the economy and gives the state more resources to be spent on other classes. 'Rent-seekers' are converted into entrepreneurs, not destroyed. Former predators who play the new game well need not lose, and those who do lose need not be so numerous that their opposition can only be overcome by an autocratic style of policymaking.

161

In addition, the state does not eliminate all its support for business, but instead puts more effective conditions on its support. It does not cut off business access to policymakers, but rather strengthens the latter's negotiating position. Negotiation, unlike 'insulation', means carrots as well as sticks, carrots that may be critical for giving business the confidence and capacity to make a positive response to reforms.

Broadening Support. By helping the private sector respond well to reforms, successful reformers increased their capacity to respond to the needs of broader society. Some developed pro-active policies to address social needs in order to pre-empt social protests. When social protests did erupt, these governments may have repressed them harshly, but they also usually responded with policies to improve the situation of protestors. Whether dictatorships or democracies, they tended to be responsive to social demands.

Also, they avoided radical changes like slashing consumer subsidies overnight. They built their legitimacy by demonstrating a sense of obligation to abide by tacit social compromises. Acquiescence by most of society indicates a tacit coalition in the sense that people remain inactive in part out of satisfaction of some of their needs and out of confidence in reforms, not only out of fear of the state. Coercion alone does not keep people quiet, at least not after their pain reaches a certain point, or after reforms violate what they consider inalienable rights. While formal pacts may be too hard for most developing countries to sustain, government policies which spread costs and benefits and build trust, represent an informal pact. To avoid provoking fierce opposition, successful adjusters avoid rupturing such pacts.[29]

In countries that have adjusted successfully, middle class groups, like the rich and the poor, have also been helped by the state in adjusting, and been given reason to believe the whole country would benefit, themselves included. Where government employment has been cut back, the state has simultaneously taken steps to promote small and medium firms and farms, which do not automatically prosper from the freeing of market forces. Formal sector workers who are asked to accept deregulation of the labor market are compensated by state spending on subsidies or social safety nets. Wealth-sharing mechanisms ensure workers' wages will rise along with profits.[30] Social mobility is preserved by growth.

In sum, building a coalition means finding a compromise that asks all groups to give up some security in return for some assurances that the state will not abandon them entirely to the market. It means avoiding both economic orthodoxy and economic populism. It does not mean creation of a society-wide consensus, or the elimination of conflict. There are still losers. But within each sector of society, some economic actors are given reason for confidence that they may benefit from reforms.

Coalition building also means strategic economic policymaking on the part of government. It means avoiding orthodox measures that unnecessarily alienate potential supporters, as well as engaging in some economically 'inefficient' spending that helps to persuade swing groups to have patience. Most groups are not lined up clearly 'for' or 'against' reforms. Rather, heterogeneous groups at both the elite and mass level have mixed interests and beliefs, favoring some aspects of reform, but not others. Groups are not certain where their best interests lie. They are open to persuasion, to leadership.

Coalition building means narrowing and isolating the most hardcore opposition. It means divide and conquer, and all the classic strategic moves that politicians normally engage in, so long as they neither overestimate their ability to go without support, nor underestimate their chances of making reform popular.

REVISIONS IN THE BANK'S APPROACH

Although neoliberal dogma does not dominate Bank thinking in the mid-1990s as much as it did in the 1980s, it has left a powerful residue. In particular, disdain for the potential of the state and faith in the justice of the market remain fundamental truths in the worldview of many Bank economists, retaining their influence over what Bank economists assume to be possible and necessary. In general, Bank publications still give the impression that it is neither possible nor necessary to solve the political problems that weaken reform by making reform more popular and building broader support, and that it is both possible and necessary, however, to carry out bold and comprehensive reforms that are very unpopular, but will cut down the opposition and eventually produce support. Neoliberals write more assuredly than ever about a basic core of reforms on which all reasonable economists agree. The meaning of 'real reforms' is so obvious as to need no explanation. Skeptics of the radical, high-cost, neoliberal approach are still members of a ridiculed minority.[31]

163

The Bank has made four major revisions in its approach to structural adjustment lending: cushioning the costs of adjustment, participation, governance and ownership. None of these fundamentally challenge the assumptions underlying neoliberal political theories. Social Investment Funds (SIFs) and participation do not indicate any recognition that market reforms themselves need basic revisions, or that empowerment of weaker groups could play an important part in solving the politics of reform. Institutional reform for the improvement of governance is not seen as requiring empowerment of the public and is not aimed at making the state more capable of taking an activist economic role. While the Bank talks more about the need for dialogue to convince governments to become more committed, conditionality continues, and it remains unclear how genuine dialogue can be when the Bank still believes countries have only two choices: the Bank's way or failure.[32]

Cushioning the Costs of Adjustment

During the years of neoliberal ascendance, the Bank told developing countries they would be rewarded with rapid recovery and acceleration of growth if they paid the high short-term costs of reform. By the early 1990s, the Bank's chief economist was saying that such expectations had been 'patently unrealistic'. Now developing countries are told to prepare for the 'long haul'. Governments must be careful not to expand consumption too rapidly at the first sign of growth, lest hard-earned stability be undone.

Because of the revised estimated time of arrival of reform's benefits, the Bank has been compelled to develop programs called Social Investment Funds, to protect societies' most vulnerable groups. The Bank has also admitted that its preoccupation with structural adjustment led it to give less priority to the fight against poverty, and so it has recently raised the share of social sector lending. In addition, the Bank has eased or dropped its opposition to social spending that neoliberals had previously proscribed as inimical to reform, such as adjustment assistance, public works projects, subsidies for staple goods, policies to promote food security and efficient import substitution. Not only are more activist social policies now encouraged, but they are retroactively declared to have been part of the consensus neoliberal package all along.

In addition, it has become more acceptable to bargain with

labor, rather than take a hard line of no concessions. The power of labor to block reforms by making unreasonable demands was never really as great as many expected, especially outside the public sector. Repression of labor organizations, encouraged by the neoliberal emphasis on 'labor market liberalization', was never necessary to make way for reform. Real wages have been cut with little resistance from workers, at least while social wages stayed above subsistence levels. Moreover, the Bank has begun to recognize the potential for enlisting workers' support for fighting inflation by negotiating social pacts built on price controls, which neoliberals had previously opposed.

But the Bank still rejects the critique of structural adjustment put forward by UNICEF economists in 1987,[33] rejecting the claim that structural adjustment has caused increased poverty, and it still expects the weaker groups in society eventually to make the greatest relative gains from adjustment. It still insists that addressing poverty does not require any revision in the basic design of adjustment policies.[34] The only way it sees to make adjustment less painful and more equitable is via supplemental programs like the SIFs, not by state actions to shape a more inclusive development strategy. It has not expanded its definition of structural adjustment beyond economic liberalization to include state actions to reallocate resources, such as technology diffusion and reform of land, tax, credit and educational finance. Its support for cushioning the costs of adjustment is strictly limited to helping the most vulnerable groups. Its renewed attention to the poor and its support for more participation by the poor do not indicate any new hope that broader support for reform can be built by making reform more equitable or less painful.

The Bank still draws a distinction between economic liberalization, which it considers apolitical, and state activism, which it sees as inevitably favoring some groups or firms over others. It believes that the more that activist policies are reduced the less distorted prices will be, and the less the overall costs to the economy. It also suspects that the less the state is involved, the less inequitable development will be. It went to great lengths in its recent study of East Asian successes to deny that activist state interventions, such as industrial policies, played a positive role in the rapid growth of those countries. It did not even consider the possibility that such policies might have made reforms easier.

But government involvement in restructuring can directly reduce the costs of reform. The less a government provides help for the private sector to respond to price changes with an increase in supply, the more adjustment must take place via cuts in demand and imports, and the more widespread, deep and enduring are the costs in wage cuts and unemployment. Middle-class and poor groups that might provide support for reforms that produced less harsh, enduring recessions are made to suffer along with the major opponents and main targets of reform, when the private sector is abandoned to the market. The priority given to overcoming opposition, by raising overall costs, hurts those whose support reformers do not consider critical or winnable, but whose support may be both critical and winnable. This is the reason many see a more '*dirigiste*' approach to adjustment as not only economically more effective, but also as distributionally more equitable and politically more viable. Governments more concerned with preserving broad support have good reason to manage restructuring. But that option remains outside the bounds of what the Bank finds acceptable.[35]

Although it calls Social Investment Funds 'compensatory programs' aimed at helping those adversely affected by reforms, it still rejects compensation for all but those most highly vulnerable. These groups are not really the most adversely affected, but rather they have the least ability to survive any costs. In relative terms, the most adversely affected have been middle-class groups that have fallen into poverty and have become the 'new poor'. The Bank has not considered compensation for these groups affordable or desirable. Such compensation, in the current view, would reduce resources for fighting poverty as well as weaken workers' incentives to shift activities, thus slowing restructuring and raising the total cost of reform.[36]

In part, this attitude to the 'new poor' may derive from their inclusion by neoliberals in the category of 'previously privileged classes', that is, all those groups that were favored by government policies under the old regime, at the expense of those not so favored. As losers of previous privileges that were not deserved, the 'new poor' do not seem to qualify for much sympathy or help. It is up to them, in the neoliberal view, to get along without those undeserved benefits, to find new ways of making a living that the market values more highly. Because their resistance to reform is seen as illegitimate, reformers feel less duty to respond through bargaining and compromise.

Perhaps a more important reason, however, for restricting to a minimum the groups that government helps, is the compulsion to draw a sharp line between politics and economics. Leaving market justice to determine the fate of economic actors allows reformers to avoid the messy political process of deciding who the state should help, and how. Once governments go beyond trying to protect the most vulnerable, where does the line get drawn? Again, a major motive is fear that allowing politics into policymaking will lead to populism. Pessimism about the capacity of developing states to act responsibly remains strong at the Bank. Letting the market make distributional decisions lets weak states avoid difficult political tasks, but it may end up creating harder ones.

Participation, Not Empowerment

The irrelevance of the poor to the problem of overcoming opposition to reform remains a widely held assumption. The poor are too weak and dispersed to provide an adequate political base. Rather than making reform more politically viable, raising spending on the poor may raise opposition among middle-class groups who feel they are paying for it.[37] A few voices within the Bank maintain that grass-roots movements can contribute to a more accountable and less polarized national political system. They are more confident than neoliberals of the potential for making empowerment of the poor a base from which to build a larger movement, and of the positive role that can be played by interest groups and political parties in reforming the state.[38]

But for the most part, the strong doubts remain that reforms can be made more popular, or that democracy in a developing-country context can be made to favor the weak rather than the already powerful. The Bank's support for Social Investment Funds is aimed primarily at substituting NGOs for the state, as a more reliable channel for funneling funds to cushion the transitional costs of economic liberalization. Its support for NGOs' efforts to boost participation of the poor in grass-roots organizations is aimed primarily at improving the design and sustainability of projects, improving public relations and perhaps coopting NGO critics. The Bank does not see grass-roots empowerment as crucial for shifting the balance of social forces in society and for pushing the state toward coalition building. It discourages NGOs from mobilizing GROs to challenge the power structures that keep them poor. Social Investment Funds are not indicative of the Bank's commitment to empower the poor and their allies to make the state more accountable and effective at attacking the

167

roots of poverty. And 'it is extremely difficult to imagine an effective anti-poverty strategy in developing-country conditions without extensive interventions (by the state)'.[39]

Neoliberals might take more interest in politically mobilizing the poor, whom they expect to benefit from reform, if they felt there were much hope that allying them with the middle class would enable them to counter demands by the wealthy. Unfortunately middle classes, often dependent on the state, are the biggest losers from radical reduction of the state. For reforms to work, many middle-class groups must give up an 'artificially' high living standard, and many must move into other activities. This entails inevitable costs. In the neoliberal view, even if the middle classes were persuaded they might benefit eventually, in the meantime they have no choice but to resist. Because reforms aimed at disciplining and extracting resources from the privileged hurt the middle class as much or more, the latter cannot be expected to support the effort. Of course, this depends on how inevitable it is that economically viable reforms must take a heavy toll on the middle classes and offer them few immediate opportunities.

Neoliberals see a second obstacle to a reform alliance between the poor and middle classes. The sharp distinction often drawn between the poor and middle classes may be exaggerated. Their fates are tied together in many ways, economically and through family connections. Their incomes tend to rise and fall together.[40] When middle-class wages fall, the poor do not necessarily find their employment opportunities improving. When governments help the poor, benefits also leak to the middle classes as well.

When governments help the poor in ways that hurt the middle class, such as by raising their taxes, the middle class may respond negatively, but that response does not follow so automatically as it would in public-choice theory. It depends on many factors. Does help for the poor increase customers, consumer goods or the quality of life for middle classes? Does the government succeed at getting the rich to pay their fair share, and so moderate the costs to the middle class? Is government popular? Does help for the poor seem part of a genuine commitment to making society more fair and the nation stronger? Self-interested individuals can care about their country as well as themselves. Enhancing government's legitimacy can increase its power.

Whether or not middle classes see their interests more closely linked to status quo elites or to progress for the poor depends in part on whether the poor seem strong enough to help middle classes challenge the status quo. When middle classes gain enough influence in government to challenge the dominance of the wealthy, state policies tend to be more beneficial to the poor than otherwise. Without managing reforms so that middle classes receive some protection along with the poor, the poor will lack the ally it needs to bring about real change. Without a strong middle, the polarized society cannot make compromises.

Governance: To Make Democracy Safe for Reform

The growing emphasis on promoting 'governance' indicates a realization of the need for a more capable and accountable state. However, governance aims primarily at improving implementation, without revising the substance of reforms.[41] Hence a more capable state must not compromise on the design of reform for political purposes, such as broadening support. It also implies that broader support does not contribute to making the state stronger and more accountable. Here, accountability means improved executive control over the bureaucracy, not responsiveness of government to the needs of the majority. Governance aims at making the bureaucracy a more functional and obedient tool of the cadre.

The global trend towards democratization poses problems for the Bank. The Bank cannot argue that democracy should be delayed, and where the Bank's authoritarian clients are weakening, it must make overtures to new democratic forces. The Bank has to argue that democracy will be good for economic reforms, at least on balance. It naturally wants to deny that economic reforms hurt chances of democratization, as it believes it must resist calls to compromise on its economic approach, as some critics ask it to do, for the sake of helping democracy.[42]

In a recent World Bank publication,[43] Haggard and Webb explain how insulating policymaking for the sake of reform in developing countries is not much different from making Central Banks independent in the industrialized democracies. While admitting that the Bank sees conflicts between pluralist politics and growth-promoting economic policies, the book emphasizes how particular ways of arranging pluralist politics can make democracy more supportive of reform. Little is said about how economic reforms might be made more popular, making leaders more willing to face popular elections. Little evidence is given of publics voting for full-fledged reform or of democratic countries carrying out reform. Except for Spain, in all the cases of countries cited in this book, either reforms are partial, democracy is partial, or both. Spain may be an exception precisely because democratization was put before economic reform, and economic reform was accompanied by coalition building.

For the most part, the political scientists the Bank listens to reinforce its fear of democracy. Most academics see a sharp trade-off between democracy and economic reform and doubt that any alternative economic approach can make reform less costly or more compatible with democracy. They expect that democratization in developing countries can only strengthen those already powerful, organized interests that block reform. Most academics see a need to 'modify' democracy to make it facilitate reform. Modification aims at reconciling insulation and participation. It means the creation of a 'two-track democracy', one that keeps electoral politics separate from policymaking.[44]

The important point is that neither the need to strengthen the state to carry out reforms, nor the imperative of democratization requires major revisions in the neoliberal economic approach. They are deemed political problems, to be solved by political means, not by using economic policies to help build coalitions. Where society has been polarized, moderation of political conflict can be achieved by institutional engineering, such as building the right kind of party system, or rationalizing the bureaucracy. The redesign of institutions is emphasized above the redesign of the economic approach, for which little room is seen. The fate of democracies is said to depend on political, not economic factors. Political scientists provide political solutions for economists who do not want their economic designs changed to help solve political problems, a tendency noted by Albert Hirschman 25 years ago when public choice theory was first gaining popularity.[45] If only countries could insulate a cadre of technocrats long enough to launch painful enough reforms, then in the consolidation stage policymakers could become more accountable and support could be built.

This formulation begs the question of how insulation, while initiating reforms, affects chances for coalition building during consolidation. The way stabilization is achieved in the short term has a strong effect on how well it can be sustained. Where technocratic cadres have used their autonomy to push radically anti-statist, unpopular policies, often they have done long-term damage to the state, the infrastructure, economic actors' capacity to respond and the public's trust in government. Rather than reduce corruption and patronage, neoliberalism may increase them. The radical approach also incurs a greater risk of recovery coming after a long delay. For many developing countries, the 'lost decade' of the 1980s left behind a 'lost generation' of unhealthy, uneducated, underclass groups who can contribute little and cost society a lot. The accumulated social debt surely makes 'consolidation' more difficult.

Insulation is also no solution in the short term when reforms provoke a negative political response that cripples investment. Even if the broader public remains quiet, investors may not trust a government that takes an economic approach requiring the unlimited exercise of state power. The revolution from above can backfire when the cadre gets the policy wrong, but keeps on pushing it with nobody to stop them. Even insulation of central banks is by no means clearly the best way to make monetary policy. More democratic policymaking can sometimes produce more pragmatic policies. But the pragmatic policy platform has been casually dismissed as no different, or if different, not a viable alternative.

The suggestion that insulation in reforming countries can be compared to institutions that try to rationalize policymaking in industrialized democracies also needs closer scrutiny. The stability of 'two-track democracy' in divided developing countries may be more problematic than the stability of representative democracies in the industrialized countries. Democracy in the industrialized countries is not doing so well either, but at least it enjoys a degree of legitimacy salvaged by an image that it responds to the will of the majority.

Dialogue and Ownership

As long as the Bank resists compromise and insists that it knows what must be done, it cannot pretend it wants real dialogue. In some cases dialogue is frustrated by the absence of developing countries with enough backing to follow through on agreements. It is doubtful that the Bank would share responsibility for the design of reforms. In most cases, the original reform plans are written by the Bank, rather than by the country. One of the architects of structual adjustment loans frankly admits that he doubts the usefulness of dialogue, which he says has been tried before, and failed.[46]

171

The Bank has increased the conditions that it puts on loans, demanding that borrowers do everything all at once. This proliferation of policy conditions stems in part from institutional flaws that the Bank has recognized, but been unable to correct. But it also stems from the still widely-held theory that overkill, that is, a sharp, complete break from past policies, though costly, could raise reform's credibility and make reforms 'irreversible'. In the targets it sets for measuring implementation of particular reforms, the Bank also tends to 'overshoot', that is, to set targets even higher than it wants borrowers to reach, because it assumes they will aim to do the least necessary to get by.

Besides failing to change its high-pressure tactics, the Bank has made few positive moves to encourage commitment. It does not consider how its tactics create distrust, or how measures to raise governments' trust in the Bank might raise their commitment to reform. When the Bank encourages countries to take high risks for high pay-offs, and the gamble fails, governments pay the price. The Bank provides no help to reward countries for the risks they take, even when failures are due to the Bank's miscalculations. Lack of confidence in the Bank's solutions or in its dependability has often contributed to a country's costly delay in taking adjustment actions. But the Bank sees the tendency to delay only as a matter of weak political will, and so must stick to a tough approach, which may contribute to countries' avoidance of adjustment in the first place.[47]

EMPOWERMENT WITHOUT ADJUSTMENT?

Northern NGOs have been among the most ardent advocates of grass-roots empowerment. Their substantial experience working among peasants and the urban poor in developing countries has convinced them that reform policies would be better designed if excluded groups were organized and given more voice. The poor understand best their own problems and needs. Furthermore, they understand the limits to what can be implemented, or the missing factors needed to make implementation possible. Therefore, their input to the formulation of reforms will make policies more realistic, flexible and likely to gain the popular commitment needed to sustain them. And their organization and participation will make them more self-reliant and politically powerful.

Many advocates of grass-roots empowerment go further, and argue that all foreign assistance should be directed toward small-

scale projects of local communities, bypassing governments when-
ever possible. When donor contributions to Social Investment
Funds must be funneled through governments, the agencies
responsible for disbursing them should be insulated from politics.
Like the Bank, NGOs seek solutions which depend on government as little as possible.

Above all, many NGOs argue, the World Bank must get out of
the business of structural adjustment lending, which they blame for
causing much of the suffering that grass-roots empowerment tries
to counter. While acknowledging that some adjustment is unavoidable for countries with chronic balance-of-payments problems, they
attribute these problems primarily to inequities in the international
system of trade and finance. Their solution would be debt relief and
the opening of rich countries' markets to poor countries' exports.
Advocates of grass-roots empowerment have more in common with
promoters of structural adjustment than many of them may realize.
Both aim to improve the effectiveness with which foreign assistance
brings about a redistribution and more productive and equitable
use of developing countries' resources. But neither sees the other's
project as necessary to its own. Promoters of adjustment pressure
the state to take on *rentiers* who have monopolized resources, but
they see no need to empower the poor to help them do so. Grass-
roots organizers would empower the poor, but see no need for help
from the state, or from external actors pressuring the state, to help
the poor gain power. Like the Bank, NGOs do not have a strategy
for fixing the state to make it work for broader interests. Rather,
they seem to expect some kind of bloodless revolution to take place
at some future time.

What Plan for Political Scaling-up?

At least the NGOs have not explained how grass-roots empowerment will expand past the point at which privileged interests see
pressures from below threatening their control over resources. Nor
have NGOs addressed what kind of allies the poor could find
among economically or politically stronger groups, and what they
would offer and ask in any coalition. Without a coalition, empowerment will lead to conflict rather than to democracy. Unless some
clear mutual understanding is reached, stronger groups will resist
compromise with weaker ones. Even when a positive-sum economic
agreement is possible, the strong will fear the increasing power of
the weak, which has to come at the expense of their own power, in

relative terms. Democracy requires a balance between pressures from below and security for elites. Cross-class political parties, or party coalitions, centered around the middle classes, have best achieved this balance. Without allies in other classes or in the state to help them, grass-roots organizations have been vulnerable to state efforts to keep them fragmented.[48]

NGO agendas depend on building coalitions and fixing the state. Redistribution to effectively address the needs of the poor requires a strong state, both to extract resources and to ensure that predators are turned into entrepreneurs who will contribute to sustainable growth. Improvement of the economy is a prerequisite for broadening participation by the poor, who are too preoccupied with survival to expand their political activities much. A strong state both requires support from a broad coalition and acts as a key partner in maintaining that coalition. Yet NGOs have no clear plan for building coalitions or strengthening the state.

This is understandable. Many of the GROs promoted by NGOs arose in the wake of the breakdown of the state, as alternatives to the state. Overborrowing, mismanagement, world recession and neoliberal reforms left many states bankrupt, unable to help those groups crushed by economic crises. NGOs have promoted self-help first to enable abandoned groups to survive this catastrophe. Not only have states not helped, but often they have grown more corrupt and incoherent. There is a strong temptation to give up on fixing government, and to concentrate instead on providing alternative means of making progress. To the extent that this helps create an active, organized civil society, as a necessary foundation for rebuilding a more accountable state, empowerment of GROs serves a vital purpose, beyond survival.

However, it may be misleading to call GROs the building ground of a new civil society, if these groups prove content to ignore national politics and to leave the government broken and/or captured. GROs risk avoiding the work of building links to political parties or of engaging the political system at the national level. Aid that helps GROs to get along without confronting the state allows them to avoid the historical role that social groups have often played in making the state more accountable and capable. Putting off that task indefinitely would be a mistake, for the poor cannot benefit nearly as much from self-help and aid as they could from helping to rebuild the state and increasing their influence on national policies.[49]

More Money for Leverage, Not Less

It also may be counterproductive for NGOs to call for all aid to go to small-scale projects. NGOs have rightly criticized the way the Bank has pushed money, but may be wrong to think that developing countries need less aid, not more. In so far as program lending puts pressure on governments to take on predators, and helps them do so, it can help the poor. If program loans are sufficient to ease political and foreign exchange constraints, and thus facilitate structural adjustment and sustained recovery, the benefits could dwarf what aid for local projects could produce. The challenge is to make adjustment work, and to ensure that its benefits are shared. To a great extent, these are interdependent goals, connected by the importance of the political response to adjustment.[50]

Helleiner has presented compelling evidence that capacity to maintain or raise imports has been among the most important determinants of the success of adjustment. Summers admits that the Bank was slow to catch on to the nasty interaction that took place in countries that sharply devalued in the context of a large debt overhang. Cline finds that debt relief has often been critical for recovery in countries where doubts about whether the debt crisis was over prevented investors from trusting the government to stick to reforms. When the Bank and the US government both demand that the IMF be more generous, NGOs should not be calling for less large-scale aid.[51]

Reforming Rather than Rejecting Conditionality

Therefore, NGOs should recognize the critical importance of large-scale loans and the need to place conditions on such loans. It is no solution to tell the Bank it can stop interfering if it stops lending. Rather than attacking policy-based lending, NGOs ought to question the ideological and ineffective way in which structural adjustment has been promoted. Rather than oppose structural adjustment *per se*, they should advocate an alternative approach that is more participatory, redistributive and likely to make the state stronger and more accountable.

Giving up program lending that conditions loans on policy reforms does not help to achieve that goal. Bank promoters of reform should be seen as potential, and sometimes actual, allies of NGOs in pressuring developing governments to become more progressive. Conditionality can keep pressure on captured states to break free from the grip of domestic elites. Bailing them out with unconditional debt relief might do little to stimulate change or help the excluded. Debt relief no doubt is desperately needed by some countries, but it should go most generously to those governments that move toward opening up the political process to seek broader input and support for policy reform.

Conditionality can also be used to make adjustment more equitable. Adjustment need not have a regressive impact, as believed by those NGOs that have campaigned for an end to program lending. Orthodox, neoliberal reforms are regressive, but the neoliberal economic approach to adjustment is not the only one. Elements of economic liberalization are no doubt important means toward adjustment in most cases, but they are only partial means. It is when neoliberals act as though all those elements are necessary, and together sufficient, that much damage has been done. Frequent reference to reforms as a 'market transition' imply that the market is the end, rather than one kind of means. Rather, structural change to make growth more sustainable and rapid is the purpose of adjustment, and much evidence suggests that a more state-led and equitable economic approach works better towards that end than neoliberalism does.

NGOs who reject both the market and the state are caught in a contradiction. NGOs know the state has not been a friend to the poor in the past, and most don't expect very much from it now. Yet many view the introduction of market forces, which reduce the discretionary power of the state, as an unalloyed evil. They focus most of their anger at international market forces that hold down both developing-country states and their people. They give less attention to those forces that the poor tend to identify as their most important enemies: domestic elites and the governments they dominate. NGOs' emphasis on increasing the self-reliance of GROs may eventually contribute to empowerment, but in the meantime, GROs do not want to be left alone to fight against overwhelming odds. They want and need external help to pressure governments to break free from elite domination. NGOs' emphasis on external enemies makes them less than eager to make common cause with international institutions that exalt the market, even if together, NGOs and the Bank could more effectively help the poor confront their domestic enemies.

The more rejectionist NGO critics mirror neoliberal ideologues within the Bank. Neoliberals expect the distributional impact of reforms to be beneficial overall, and that the painful costs of adjustment will produce an economic breakthrough. Many NGO critics blame increases in poverty mainly on adjustment and expect all the pain to lead nowhere. In the end, both groups share the belief that structural adjustment means economic liberalization and that there are no less painful or more equitable approaches to adjustment.

By rejecting structural adjustment *per se*, some NGOs hurt their own credibility and leave themselves out of a critical debate. Instead, they should try to champion those economists within the Bank, as well as academics outside it, who have criticized the neoliberal approach and argued that alternative approaches to adjustment are not only available, but have proven successful. A large part of the Bank's power derives precisely from its capacity to trivialize critics and to promote an image of consensus among all reasonable economists. Although Bank management has been able to admit mistakes to some degree, it maintains the fiction that it knows the correct answers and that disagreements are minor. Rather than joining Bank management in trivializing disagreements within the Bank, NGOs should work to publicize them, translating them into plain language.

LEAVING THE PAST BEHIND AND GETTING BACK TO THE BASICS

The World Bank cannot lend billions of dollars to developing countries without influencing their domestic politics. The only question is how it will influence them. Will it affect them in a way that contributes to positive political changes that enable countries to pursue more equitable and sustainable growth? Or will it affect them in a way that contributes to the concentration of power and the polarization of society?

The neoliberals who launched radical market reforms in the name of structural adjustment clearly designed their economic strategy to help bring about political changes they considered critical to economic success. They aimed at bringing down those selfish elites who were blocking economic growth, by knocking out from under them their main prop, state economic interventionism. Neoliberals aimed at supporting a progressive shift in

the balance of power among domestic social forces, as a necessary requirement for freeing repressed entrepreneurialism.[52] But
they encouraged coercive methods for achieving this end, either
explicitly or by implication. Those methods have not worked.
Aggressive financial pressure, empowerment of an insulated cadre
of neoliberal technocrats, and radical reduction of the state's role
in the economy have not brought about a progressive realignment
of forces within developing countries. Rather, in most countries,
the neoliberal strategy has left the economy in trouble and added
to the polarization of society.

Still, the neoliberals had the right idea in thinking of the
solution to economic problems in terms of a power struggle.
Their mistake was to overestimate the power of coercion and to
underestimate the power of persuasion and the power of material
rewards, at both the national and international levels. Also, they
relied too much on deductive economic theories to tell them how
economic policy reforms would affect the distribution of power.
They mistakenly expected that economic measures could
indirectly bring a major shift in the balance of social forces.

In order to promote positive political change, the Bank should
aim more directly at helping to shift the balance of forces in
developing countries. It should aim to support those elites who
favor class compromise and to help empower the weak. It can do
so without discriminating against countries according to their
political systems and with purely technical economic justifications
for its actions.

The Bank should use strong persuasion and differential
rewards to push countries to pursue three main priorities: to
seek and demonstrate broader support for reforms; to undertake more overtly redistributive reforms; and to maintain strict
compliance with the minimum basic requirements of economic
health, narrowly defined. These actions can lure governments to
look beyond their narrow support base, and can help empower
the weak to pressure governments to do so and reward those
that do.

To the extent that governments make efforts to pursue these
three aims, they should enjoy generous support from the Bank. No
further conditions should be placed on their economic policies.
They should be required to design their own reforms. The Bank
should take no responsibility for deciding the timing, speed, scope,
sequencing or market-friendliness of reforms. It can give its best
advice on the expected impacts of various choices. But it should
expand its definition of structural adjustment so that it can support

more varied economic approaches. The generosity of support for reforms should be determined according to how economically essential and distributionally progressive they are, and how wide a popular endorsement the government has gained for them.

Countries that choose not to demonstrate broader ownership or to undertake progressive reforms or to abide by economic common sense, can simply be left alone. The IMF can carry out the obligation of donor countries to provide balance-of-payments support to such countries, but should provide nothing more, and should stay out of structural adjustment.

Finally, the Bank and donor countries should recognize that developing-country governments that adopt progressive structural reforms are taking risks that serve the interests of donors, and that they deserve some assurance that they will be rewarded for taking these risks. The aid relationship should be treated more explicitly as part of a broader effort at international cooperation, in which donors, as well as recipients, have obligations.

Broadening the Meaning of Ownership

Opening a real dialogue means the Bank must relax its high-pressure tactics, which do not work well anyway. It can continue to condition loans on countries' choices, but it does not need to sacrifice all flexibility to the fear that countries will use funds only to avoid reforms. That problem explains only a minority of cases of weak adjustment, and is not nearly so difficult to identify and sanction as hardliners like to claim.

The Bank might reduce its fear of moral hazard by pushing harder for states to build coalitions and to take on special interests. That is part of the appeal of the effort to increase government's 'ownership' of reforms. Landell-Mills, Johnson, Gulhati, Jaycox and others at the Bank and the IMF have argued that governments should be required to consult with groups whose support is needed for carrying out reforms, and to demonstrate their support, whether by elections, referendums, votes in parliament, tripartite negotiations, public hearings or otherwise.[53]

In a sense, it is not interference for the Bank to ask a government to show that it has consulted and gained approval for its reform plan from key constituencies. It is part of a banker's job to investigate a borrower's capacity to use funds as intended. But in another sense, it does mean taking sides, because governments would be pushed to opt for involving more groups, and thus to risk the wrath of already well-connected interests who do not want to share their access to government with other groups, as that may force them to compete harder for their profits.[54]

Requiring demonstration of ownership can also be seen as a kind of state-strengthening, rather than state-weakening, conditionality, as neoliberalism has proven to be. By encouraging a government to broaden its support, ownership can strengthen a state's ability to undertake a more activist economic approach, with less risk that activism will lead to capture. More activist reforms which are *more* politically difficult, in that they require a strong state, can make the impact of reforms less costly and thus make the task of sustaining them *less* politically difficult. Structural change which challenges vested interests can speed the supply response to adjustment, and thus require less cutting of demand, making adjustment less harsh.

It has been argued convincingly by economists within the Bank that the success of reform in East Asia has been due in great part to a certain kind of ownership. Despite their authoritarian regimes, most East Asian countries have developed 'deliberation councils' or other forms of regular consultations with representatives of both business and labor. These institutions give states a way to convince elites they will benefit from reforms. They facilitate communication and cooperation among state, business and labor groups, reducing the risk each feels in making compromises. By institutionalizing the sharing of rents, such compromises reduce the incentives for rent-seeking and raise private-sector confidence in the state. Support for reform from all sectors of society makes the state's commitment to reform more credible, and so reduces the fear of external lenders that their funds will be used to avoid reform.[55]

Without doubt, some developing-country regimes will resent and resist pressure on them to demonstrate broader support for their policies. Some have good reasons to fear political opening. But many governments might be persuaded that political opening could make them more secure, rather than less, especially if the international community provides extra finance in return. Analysts often lament how useless it is for outsiders to try to push governments to open up, but they may underestimate the power of persuasion, for good and for ill.

The Bank on its own can help reverse some of the damage that was done when neoliberals helped concentrate power in financial ministries, by reaching out and establishing stronger relations with other government departments. The Bank could also outline areas where it sees room for discretion, rather than discouraging all discretionary policies as contrary to ultimate objectives. It could distinguish between those policies which are most harmful and in need of reform, and other 'inefficient', but politically useful, policies that could be lived with.

More Support for More Redistributive Adjustment

Secondly, the Bank could put much more pressure on governments to pursue redistributive strategies of growth. It has evidence showing extreme inequality constitutes a major obstacle to sustainable growth. It can justify pushing aggressive anti-poverty actions as critical for the health of a country's economy, not just for the health of the poor. While excessive attention to redistribution can hurt growth, so can excessive neglect. Especially since the Bank contributed to this neglect, and admits to having done so, it should share responsibility for achieving a better balance. In so doing, it would be helping redistribute resources towards the excluded, thereby boosting their political power. By promoting redistributive development, the Bank could probably contribute more to democratization than by any political conditionality. Under conditions of extreme inequality, democracy tends to be fragile.

The Bank's extreme concern about not interfering in countries' politics implies that it has not been interfering all along. But any set of economic policies the Bank gets a country to adopt necessarily affects the balance of social forces within that country, often quite dramatically. Even when the Bank refrains from taking positions on policies with distributional impacts, such as taxing and spending, it does not thereby avoid interfering. As long as it lends to a government, by default its neutrality on distributional questions amounts to support for the status quo.[56] Since the Bank has already declared poverty reduction the proper measure of its success, why can it not openly promote the redistribution of resources which it expects to result from neoliberalism, but which probably will not happen without deliberate government actions?

Global integration and interdependence are inexorable forces that increasingly compel donors to urge developing countries to extend greater social rights to their people. But donors can do so in more and less objectionable ways. For example, loans conditioned on states taking specific actions to fight poverty can be negotiated separately from balance-of-payments lending. Countries can be given the choice of getting more help in return for tolerating more intrusive conditionality, or getting more freedom in return for loans on less generous terms. Many might choose the former. Discussions at the 1995 Social Summit in Copenhagen indicate that most developing counties would raise spending to improve the productivity of the poor, if donors offered truly new funds earmarked for that purpose. Pushing for greater redistribution need not mean threatening to withdraw lending, but it does mean giving greater priority to pro-poor lending. Mahbub Ul Haq, a long-time champion of developing countries' views, argues there has been too little interference of this kind, not too much.[57]

Greater pressure for fighting poverty can also be justified on strictly technical grounds. Much recent evidence has been found to support the notion that inequality may be the root obstacle to growth in many developing countries.[58] This notion is not entirely new, but mainstream thinking has come a long way to get to it. Redistribution has gone from being an obstacle to growth, to a potential by-product of growth, to being a key to adjustment and sustainable growth.

Countries with more equitable social structures in East Asia have done better in part because they have filled capitalists' need for healthy, educated, skilled, productively employed workers with rising real wages, access to a share of productive assets, chances to become small-to-medium entrepreneurs and faith in the economic system. The Bank's study of the East Asian Miracle[59] gives plenty of play to the essential role of governments in improving the quality of 'human capital', but not much to how governments have had to interfere with 'property rights' in order to do so. The use of capital controls and foreign investment controls are only the most obvious examples.

Narrowing the Definition of Minimum Requirements and Expanding the Definition of Structural Adjustment

Before the Bank can identify the minimum requirements for restoring economic health, it must first develop a more precise definition of the aims of structural adjustment. The aims of structural adjustment need to be redefined in a more concrete, measurable way. The Bank has devised no composite set of measures to evaluate the success of adjustment attempts. It either looks at individual indicators of the benefits that structural changes are supposed to produce, like faster growth, or it looks at degree of implementation of the policy reforms which are expected to bring about structural changes.[60]

Identification of the minimum policy reforms necessary for making structural progress, for reducing constraints and increasing flexibility, means identifying policy changes which can address some of these problems without making others worse. Ideally, it would mean an improved understanding of which constraints are the most critical in each country. The Bank needs to suggest priorities in each country, rather than calling all reforms equally necessary. By indicating which issues are most critical, it could make governments more willing to act than when they are told they must do everything at once.

If the Bank were more willing to admit the limits to its knowledge, it could play a more useful role in elaborating alternative policy choices and studying their likely effects, but allowing governments to choose the approach they think will best balance their economic and political needs. Developing countries should be allowed to make their own mistakes. Reform is ultimately an experiment, and they have already paid for many of the Bank's mistakes.

In particular, the Bank should leave it to borrowing governments to decide whether they feel their states are capable of using more activist approaches to reform. Instead of continuing to defend the ideology that the least state is best, the Bank could explain the positive roles states might play. It might even go so far as to strengthen the state's capacity to carry out efficient subsidizing of credit to firms that need and deserve help and to adopt some kind of 'industrial policy'. It has already admitted that states may have to act as bankers until conditions are more suitable for financial liberalization.[61]

CONCLUSION

Developing states that pursue activist economic policies can best facilitate cross-class coalition building, thereby developing the implicit compromises among major social groups that can best hold activist states accountable and make them effective. Together, activist states and broad social coalitions can best carry out the difficult structural reforms necessary for accelerating sustainable growth and reducing poverty in developing countries.

Neoliberals who led the World Bank's original effort to promote radical market reforms in the mid-1980s identified activ-

183

ist policies as the main source of developing countries' economic miseries. They concluded that developing countries had proven themselves incapable of carrying out activist policies in a responsible way. Attempting an activist economic strategy in the context of the developing world would almost always, in their view, lead to excessive and self-destructive proliferation and politicization of policy interventions.

Neoliberals also discounted the importance of coalition building. They had a clear idea of the political approach they felt developing countries needed to follow to carry out market reforms, and that approach did not include compromise or coalition building. Rather it entailed the concentration of policy-making power within a small cadre of neoliberal technocrats, who would carry out a 'revolution from above'. The Bank would help these technocrats increase their influence by using high-pressure tactics in its bargaining with developing-country governments.

While neoliberals are no longer ascendant at the Bank, their influence is still strong. Despite many changes in its original strategy, the Bank has not questioned core neoliberal political assumptions nor how policy-based lending could support coalition building in developing countries.

Northern NGOs who have criticized the Bank's approach and tried to push the Bank toward an alternative approach have yet to articulate a strategy for building cross-class coalitions. NGOs emphasize the need for grass-roots empowerment, but have not explained how empowerment will expand past the point at which privileged interests feel their control over resources is threatened. NGOs have not yet addressed what kind of allies the poor can find among economically and politically stronger groups, nor what the poor might offer, and ask, of such groups in return for joining an alliance. Without a coalition, empowerment will increase conflict rather than democracy.

Some NGOs go to the opposite extreme from neoliberals in their economic proposals. They discount the importance of structural economic reforms and call for all foreign aid to fund small-scale projects chosen by grass-roots groups. Rather than seeking more effective use of large loans, they would resolve the conditionality dilemma by eliminating policy-based lending. However, the chances for reducing poverty and for the poor to find allies, depend on structural policy reforms. Most NGOs do not recognize that Bank promoters of policy reform can be, and at times have been, their allies, in so far as policy reforms have leveraged privileged groups' contribution to economic growth and the government's capacity to spread growth. NGOs make the same mistake as neo-liberals by equating policy reform with neoliberalism.

Also, like neoliberals, many NGOs search for economic solutions that bypass the state. They doubt the state can become accountable and able to play an effective activist economic role. Their avoidance of the state accounts in part for their neglect of cross-class coalitions. Their skepticism about chances for coalition building also may derive from their distrust of the Bank and developing-country allies. Building greater trust and cooperation between NGOs and the Bank could contribute to building broader coalitions within developing countries.

A combination of empowerment and adjustment could produce positive political effects that make an indirect economic contribution many times greater than the monetary value of aid. No amount of aid can compare with the domestic resources of developing countries that have been neglected, hoarded or wasted.[62] If foreign aid can serve as a *catalyst* for coalition building, it might help developing countries to increase their mobilization, distribution and productive use of these resources. It could have a much greater impact than most donor-country politicians and publics realize.

Notes

1. S. Please, 'From Structural Adjustment to Structural Transformation' in W. van der Geest (ed.), *Negotiating Structural Adjustment in Africa* (London: James Curry, 1994) pp. 14–24.
2. J.G. Ruggie, 'Political Structure and Change in the International Economic Order: The North-South Dimension' in J.G. Ruggie (ed.), *Antinomies of Interdependence: National Welfare and the International Division of Labor* (New York: Columbia University Press, 1983) pp. 423–87.
3. There is a large literature describing structural imbalances or constraints. See O. Rosales, 'An Assessment of the Structuralist Paradigm for Latin American Development and the Prospects for Its Renovation' *CEPAL Review*, no. 34 (April 1988) pp. 19–36; D. Senghaas, 'European Development and the Third World: An Assessment' *Review* (of the Fernand Brandel Center for the Study of Economics, History, and Civilizations), vol. 11, no. 1 (Winter 1988) pp. 127–40.
4. Among those neoliberals who most influenced the Bank in this period, Colclough lists Lal, Krueger, Little, Bauer, Balassa and Berg, although the latter two do not qualify in terms of subscribing to the neoliberal political theory described here. Neoliberals have also been called market fundamentalists, pricist fanatics, anti-statists and purveyors of the

new orthodoxy, the new political economy and state minimalism. See C. Colclough, 'Structuralism versus Neo-liberalism: An Introduction' in C. Colclough and J. Manor (eds), *States or Markets? Neo-liberalism and the Development Policy Debate* (Oxford: Clarendon Press, 1991) pp. 1–25.

5. M. Grindle discusses this aspect of neoliberal theory in 'The New Political Economy: Positive Economics and Negative Politics' *Policy, Planning and Research Papers*, WPS 304 (Washingotn, DC: World Bank, December 1989).

6. Colclough, 'Structuralism versus Neo-liberalism', p. 7.

7. M. Goldman, 'The Chinese Model: The Solution to Russia's Economic Ills?' in *Current History*, vol. 92, no. 576 (October 1993) pp. 320–4.

8. R.N. Cooper, *Economic Stabilization and Debt in Developing Countries* (Cambridge, Mass: MIT Press, 1992); S. Fischer, 'Issues in Medium-Term Macroeconomic Adjustment' in *World Bank Research Observer*, vol. 1, no. 2 (1986) pp. 163–82; A.O. Krueger, 'Interactions between Inflation and Trade Regime Objectives in Stabilization Programs' in W. Cline and S. Weintraub (eds), *Economic Stabilization in Developing Countries* (Washington, DC: Brookings Institution, 1981); Yagci *et al.*, 'Structural Adjustment Lending: An Evaluation of Program Design', *World Bank Staff Working Paper No. 735* (1985).

9. Fischer, 'Issues in Medium-Term Macroeconomic Adjustment' pp. 163–82; Krueger, 'Interactions between Inflation and Trade Regime Objectives' pp. 83–117; M. Mussa, 'The Adjustment Process and the Timing of Trade Liberalization', National Bureau of Economic Research, Working Paper Series, no. 1458 (September 1984); V. Thomas, *Best Practices in Trade Policy Reform* (New York and Oxford: Oxford University Press, 1991).

10. U. Hiemenz and R.J. Langhammer, 'Liberalization and the Successful Integration of Developing Countries into the World Economy' in G.T. Renshaw (ed.), *Market Liberalization, Equity and Development* (Geneva: International Labour Organisation, 1989) pp. 105–39.

11. Russia's radical reformer, Yegor Gaidar, expressed this theory of reform succinctly: 'It is a very serious risk to do nothing. It is a serious risk to do anything unpopular. It is a serious risk to do anything popular, because everyone knows that anything popular leads you nowhere.' *Christian Science Monitor*, December 16, 1991, p. 7.

12. Lal, who had a high position at the Bank at the time, called for 'a courageous, ruthless and perhaps undemocratic government ... to ride roughshod over ... special interest groups'. See D. Lal, *The Poverty of Development Economics* (Cambridge, Mass: Harvard University Press, 1983) p. 33. That efforts were made to put the 'cadre strategy' into practice has been noted by several observers. See D. Gordon, 'Sustaining Economic Reform in Sub-Saharan Africa: Issues and Implications for USAID', Working Paper No. 6, *Implementing Policy Change* (Washington, DC: Management Systems International,

1994); P. Mosley, J. Toye and J. Harrigan, *Aid and Power: The World Bank and Policy-Based Lending* (London and New York: Routledge, 1991); B. Rich, *Mortgaging the Earth: The World Bank, Environmental Impoverishment and the Crisis of Development* (Boston: Beacon Press, 1994).

13. To be sure, reforms that are partial, piecemeal, inconsistent and weak may achieve little. But any reforms that are not radical tend to get labelled in this way.

14. S. Haggard, *Pathways from the Periphery: The Politics of Growth in the NICs* (Ithaca: Cornell University Press, 1990) p. 267.

15. A. Pickel, 'Authoritarianism or Democracy: Marketization as a Political Problem' in *Policy Sciences*, vol. 26, no. 3 (1993) pp. 139–63.

16. Yagci *et al.*, 'Structural Adjustment Lending: An Evaluation of Program Design'; S. Dell, *International Development Policies: Perspectives for Industrial Countries* (Durham: Duke University Press, 1990); T. Killick, 'Issues Arising from the Spread of Obligatory Adjustment' in G. Bird (ed.), *Third World Debt: The Search for a Solution* (Aldershot: Edward Elgar, 1989).

17. J.D. Sachs, 'Strengthening IMF Programs in Highly Indebted Countries' in C. Gwin and R.E. Feinberg (eds), *Pulling Together: The International Monetary Fund in a Multipolar World* (New Brunswick, NJ: Transaction Books, 1989) pp. 101–22.

18. L. Summers and L. Pritchett, 'The Structural Adjustment Debate' in *American Economic Review*, vol. 83 (May 1993) pp. 383–9.

19. M. Bruno, *Crisis, Stabilization and Economic Reform: Therapy by Consensus* (New York: Oxford University Press, 1993).

20. R. Dornbusch, 'From Stabilization to Growth' in R. Dornbusch, *Stabilization, Debt and Reform: Policy Analysis for Developing Countries* (Englewood Cliffs, NJ: Prentice Hall, 1993) pp. 32–60.

21. R.H. Green, 'The IMF and the World Bank in Africa: How Much Learning?' in T. Callaghy and J. Ravenhill (eds), *Hemmed In: Responses to Africa's Economic Decline* (New York: Columbia University Press, 1994 pp. 54–89); D. Mathieson and L. Rojas-Suarez 'Liberalizing the Capital Account' in *Finance and Development* vol. 29, no. 4 (December 1992) pp. 41–3.

22. L. Serven and A. Solimano, 'Debt Crisis, Adjustment Policies and Capital Formation in Developing Countries: Where Do We Stand?' in *World Development*, vol. 21, no. 1 (1992) pp. 127–40.

23. L.C.B. Pereira, 'Economic Reforms and Economic Growth: Efficiency and Politics in Latin America' in L.C.B. Pereira, J.A. Maravall and A. Przeworski, *Economic Reforms in New Democracies: A Social-Democratic Approach* (Cambridge: Cambridge University Press, 1993) pp. 15–76; H. Reisen, 'Financial Opening and Capital Flows' in C. Bradford (ed.), *Mobilising International Investment for Latin America* (Paris: OECD, 1992) pp. 143–52.

24. Johnson calls this one of the major mistakes made; see O. Johnson, 'Managing Adjustment Costs: Political Authority and the Implemen-

tation of Adjustment Programs, with Special Reference to African Countries' in *World Development*, vol. 22, no. 3 (March 1994) pp. 399–411.

25. C. Conaghan, J. Malloy and L. Abugattas, 'Business and the Boys: The Politics of Neoliberalism in the Central Andes' in *Latin American Research Review*, vol. 25, no. 2 (1990) pp. 3–30; W. Adams and J.W. Brock, *Adam Smith Goes to Moscow: A Dialogue on Radical Reform* (Princeton: Princeton University Press, 1993).

26. T. Callaghy, 'Vision and Politics in the Transformation of the Global Political Economy: Lessons from the Second and Third World' in R.O. Slater, Barry M. Schultz and Steven R. Dorr (eds), *Global Transformation and the Third World* (Boulder: Lynne Rienner, 1993 and London: Adamantine Press, 1993) pp. 161–257.

27. Christian Morrison, Jean-Dominique Lafay and Sebastian Dessus, 'Adjustment Programmes and Politico-Economic Interactions in Developing Countries: Lessons from an Empirical Analysis of Africa in the 1980s' in Giovanni A. Cornia and Gerald K. Helleiner (eds), *From Adjustment to Development in Africa: Conflict, Controversy, Convergence, Consensus* (New York: St Martins Press, 1994) pp. 174–91; J. Walton and D. Seddon, *Free Markets and Food Riots: The Politics of Global Adjustment* (Oxford and Cambridge: Basil Blackwell, 1994).

28. Adjustment has been most sustained and successful in South Korea and Taiwan, but Indonesia, Thailand, Sri Lanka, China, Hungary, Spain, Botswana, Mauritius, Colombia, Costa Rica and post-1984 Chile have also achieved important structural changes. How to define successful adjustment is taken up in the last section of this paper. The examples of 'successes' listed here are not meant to imply that successes have 'consolidated' adjustment, or that stumblers are necessarily headed for ultimate failure. Rather, successes are those moving in the right direction, carrying out structural changes that make their economies stronger and more flexible, while stumblers are those that have made little structural progress, or whose progress has come by running up 'debts' that will undermine it. Furthermore, success must be measured relative to a country's starting point, not by whether it is becoming the next South Korea. It is a success if it overcomes some of the structural problems holding it back and builds a solid foundation for future changes. Adjustment should be seen as a process of continuous adaptation that never reaches an endpoint. See T. Killick, *The Adaptive Economy: Adjustment Policies in Small, Low-Income Countries* (Washington, DC: The World Bank, 1994).

29. Walton and Seddon, *Free Markets and Food Riots* (1994).

30. J.E. Campos, 'Leadership and the Principle of Shared Growth: Insights into the Asian Miracle' in *Asian Journal of Political Science*, vol. 1, no. 2 (1993) pp. 1–38.

31. J. Bhagwati, 'Shock Treatments: Review of J. Sachs, Poland's Jump to the Market Economy', *The New Republic*, vol. 210, no. 13 (March

28, 1994) pp. 39–43; V. Milor, *Changing Political Economies: Privatization in Post-Communist and Reforming States* (Boulder: Lynne Rienner, 1994).

32. In practice, there is no doubt much variation in the degree to which Bank missions take a hardline approach with particular countries. Some missions have always taken an open-minded approach to negotiations and encouraged countries to propose their own alternatives. It is hard to tell, however, what share of missions has taken a more open approach, or whether it is a growing trend. It is clear, though, that missions often get overruled by management, which feels they are not tough enough. And there has been no general directive from above notifying missions of any change in the guidelines for negotiations. It has not been made a part of official policy that missions should be prepared to accept certain compromises.

33. G. Cornia, R. Jolly and F. Stewart, *Adjustment with a Human Face* (Oxford: Clarendon Press, 1987).

34. F. Stewart, 'Many Faces of Adjustment' in P. Mosley (ed.), *Development Finance and Policy Reform: Essays in the Theory and Practice of Conditionality in LDCs* (St Martins Press, 1992) pp. 176–231.

35. A. Amsden, J. Kochanowicz and L. Taylor, *The Market Meets Its Match: Restructuring the Economies of Eastern Europe* (Cambridge: Harvard University Press, 1994).

36. D. Kingsbury, *Compensatory Social Programs and Structural Adjustment: A Review of Experience* (Washington, DC: USAID, 1994).

37. F. Bourguignon and G. Morrison, *Adjustment and Equity in Developing Countries* (Paris: OECD, 1992); J. Nelson, 'Poverty, Equity and the Politics of Adjustment' in S. Haggard and R. Kaufman (eds), *The Politics of Economic Adjustment: International Constraints, Distributional Conflicts and the State* (Princeton: Princeton University Press, 1992) pp. 221–69.

38. R. Gulhati, 'Imposing Conditions on Aid' in U. Kirdar (ed.), *A World Fit For People* (New York: New York University Press, 1994 pp. 200–10); E.V.K. Jaycox, *Capacity-Building: The Missing Link in African Development* (Reston, VA: African American Institute, 1993); Johnson, 'Managing Adjustment Costs'; P. Landell-Mills and I. Serageldin 'Governance and the External Factor' in *Proceedings of the World Bank Annual Conference on Development Economics, 1991* (Washington, DC: World Bank, 1992) pp. 303–20.

39. T. Killick, 'Structural Adjustment and Poverty Alleviation: An Interpretive Survey' in *Development and Change*, vol. 26 (1995) p. 325.

40. P. Gibbon, 'The World Bank and the New Politics of Aid' European Journal of Development Research, vol. 5 (June 1993) pp. 35–62; T. Skalnes, 'The State, Interest Groups and Structural Adjustment in Zimbabwe' in *Journal of Development Studies*, vol. 29, no. 3 (April 1993) pp. 401–28; Walton and Seddon, *Free Markets and Food Riots*.

41. L.L. Frischtak, 'Governance Capacity and Economic Reform in Developing Countries', *World Bank Technical Paper No. 254* (1994).

42. A. Sen, 'Markets and Freedoms: Achievements and Limitations of the Market Mechanism in Promoting Individual Freedoms' in *Oxford Economic Papers*, vol. 45 (October 1993) pp. 519–41; A. Kohli, 'Democracy and Economic Orthodoxy: Trends in Developing Countries' in *Third World Quarterly*, vol. 14, no. 1 (November 1993) pp. 668–89.

43. S. Haggard and S.B. Webb (eds), *Voting for Reform: Democracy, Political Liberalization, and Economic Adjustment* (New York: Oxford University Press, for the World Bank, 1994).

44. L. Armijo, T. Biersteker and A. Lowenthal, 'The Problems of Simultaneous Transitions' in *The Journal of Democracy*, vol. 5, no. 4 (1994) pp. 161–75; S. Haggard and R. Kaufman, 'The Challenges of Consolidation' in *Journal of Democracy*, vol. 5, no. 4 (1994) pp. 5–16; C. Graham, *Safety Nets, Politics and the Poor: Transitions to Market Economies* (Washington, DC: Brookings Institution, 1994); Kohli, 'Democracy and Economic Orthodoxy'.

45. K. Remmer, 'Democracy and Economic Crisis: The Latin American Experience' in *World Politics*, vol. 42, no. 3 (April 1990) pp. 315–35; S.P. Huntington, *The Third Wave: Democratization in the Late Twentieth Century* (Norman: University of Oklahoma Press, 1991).

46. S. Please, 'Beyond Structural Adjustment in Africa' in *Development Policy Review*, vol. 10, no. 3 (September 1992) pp. 289–307.

47. Graham Bird notes the same dynamic between the IMF and its clients; see G. Bird, *IMF Lending to Developing Countries: Issues and Evidence* (London and New York: Routledge, 1995).

48. A. Fowler, 'The Role of NGOs in Changing State-Society Relations: Perspectives from Eastern and Southern Africa' in *Development Policy Review*, vol. 9 (March 1991) pp. 53–84; D. Rueschemeyer, E.H. Stephens, and J.D. Stephens, *Capitalist Development and Democracy* (Chicago: University of Chicago Press, 1992).

49. D. Brautigam, 'Governance, Economy and Foreign Aid' in *Studies in Comparative International Development*, vol. 27, no. 3 (1992) pp. 3–25; J. Clark, *Democratizing Development: The Role of Voluntary Organizations* (West Hartford: Kumarian Press, 1991).

50. Woodward argues that the high costs of reform are mainly due to their not working; see D. Woodward, *Debt, Adjustment and Poverty in Developing Countries* (New York: St Martins Press, 1992).

51. See W. Cline, *International Debt Re-examined* (Washington, DC: Institute of International Economics, 1995); G.K. Helleiner, 'The IMF, the World Bank, and Africa's Adjustment and External Debt Problems: An Unofficial View' in *World Development*, vol. 20, no. 6 (June 1992) pp. 779–92; Summers and Pritchett, 'The Structural Adjustment Debate'.

52. Some neoliberals had no conscious political strategy at all, but simply were true believers in the promise of market reforms to redistribute rewards to members of every class that took advantage of the opportunities provided by price reforms. Since weaker classes were the most deprived of opportunities under statist regimes, many neoliberals

assumed that the opening of markets would reward them the most, in relative terms.

53. Gulhati, 'Imposing Conditions on Aid'; Jaycox, *Capacity-Building: The Missing Link in African Development*; Johnson, 'Managing Adjustment Costs'; Landell-Mills and Serageldin, 'Governance and the External Factor'.

54. M. Moore, 'Declining to Learn from the East? The World Bank on 'Governance and Development' *Institute for Development Studies (IDS) Bulletin*, vol. 24, no. 1 (January 1993) pp. 39–50; M. Moore and M. Robinson, 'Can Foreign Aid Be Used to Promote Good Government in Developing Countries?' in *Ethics and International Affairs*, vol. 8 (1994) pp. 141–58.

55. R. Bates, 'Comment' in J. Williamson (ed.), *The Political Economy of Policy Reform* (Washington, DC: Institute of International Economics, 1993) pp. 29–34; J. Nelson, 'Consolidating Economic Adjustment: Aspects of the Political Economy of Sustained Reform' in P. Mosley (ed.), *Development Finance and Policy Reform: Essays in the Theory and Practice of Conditionality in LDCs* (St Martins Press, 1992) pp. 105–28.

56. T. Killick, T. Addison and L. Demery, 'Poverty, Adjustment and the IMF' in K. Haq and U. Kirdar (eds), *Human Development, Adjustment and Growth* (Islamabad, Pakistan: North-South Roundtable, 1987) pp. 112–37.

57. M. Ul Haq, 'From Dialogue to Action' in K. Haq and U. Kirdar (eds), *Human Development, Adjustment and Growth* (Islamabad, Pakistan: North-South Roundtable, 1987) pp. 14–20.

58. T. Perrson and G. Tabellini, 'Is Inequality Harmful for Growth?' in *American Economic Review*, vol. 84, no. 3 (June 1994) pp. 600–21.

59. World Bank, *The East Asian Miracle: Economic Growth and Public Policy* (New York: Oxford University Press, 1993).

60. Using implementation as a measure of success has produced an ever-changing list of successful 'models'. True believers are so certain that the implementation of market reforms guarantees future success that they would rather judge reform efforts by policy outputs than by policy outcomes. See Williamson, 'In Search of A Manual for Technopols'. By such teleological reasoning, Mexico was being hailed by many as the model to be emulated in 1993, at the same time that the United Nations Development Programme (UNDP) was putting Mexico on its early warning list of 17 countries that were at risk of falling apart. See UNDP, *Human Development Report 1993* (New York: Oxford University Press, 1993).

61. A. Amsden, 'A Theory of Government Intervention' in L. Putterman (ed.), *State and Market in Development: Synergy or Rivalry?* (Boulder: Lynne Rienner, 1992) pp. 53–84.

62. M. Ul Haq, 'From Dialogue to Action'; and M. Stiefel, *A Voice for the Excluded: Popular Participation in Development: Utopia or Necessity?* (London: Zed Books, 1994).

Glossary

African, Caribbean and Pacific (ACP) Countries – Countries entitled to tariff concessions and official development assistance under the Lomé Conventions. As of 1992, some 65 developing countries received European Community (EC) foreign aid in the form of capital investment, debt relief, duty reductions, subsidies, or technical assistance.

African Development Bank (AfDB) – An international development finance institution owned by 76 member-governments, including 51 regional members from Africa and 25 non-regional, mostly industrialized nations. Headquartered in Abidjan, Cote d'Ivoire, the Bank was founded as a purely African self-help initiative in 1963 and began with only $250 million in capital, none of which came from the world's industrialized nations. In 1982, the AfDB accepted developed countries as members.

Agenda 21 – The main strategy document for environmentally responsible development for the next century from the United Nations Conference on Environment and Development (UNCED) in Rio de Janeiro, June 1992. Agenda 21 is an action plan covering over 100 program areas and includes commitments of international aid to protect natural habitats and biodiversity and to alleviate poverty.

Asian Development Bank (AsDB) – An international development finance institution owned by 52 member-governments, including 19 industrialized nations in Europe, North America, Asia and the Pacific, and 33 developing nations. The Bank, which is headquartered in Manila, was created in 1966 on recommendation of the United Nations Economic Commission for Asia and the Far East to accelerate economic development in the developing countries of Asia.

Beggar-thy-neighbor policies – Economic policies by one country to improve its domestic economy, but which have adverse effects on other economies, such as competitive devaluations and tariffs.

Balance-of-payments deficit/surplus – The balance-of-payments consists of the current account (flows of goods and services) and the capital account (flows of financial assets). A country is said to have a balance-of-payments deficit when its income (credits from exports, cash inflows, loans, etc.) is less than its payments (debits from imports, cash outflows, debt repayments, etc.). A balance-of-payments surplus occurs when income is greater than payments.

Brady Plan – Named after a March 1989 initiative by then US Secretary of Treasury, Nicholas Brady, who proposed that countries with sound adjustment programs should get access to debt reduction for commercial bank debt facilities supported by international financial institutions and official creditors.

Bretton Woods institutions (BWIs) – The institutions founded at the conference of Bretton Woods, New Hampshire, in 1944, namely, the World Bank and the International Monetary Fund (IMF).

Committee of Twenty (C–20) – Established by the IMF's Board of Governors in light of the events following August 15, 1971, when US President Richard Nixon suspended the convertibility of dollars into gold. The committee consisted of one member appointed by each country or group of countries which appoints or elects an Executive Director of the Fund. The Committee decided to let a new monetary system evolve gradually out of existing arrangements and completed its work in 1974.

Concessionality versus Conditionality – A description of lending conditions which reduce the burden to the borrower, like a low interest rate. Concessionality should not be confused with conditionality, which is a description of requirements for borrowers to receive loans.

Council of Europe – A regional body composed of 21 European states created by the Statute of the Council signed at London in 1949. The Council of Europe was established to facilitate economic and political cooperation in western Europe. The European Commission on Human Rights and the European Court of Human Rights are affiliates of the Council. The Council of Europe should not be confused with the European Council of Ministers, which is the decision-making body of the 12 member-states of the European Community.

Countervailing powers – A concept introduced by economist John Kenneth Galbraith suggesting that restraints on large corporations come not from competitors on the same side of the market, but from countervailing powers on the opposite side of the market, such as large labor unions.

Debt crisis – Extreme difficulties of many developing countries to repay their loans since 1982, caused mainly by drastically increasing interest rates in the hard-currency creditor countries and a slowing of the world economy, which led to lower exports.

Debt Reduction Program – Operational guidelines by the World Bank, adopted in 1989, to provide support over three years to developing countries for the reduction of their debt and their debt-servicing payments. A $100 million fund has been established by the International Development Association to help severely indebted, low-income countries reduce their commercial debt.

Debt-swap – The sale of a country's outstanding loans to a third party, at a discount and converted into the debtor's local currency. In the case of a debt for equity swap, the third party is typically a transnational corporation which then uses the repayment in local currency for investment in the debtor country.

Debt write-down – An internal decision of a bank to reassess the value of an outstanding loan and adjust its internal accounts to reflect reduced expectation of full repayment. The debt is written-down in the bank's books, but the debtor country is not forgiven its debt or required to repay less.

Deflation – The opposite of inflation, that is, a sustained fall in the general price level. The term deflation is also used, although incorrectly, to describe a sustained reduction in the rate of inflation, that is, a slower increase in the general price level.

Depreciation/devaluation – A decrease in the value of a currency. If the exchange rate is defined in terms of foreign currency over domestic currency, then a devaluation of the domestic currency implies a decrease of the exchange rate. If the exchange rate is defined in terms of domestic currency over foreign currency, then a devaluation of the domestic currency implies an increase of the exchange rate.

Development (equitable, sustainable and participatory) – A healthy growing economy which (1) distributes the benefits widely, (2) meets the needs of the present generation without compromising the needs of future generations, and (3) provides for human rights and freedoms, effective governance and increasing democratization.

Development Committee – Officially the 'Joint Ministerial Committee of the Boards of Governors of the World Bank and the IMF on the Transfer of Real Resources to Developing Countries'. Established in October 1974, it currently consists of 24 members, generally Ministers of Finance, appointed in turn to successive periods of two years by one of the countries or groups of countries that designates a member of the World Bank's or the IMF's Board of Executive Directors. The Committee advises and reports to the Boards of Governors of the Bank and the IMF.

Economic Community of West African States (ECOWAS) – Also known as the Economic Community of West Africa, a regional intergovernmental organization of 16 Sub-Saharan African countries: Benin, Burkina Faso, Cape Verde, Cote d'Ivoire, Gambia, Ghana, Guinea, Guinea-Bissau, Liberia, Mali, Mauritania, Niger, Nigeria, Senegal, Sierra Leone and Togo. Created by the treaty of Lagos, Nigeria, in 1975, ECOWAS was established to promote uniform economic policies and eliminate regional trade barriers. Internal tariffs on most raw materials and handicrafts were removed in 1990.

Enhanced Structural Adjustment Facility (ESAF) – Introduced in 1988, ESAF is disbursed by the IMF as a trustee. Objectives, eligibility, terms and basic program features of ESAF parallel those of the Structural Adjustment Facility (SAF), but the adjustment measures are less stringent than those of the SAF. A detailed policy framework paper is prepared each year.

Enhanced Toronto Terms – See: Toronto Terms.

European Bank for Reconstruction and Development (EBRD) – Also known as the European Bank, a development bank created in Paris in 1990. The EBRD was established by the European Community and other countries around the globe to finance the economic development of the former Soviet Union and the countries of Eastern Europe.

Executive Director – The Executive Directors represent the member governments of the World Bank. According to the Articles of Agreement, the five largest shareholders – the United States, Japan, Germany, France, and the United Kingdom – each appoint one Executive Director. The other countries are grouped into 19 constituencies, each of which is represented by an Executive Director elected by a country or a group of countries. The same arrangements apply to the Executive Directors of the IMF and generally, the regional development banks.

Extended Fund Facility (EFF) – A program of the IMF that aims to overcome structural balance-of-payments deficits. This program generally lasts for three years, although it may be lengthened to four years. The program identifies policies and measures in detail for the first year. Resources are provided in the form of extended arrangements that include performance criteria and drawings in installments. Repurchases are made in four to ten years.

Externality – A positive or negative spill-over effect from consumption or production which is not reflected in any price. No markets exist which are able to define and enforce property rights over these externalities (such as clean air).

Foreign direct investment – Investment abroad, usually by transnational corporations, involving an element of control by the investor over the corporation in which the investment is made.

Foreign portfolio investment – Investment abroad, mainly in financial (including monetary) assets, in which the investment is too small to give an investor partial or total control of a company.

G–7 – Group of Seven; the seven major industrial countries (Canada, France, Italy, Germany, Japan, the United Kingdom, and the United States) whose heads of government and economic ministers meet annually at economic summits to coordinate macroeconomic policies, especially exchange-rate policies.

G–24 – Group of 24; formed at the 1972 Lima meeting to represent the interests of the developing countries in negotiations on international monetary affairs. The Group's members are: Algeria, Argentina, Brazil, Colombia, Cote d'Ivoire, Egypt, Ethiopia, Gabon, Ghana, Guatemala, India, Iran, Lebanon, Mexico, Nigeria, Pakistan, Peru, Philippines, Sri Lanka, Syria, Trinidad and Tobago, Venezuela and Zaire. China attends as an invitee.

General Agreement on Tariffs and Trade (GATT) – An agreement signed at the 1947 Geneva Conference on multilateral trade. It set out rules of conduct, provided a forum for multilateral negotiations regarding the solution of trade problems and aimed to eliminate tariffs and other barriers to trade.

Generalized System of Preferences (GSP) – Introduced in 1971, the system implies that some exports from developing countries are given preferential access to the markets of industrial countries.

Global Environment Facility (GEF) – An entity that provides grants and concessional funds to developing countries for projects and activities that aim to protect the environment. The GEF Secretariat is functionally independent but administratively supported by the World Bank. The UNDP is responsible for technical assistance activities and UNEP provides the secretariat for the Scientific and Technical Advisory Panel, made up of 15 international environmental experts.

Good governance – Governance which (1) distinguishes clearly between what is public and what is private, (2) implies accountability, (3) is based on the rule of law and (4) implies transparent information and decision making.

Great Depression – The most severe economic contraction of the world economy in recorded history. In the United States, for example, real GDP fell by 30 per cent and unemployment increased to over 25 per cent of the labor force in the four years after the stock market crash of 1929.

Gross domestic product (GDP) – GDP is the value of all final goods and services produced in the country within a given period.

Gross national product (GNP) – GNP is the value of all final goods and services produced by domestically owned factors of production, whether inside or outside the national borders, within a given period.

Human capital – Investments in people (human resources) to improve their productivity, especially education and job training.

Human development index (HDI) – A composite measure of human development containing indicators representing three equally weighted dimensions of human development: life expectancy at birth, adult literacy and mean years of schooling, and income per capita in purchasing power parity dollars.

Import substitution policy – A policy of replacing imports with domestic products, which involves charging higher import duties and/or restricting imports through quotas or outright bans.

Immiserization – A steady decline in economic welfare. The term was first used by Karl Marx, who predicted increasing misery for the proletariat, leading to class consciousness and an overthrow of capitalism through socialist revolution.

Infant industry – An industry in its early stages of development whose share of the domestic market is still small due to competition from overseas competitors.

Inspection Panel – The Inspection Panel is an independent forum established by the Executive Directors of the World Bank and the International Development Association (IDA) in 1993. The purpose of the panel is to provide directly and adversely affected people of a Bank-financed project with a forum to investigate whether or not the Bank acted in accordance with its own policies and procedures.

Inter-American Development Bank (IDB) – An international financial institution created in 1959 to help accelerate the economic and social development of its member countries in Latin America and the Caribbean. The Bank is owned by its 46 member countries, including 28 regional members from the Western Hemisphere and 18 non-regional members from Europe, Asia and the Middle East. The Bank's headquarters are in Washington, DC.

International Bank for Reconstruction and Development (IBRD) – Commonly referred to as the World Bank, founded in 1944 at Bretton Woods. A lending institution whose official aim is to promote long-term economic growth that reduces poverty in developing countries. (See also: World Bank Group.)

International Development Association (IDA) – An affiliate of the World Bank Group established in 1960 to promote economic development in the world's poorest countries.

International Finance Corporation (IFC) – The World Bank Group's investment bank for developing countries, established in 1956. It lends directly to private companies and makes equity investments in them, without guarantees from governments.

International Labour Organisation (ILO) – Established in 1919 by the Treaty of Versailles, the ILO became a specialized agency of the United Nations in 1946. The ILO promotes international cooperation regarding policies designed to achieve full employment, improve working conditions, extend social security and raise general living standards.

International Monetary Fund (IMF) – Established in December 1945 following ratification of the Articles of Agreement of the Fund, formulated at the Bretton Woods conference in 1944. The Fund became a specialized agency of the United Nations in 1947 and acts as a monitor of the world's currencies by helping to maintain an orderly system of payments between all countries. To this end, it lends money to its members facing serious balance-of-payments deficits, subject to a variety of conditions.

International Trade Organization (ITO) – In 1947, the United Nations Economic and Social Council (ECOSOC) convened an International Conference on Trade and Development in Havana, Cuba, which drew up the Havana Charter, proposing the establishment of an International Trade Organization under the aegis of the United Nations. Although 50 countries signed the Havana Charter, it failed to receive the necessary number of ratifications and the idea of a permanent UN trade body was never realized. (See also GATT, UNCTAD and WTO.)

Keynes Plan – Proposals of the UK treasury to establish an International Clearing Union which received consideration at the Bretton Woods conference in 1944. As John Maynard Keynes (1883-1946) was primarily responsible for their formulation, these proposals were collectively referred to as the Keynes Plan.

Lender of Last Resort – A country's ultimate lender, providing credit or guarantees to the country's national banking system. For example, in the United States, the Federal Reserve System, acting principally through the regional Federal Reserve Banks, is the lender of last resort.

Liberal/neoliberal school – The idea central to liberalism is that people be allowed to pursue their own interests and desires, constrained only by rules which prevent their encroachment of the liberty of others. In economic theory, the prescription is therefore to minimize the role of government. The neoliberal school emerged in response to the structuralist school of economics, which claimed a positive role for the state in managing economic affairs. Neoliberal policies have been dominant in the structural adjustment programs implemented after the debt crisis of 1982.

Lomé Convention – A trade and economic cooperation convention signed first in 1975 at Lomé, the capital of Togo, by European Community (EC) member countries and 46 African, Caribbean and Pacific (ACP) developing countries. The most recent Lomé Convention (Lomé IV) was concluded in 1989 and expires in 1999.

London Club – *Ad hoc* meetings of commercial bankers to restructure loans owed by governments and private entities in countries experiencing payment difficulties. London Club-member commercial banks often require that sovereign debtors have an IMF arrangement and a debt rescheduling arrangement in place through the Paris Club (see below).

Marshall Aid – Named after US Secretary of State, General Marshall, the aid given by the United States and Canada to Western European countries to restore their economies after World War II; also known as the Marshall Plan or European Recovery Programme.

Mixed economy – A system which combines competitive private enterprise with some degree of government activity. While the allocation of resources is dominated by individual actions through the price mechanism, the government plays some role in determining the level of aggregate demand by means of fiscal and monetary policy.

Monetarism – A school of economic thought which argues that monetary factors are the principal cause of instability in the economy. In particular, monetarists believe that an increase in the supply of money will generate inflation rather than employment.

Most favored nation status – The result of the GATT (or any other trade agreement) whereby all contracting parties promise to treat each other in trade as favorably as they do any other country. Exceptions are customs unions and free-trade agreements.

Multi-Fibre Arrangement (MFA) – A set of complicated multilateral umbrella agreements which set limits on the flow of textiles and clothing produced in the developing countries for sale in the developed countries. The application of import quotas for textiles and clothing from developing countries, but not to those from other developed countries, is a clear breach of the GATT principles of non-discrimination. The fourth MFA began in 1986 and was scheduled to expire in 1991. However, the MFA became part of the Uruguay Round of GATT negotiations which concluded in April 1994, when it was agreed to give the MFA another ten years before being phased out.

Multilateral Investment Guarantee Agency (MIGA) – A member of the World Bank Group designed to help smooth the flow of foreign investment by insuring investors against non-commercial risks and providing investment advice and promotion services.

Neoclassical economics – A body of economic theory which uses the general techniques of the original nineteenth-century marginalist economists. Today, it is often combined with the liberal doctrine, which advocates the greatest possible use of markets and the forces of competition to enhance economic activity. Thus, economic policy based on neoclassical economics is often called either neoclassical or neoliberal.

Net flow of capital – The difference between total flow of capital into and out of a country or institution: the net flow of capital is the gross flow of capital out minus the gross flow of capital in.

For example, if the total amount of capital which flows into a country exceeds the total amount of capital which flows out of a country, the net flow of capital is positive and the country is said to be a net creditor country.

Official Development Assistance (ODA) – Concessional financial aid to developing countries and multilateral institutions provided by official agencies, including state and local governments. It contains a grant element of at least 25 per cent.

Organization for Economic Cooperation and Development (OECD) – Originally set up as the Organization for European Economic Cooperation (OEEC) to coordinate Marshall Plan aid in 1948, the OECD took its present form in 1961 in order to encourage economic growth and maintain financial stability among its 24 member countries: Australia, Austria, Belgium, Canada, Denmark, Finland, France, Germany, Greece, Iceland, Ireland, Italy, Japan, Luxembourg, the Netherlands, New Zealand, Norway, Portugal, Spain, Sweden, Switzerland, Turkey, the United Kingdom and the United States. Mexico joined in 1994, South Korea in 1995.

Organization of African Unity (OAU) – Established at Addis Ababa, Ethiopia, in 1963, the OAU was originally formed to encourage political cooperation among African states. More recently, it has worked for trade reform and debt relief for developing countries. All African countries are OAU members.

Organization of American States (OAS) – A mutual defense and economic association, chartered in Bogotá in 1948. With the exception of Canada, all countries in the Americas were founding OAS members. Cuba was expelled in 1972. Canada, an official observer since 1972, became a full member in 1989. The Inter-American Development Bank is the OAS multilateral development bank.

Oxfam – A global network of organizations, started in Oxford, England, that funds self-help projects in developing countries.

Participatory development – Development which includes a mechanism for enabling affected people to share in the creation of a project or program, beginning with identification all the way through to implementation and evaluation. On the national scale it implies a political system of human rights and freedoms, effective governance and increasing democratization.

Paris Club – Ad hoc meetings of OECD creditor governments since 1956 to arrange renegotiation of debt owed by official debtors to official creditors or guarantors. (See also London Club.)

Political conditionality – In this volume, political conditionality refers to a requirement by aid donors that borrowing countries alter their domestic political environment in ways that sustain economic and human development. It may take three main forms: support through technical assistance to promote human rights and democratic development, persuasion through policy dialogue, or political pressure.

Public choice theory – A branch of economics concerned with the application of economic theory to the analysis of non-market decision making, especially the economic analysis of politics.

Replenishment – The refunding of a multilateral financial institution. For example, in the tenth replenishment of the International Development Association (IDA), 34 donor nations agreed to provide a total of $18 billion for the three-year period 1994–6.

Rights Accumulation Program – Introduced by the IMF in 1990 and used for the first time in 1991, the program allows a member country with protracted arrears to the IMF to accumulate rights based on its performance within an IMF-monitored adjustment program. The accumulated rights would then be cashed as the first disbursement under a successor IMF-supported program financed from the IMF's general resources or, for eligible countries, partially from the concessional Structural Adjustment Facility (SAF) and/or Enhanced Structural Adjustment Facility (ESAF).

Sectoral adjustment loans (SECALs) – Introduced in 1980, the World Bank's provision of resources within a Structural Adjustment Program (SAP) for loans which target policy reforms at the sectoral level; see also Structural Adjustment Loan (SAL) and Structural Adjustment Program (SAP).

Social Investment Fund (SIF) – Created in the second half of the 1980s by many governments, especially in Latin America and the Caribbean, to alleviate the negative impact on the poor of the debt crisis and structural adjustment measures. Many SIFs have been transformed into permanent or semi-permanent entities to finance infrastructure and social service projects targeted to reach the very poor.

Social security – Public programs which pay regular amounts of money to workers and their families to make up for income losses associated with old age, illness, unemployment, or death.

Special drawing right (SDR) – The IMF's standard unit of account, introduced in 1969, which IMF member countries may use to settle international trade balances and debts if the member country meets a variety of conditions. The value of SDRs was originally expressed in terms of gold, but since 1974 it has been valued in its members' currencies.

Special Programme of Assistance (SPA) – The World Bank's special assistance to the poorest countries which are (1) eligible for IDA loans, (2) have a projected debt-service ratio of 30 per cent or more, (3) are implementing a policy reform program that is endorsed by the Bank, and (4) have reached agreement on a policy framework paper with the IMF.

Stand-by arrangement – A facility of the IMF permitting members to draw down emergency funds for balance-of-payments crisis. The drawdowns are available in addition to other IMF lending facilities.

Structural adjustment facility (SAF) – Introduced in 1986, the IMF's provision of resources on concessional terms (0.5 per cent interest and repayments within five to ten years) to low-income developing countries facing balance-of-payments problems, conditional on a medium-term structural adjustment program, set out in a policy framework paper (PFP). See also: Enhanced Structural Adjustment Facility (ESAF) and Extended Fund Facility (EFF).

Structural adjustment loan (SAL) – Introduced in 1979, the World Bank's provision of resources for general budget support provided the country undertake agreed-upon policy reforms; see Structural adjustment program (SAP).

Structural adjustment program (SAP) – A long-term loan from the World Bank and other multilateral development banks (MDBs) which is designed to restore equilibrium and promote economic growth. The original rationale for SAPs was that sound projects were not possible in an unsound policy environment. Thus, SAPs became an instrument to influence macroeconomic policies of developing countries, based on neoclassical economics, advocating *laissez-faire* and free trade.

Structuralist/neostructuralist school – Primarily associated with the work of the United Nations Economic Commission for Latin America and the Caribbean (UNECLAC) and its first director, Raul Prebisch, the structuralist school of economics posits a bipolar world economy, the center and the periphery, with the structure of the economy in each differing substantially. The different structures implied the need for a new long-term strategy for the development of the periphery. Neostructural thought emerged in the 1970s, concentrating more on short-term policies and the individual country's own potential.

Surveillance – IMF member governments are obligated to provide the IMF with the data necessary for the IMF to conduct accurate economic monitoring. The concept was adopted in 1977, modified in 1987 and 1988, and strengthened in April 1995 in the aftermath of the Mexican peso crisis.

Sustainable development – Development which meets the needs of the present generation without compromising the needs of future generations.

Tableau économique – The first clear illustration of the interrelatedness of the economy, developed by the intellectual leader of the French physiocratic movement, Francois Quesnay (1694–1774). The *tableau économique* gave a crude representation of: (1) the flow of money incomes among different classes of society (landowners, farmers, artisans and servants); and (2) the creation and annual circulation of the net product throughout the economy.

Terms of trade – The quotient between an index of export prices and an index for import prices. When a country's terms of trade decline, as is the case for many developing countries, it is necessary to export more in order to import the same quantity of goods and services.

Tobin tax – A proposal by US Nobel Laureate James Tobin to tax international currency transactions. Tobin's original proposal in 1978 suggested imposing a tax of .05 per cent on all short-term foreign bank accounts. In his latest proposal in UNDP's *Human Development Report 1994*, Tobin suggests a tax of .5 per cent on foreign exchange transactions.

Toronto Terms – A menu of options meant to enable reductions in the official debt of low-income, debt-distressed countries. Agreed upon in September 1988 (following agreement in principle at the economic summit held in Toronto three months earlier), the terms include reduced interest, very long grace and repayment periods, and partial write-offs of debt service obligations during the consolidation period. The terms have been enhanced by the Paris Club in 1991 (thus, Enhanced Toronto Terms), by provision of a consolidation option at market rates, with a 25-year repayment period, including a 14-year grace period.

Transnational corporation (TNC) – A large enterprise having a home base in one country but operating wholly or partially-owned subsidiaries in other countries. Such corporations expand on an international scale to take advantage of economies of scale and to benefit from near monopoly status, often to the detriment of the developing countries in which they operate.

Trinidad Terms – Proposed by John Major, then UK Chancellor of the Exchequer, at the September 1990 Commonwealth Finance Ministers' Conference. These terms would have reduced by two-thirds the stock of outstanding debt owed to Paris Club creditors. But the Trinidad Terms have not been accepted by the creditors, who agreed to adopt the Enhanced Toronto Terms in 1991; see Toronto Terms.

United Nations Conference on Trade and Development (UNCTAD) – The conference, first convened in 1964, is now a permanent organ of the UN General Assembly. All members of the United Nations or of its specialized agencies are members of the conference, which has a permanent executive organ and a permanent secretariat. Its role has been to champion the case of developing countries against the trade policies of the developed countries. UNCTAD's major success has been in securing the Generalized System of Preferences (GSP).

United Nations Declaration on the Right to Development – On December 4, 1986, the UN General Assembly adopted Resolution 41/128 which contained the Declaration on the Right to Development. The Declaration was passed by 146 votes to one (the United States), with eight abstentions (Denmark, Finland, the Federal Republic of Germany, Iceland, Israel, Japan, Sweden and the United Kingdom).

United Nations Development Programme (UNDP) – Created in 1966, it combined the UN Expanded Programme of Technical Assistance and the UN Special Fund. It is responsible for administering and coordinating development projects and technical assistance provided under the auspices of, or in collaboration with, the UN system of development agencies and organizations.

United Nations Economic and Social Council (ECOSOC) – One of the original six major organs of the United Nations. It coordinates the economic and social work of the United Nations and the specialized agencies and institutions. The Council makes recommendations and initiatives relating to all economic and social questions.

United Nations Economic Commission for Africa (UNECA) – One of the five UN regional economic commissions, created to promote global economic development. The commissions identify projects to improve economic performance in the least developed parts of each region and monitor project implementation. UNECA headquarters are in Addis Ababa, Ethiopia.

United Nations Security Council – The principal policymaking body of the United Nations on issues of international security. The Security Council's five permanent members are China, France, Russia, the United Kingdom and the United States. Ten additional members are selected by the General Assembly for rotating two-year terms. Of various UN bodies, only the Security Council has enforcement powers, which derive from its ability to organize armed forces and dispatch troops to conflicted regions around the world.

Uruguay Round – The eighth round of GATT negotiations, launched in September 1986 in Punta del Este (Uruguay) and concluded in April 1994 at Marrakesh (Morocco). The Uruguay Round dealt with unfinished business from earlier GATT rounds and new issues, such as trade in services, the protection of intellectual property rights, trade-related investment measures, and especially, the establishment of a World Trade Organization (WTO).

White Plan – Proposals for an International Stabilization Fund made by the United States at the Bretton Woods conference in 1944, and commonly called the White Plan after its chief author, Harry D. White, then Under Secretary of the US Treasury. Unlike the Keynes Plan, the White Plan did not provide for the establishment of a new international means of payment or the extension of credit facilities.

World Bank – See: International Bank for Reconstruction and Development.

World Bank Group – Consists of the International Bank for Reconstruction and Development (IBRD, commonly referred to as the World Bank), the International Finance Corporation (IFC), the International Development Association (IDA), the International Center for Settlements of Investment Disputes (ICSID), and the Multilateral Investment Guarantee Agency (MIGA). All of them are headquartered in Washington, DC.

World Trade Organization (WTO) – The WTO, successor to the GATT, is a procedural umbrella agreement to provide an institutional and organizational framework for the administration of the multilateral trade agreements concluded at GATT's Uruguay Round.

Bibliography

Adams, W. and J.W. Brock *Adam Smith Goes to Moscow: A Dialogue on Radical Reform* (Princeton: Princeton University Press, 1993).

Africa Watch *Kenya: Taking Liberties* (New York: Africa Watch, 1991).

African Development Bank (AfDB) *African Development Report 1993* (Abidjan: African Development Bank, 1993).

African Development Bank *Group Projections on Africa's External Resource Requirements and the Bank Group: A Ten Year Perspective* (Abidjan: African Development Bank, April 1993).

African National Congress *Reconstruction and Development Programme* (Johannesburg, South Africa: Umanyano Publications, 1994).

Akyüz, Yilmaz 'On Financial Openness in Developing Countries' in United Nations Conference on Trade and Development (UNCTAD) (ed.), *International Monetary and Financial Issues for the 1990s: Research Papers for the Group of Twenty-Four*, Volume II (New York: United Nations, 1993) pp. 110–24.

Amsden, A. *Asia's Next Giant: South Korea and Late Industrialization* (New York: Oxford University Press, 1989).

Amsden, A. 'A Theory of Government Intervention' in L. Putterman (ed.) *State and Market in Development: Synergy or Rivalry?* (Boulder: Lynne Rienner, 1992) pp. 53–84.

Amsden, A., J. Kochanowicz and L. Taylor *The Market Meets Its Match: Restructuring the Economies of Eastern Europe* (Cambridge: Harvard University Press, 1994).

Anand, Sudhir and Ravi M. Kanbur 'Public Policy and Basic Needs Provision: Intervention and Achievement in Sri Lanka' in Jean Dreze and Amartya Sen (eds), *The Political Economy of Hunger, Volume 3* (Oxford: Oxford University Press, 1991) pp. 59–92.

Armijo, L., T. Biersteker and A. Lowenthal 'The Problems of Simultaneous Transitions' in *The Journal of Democracy*, vol. 5, no. 4 (1994) pp. 161–75.

Ascher, W. 'On the Convergence of Efficiency and Equity via Neoclassical Prescriptions' in *Journal of Inter-American Studies and World Affairs*, vol. 31, nos. 1 & 2 (Spring 1989) pp. 49–62.

Avramovic, Dragoslav *Economic Growth and External Debt* (Baltimore: Johns Hopkins University Press, 1964).

Avramovic, D. 'Commodity Problem: What Next?' in *World Development* vol. 15, no. 5 (Special Issue, May 1987) pp. 645–56.

Bank, David L. 'Measuring Human Rights' in I. Brecher (ed.), *Human Rights, Development and Foreign Policy: Canadian Perspectives* (Halifax, Canada: Institute for Research on Public Policy, 1989) pp. 539–62.

Bates, R. 'Comment' in John Williamson (ed.) *The Political Economy of Policy Reform* (Washington, DC: Institute of International Economics, 1993) pp. 29–34.

Beckerman, Wilfred and T. Jenkinson 'What Stopped the Inflation? Unemployment or Commodity Prices' in *Economic Journal*, vol. 96 (1986) pp. 36–54.

Beckmann, David 'Recent Experience and Emerging Trends' in Samuel Paul and Arturo Israel (eds), *Nongovernmental Organizations and the World Bank* (Washington, DC: World Bank, 1991) pp. 134–54.

Berger, D. 'Wildlife as a Peoples' Resource: A First Step and the Journey Ahead', Research Memorandum 7 (Nairobi: African Centre for Technology Studies, 1993).

Bhagwati, Jagdish N. 'Dependence and Interdependence: Developing Countries in the World Economy', text of the Ernest Sturc Memorial Lecture, delivered at the School for Advanced International Studies, The Johns Hopkins University, November 5, 1987, mimeo.

Bhagwati, Jagdish N. 'Shock Treatments: Review of J. Sachs, Poland's Jump to the Market Economy' in *The New Republic*, vol. 210, no. 13 (March 28, 1994) pp. 39–43.

Bhuvan, Bhatnagar and Aubrey C. Williams 'Participatory Development and the World Bank', *World Bank Discussion Paper No. 183* (Washington, DC: World Bank, 1992).

Bird, G. *IMF Lending to Developing Countries: Issues and Evidence* (London and New York: Routledge, 1995).

Blackden, Mark C. 'Human Rights, Governance, and Development', Inter-Divisional Thematic Team on Governance, Sub-Group on Human Rights (Washington, DC: World Bank, October 1991).

Bobrow, D. and J. Dryzek *Policy Analysis by Design* (Pittsburgh: University of Pittsburgh Press, 1987).

Bourguignon, F. and G. Morrison *Adjustment and Equity in Developing Countries* (Paris: OECD, 1992).

Brautigam, D. 'Governance, Economy and Foreign Aid' in *Studies in Comparative International Development*, vol. 27, no. 3 (1992) pp. 3–25.

Bretton Woods Commission *Bretton Woods: Looking to the Future* (Washington, DC: Bretton Woods Commission, 1994).

Bruno, M. *Crisis, Stabilization and Economic Reform: Therapy by Consensus* (New York: Oxford University Press, 1993).

Bruno, M. 'Development Issues in a Changing World: New Lessons, Old Debates, Open Question', *Proceedings of the Conference on Development Economics*, 1994 (Washington, DC: World Bank) pp. 9–19.

Bulmer, M. *Social Science and Social Policy* (London: Allen and Unwin, 1986).

Burdge, R. 'A Community Guide to Social Impact Assessment', Presentation at a Workshop organized by the Environmental Evaluation Unit, University of Cape Town, Johannesburg, South Africa, July 1992.

Burdge, R. and R. Robertson 'Social Impact Assessment and the Public Involvement Process' in *Environmental Impact Assessment Review*, vol. 10 (1990) pp. 81–90.

Cahn, Jonathan 'Challenging the New Imperial Authority: The World Bank and the Democratization of Development' in *Harvard Human Rights Law Journal*, vol. 6 (1993) pp. 159–94.

Callaghy, T. 'Vision and Politics in the Transformation of the Global Political Economy: Lessons from the Second and Third World' in Robert O. Slater, Barry M. Schultz and Steven R. Dorr (eds) *Global Transformation and the Third World* (Boulder: Lynne Rienner, 1993 and London: Adamantine Press, 1993) pp. 161–257.

Campos, J.E. 'Leadership and the Principle of Shared Growth: Insights into the Asian Miracle' in *Asian Journal of Political Science*, vol. 1, no. 2 (1993) pp. 1–38.

Center for International Policy *Enforcing Human Rights: Congress and the Multilateral Banks* (Washington, DC: Center for International Policy, 1985).

Cernea, Michael M. 'Using Knowledge from Social Science in Development Projects', *World Bank Discussion Paper No. 114* (Washington, DC: World Bank, 1991).

Cernea, Michael M. 'The Sociologist's Approach to Sustainable Development' in *Finance and Development*, vol. 30, No. 4 (1993) pp. 11–13.

Chalker, Lynda *Governance Working Paper: Africa Bureau Democracy and Governance Program* (Washington, DC: US Agency for International Development, 1992).

Chandrasekhar, C.P. 'An Asian Perspective on the Human Development Report 1993' prepared for the Human Development Report Office (New Delhi: UNDP, 1993) mimeo.

Chandrasekhar, C.P. 'The Macroeconomics of Imbalance and Adjustment' in Prabhat Patnaik (ed.), *Themes in Indian Economics: Macroeconomics* (New Delhi: Oxford University Press, forthcoming).

Clark, J. *Democratizing Development: The Role of Voluntary Organizations* (West Hartford: Kumarian Press, 1991).

Cline, W. *International Debt Re-examined* (Washington, DC: Institute of International Economics, 1995).

Colclough, Christopher. 'Structuralism versus Neo-liberalism: An Introduction' in Christopher Colclough and James Manor (eds) *States or Markets? Neo-liberalism and the Development Policy Debate* (Oxford: Clarendon Press, 1991) pp. 1–25.

Commission of the European Communities *Towards a New Bretton Woods: Alternatives for the Global Economy*, Report for the FAST Programme (Brussels: Commission of the European Community, 1993).

Commonwealth Secretariat *Towards a New Bretton Woods: Challenges for the World Financial and Trading System* (London: Commonwealth Secretariat, 1983).

Conable, Barber *Managing Development: The Governance Dimension* (Washington, DC: World Bank, 1991).

Conaghan, C., J. Malloy and L. Abugattas 'Business and the Boys: The Politics of Neoliberalism in the Central Andes' in *Latin American Research Review*, vol. 25, no. 2 (1990) pp. 3–30.

Cooper, R.N. *Economic Stabilization and Debt in Developing Countries* (Cambridge, MA: MIT Press, 1992).

Cornia, Giovanni A., Richard Jolly and Frances Stewart (eds) *Adjustment With a Human Face – Protecting the Vulnerable and Promoting Growth*, A UNICEF Study (Oxford: Clarendon Press, 1987).

Council for the Environment *Integrated Environmental Management in South Africa* (Pretoria: Lotter, 1989).

Council for Scientific and Industrial Research (CSIR) *Environmental Impact Assessment: Eastern Shores of Lake St Lucia*, vol. 1, Specialist Reports; vol. 2, Reports on the Key Issues; vol. 3, Environmental Impact Report; vol. 4, Final Report (Pretoria: CSIR Environmental Services, 1993).

Craig, D. 'Social Impact Assessment: Politically Oriented Approaches and Applications' in *Environmental Impact Assessment Review*, vol. 10 (1990) pp. 37–54.

Culagovski, Jorge, Victor Gabor, Maria Cristina Germany, and Charles P. Humphreys *African Financing Needs in the 1990s*, Policy, Research, and External Affairs Working Papers, Technical Department, Africa Regional Office (Washington, DC: World Bank, 1991).

Dag Hammarskjold Foundation 'The International Monetary System and the New International Order', *Development Dialogue*, No. 2 (Uppsala: Dag Hammarskjold Foundation, 1980).

Dell, Sidney *International Development Policies: Perspectives for Industrial Countries* (Durham: Duke University Press, 1990).

Dell, Sidney 'Reforming the World Bank for the Tasks of the 1990s' Exim Bank Commencement Day Lecture (Bombay: Exim Bank, 1990).

Derman, W. and S. Whiteford (eds) *Social Impact Analysis and Development in the Third World* (Boulder: Westview Press, 1985).

Department of Environmental Affairs *The Integrated Environmental Management Guideline Series* (Pretoria: Department of Environmental Affairs, 1992).

de Vries, Barend A. *Remaking the World Bank* (Washington, DC: The Seven Locks Press, 1987).

Dias, Clarence and James Paul 'To Secure Human Rights in Development Processes and to Set Out the Human Rights Obligations of Development Agencies', Draft Charter (New York: International Center for Law in Development, 1994).

Dietz, T. 'Theory and Method in Social Impact Assessment' in *Sociological Inquiry*, vol. 57, no. 1 (1987) pp. 54–69.

Dobb, Maurice *Welfare Economics and the Economics of Socialism: Towards a Commonsense Critique* (Cambridge: Cambridge University Press, 1969).

Dornbusch, Rudiger. 'From Stabilization to Growth' in Rudiger Dornbusch (ed.) *Stabilization, Debt and Reform: Policy Analysis for Developing Countries* (New York: Harvester Wheatsheaf, 1993) pp. 32–60.

Economic and Social Commission for Asia and the Pacific (ESCAP) *Economic and Social Survey of Asia and the Pacific, Part II: Expansion of Investment and Intraregional Trade as a Vehicle for Enhancing Regional Economic Cooperation and Development in Asia and the Pacific* (New York: United Nations, 1993).

Ferguson, James *The Anti-Politics Machine: Development, Depoliticization and Bureaucratic Power in Lesotho* (Cambridge: Cambridge University Press, 1990).

Finch, David 'IMF Surveillance and the Group of 24: International Monetary and Financial Issues for the 1990s', in United Nations Conference on Aid and Development (UNCTAD) (ed.) *International Monetary and Financial Issues for the 1990s: Research Papers for the Group of 24*, vol. II (New York: United Nations, 1993) pp. 101–109.

Fischer, S. 'Issues in Medium-Term Macroeconomic Adjustment' in *World Bank Research Observer*, vol. 1, no. 2 (1986) pp. 163–82.

Fowler, Alan 'The Role of NGOs in Changing State-Society Relations: Perspectives From Eastern and Southern Africa' in *Development Policy Review*, vol. 9 (1991) pp. 53-84.

Fox, J. 'Feedback Loops and Economies of Scale: Achieving Export-Led Growth in the Caribbean Basin', USAID Document PN ABG 564 (Washington, DC: US Agency for International Development, 1990).

Freeman, R.B. 'Labor Market Institutions: Help or Hindrance to Economic Development?' in *Proceedings of the World Bank Annual Conference on Development Economics 1992* (Washington, DC: World Bank, 1992) pp. 117–44.

Freudenberg, W. and K. Keating 'Increasing the Impact of Sociology on Social Impact Assessment: Towards Ending the Inattention' in *American Sociologist*, vol. 17 (1985) pp. 71–8.

Friedman, S. 'The Elusive Community: The Dynamics of Negotiated Urban Development', Research Report no. 28 (Johannesburg: Centre for Policy Studies, 1993).

Frischtak, L.L. 'Governance Capacity and Economic Reform in Developing Countries', *World Bank Technical Paper no. 254* (1994).

Fu-Keung, D. 'Difficulties in Implementing Social Impact Assessment in China' in *Environmental Impact Assessment Review*, vol. 10, no. 1/2 (1990) pp. 113–22.

Fuggle, R. 'Integrated Environmental Management: A Framework for Minimising and Mitigating Environmental Consequences of Development Actions in the Countries of Southern Africa', Paper delivered to the Southern African Regional Commission for the Conservation and Utilisation of the Soil (Malawi, May 1990).

Gagnon, C., P. Hirsch and R. Howitt 'Can SIA Empower Communities?' in *Environmental Impact Assessment Review*, vol. 13, no. 4 (1993) pp. 229–53

Garritsen de Vries, Margaret *Balance of Payments Adjustment, 1945–1986: The IMF Experience* (Washington, DC: International Monetary Fund, 1987).

Gibbon, P. 'The World Bank and the New Politics of Aid', *European Journal of Development Research*, vol. 5 (June 1993) pp. 35–62.

Gillies, David W. 'Evaluating National Human Rights Performance' in *Bulletin of Peace Proposals*, vol. 21, no. 1 (1990) pp. 15–27.

Girvan, Norman 'Empowerment for Development: From Conditionality to Partnership' in Jo Marie Griesgraber and Bernhard G. Gunter (eds) *Rethinking Bretton Woods*, vol. 1, *Promoting Development: Effective Global Institutions for the Twenty-first Century* (London: Pluto Press with the Center of Concern, 1995) pp. 23–37.

Gold, Joseph 'Special Drawing Rights: The Role of Language', *IMF Pamphlet*, no. 15 (Washington, DC: International Monetary Fund, 1971).

Gold, Joseph 'Political Considerations Are Prohibited by Articles of Agreement when the Fund Considers Requests for Use of Resources' in *IMF Survey*, May 23, 1983, pp. 146–8.

Goldman, M. 'The Chinese Model: The Solution to Russia's Economic Ills?' in *Current History*, vol. 92, no. 576 (October 1993) pp. 320–4.

Goodin, Robert E. 'The Development Rights Trade-Off: Some Unwarranted Economic and Political Assumptions' in *Universal Human Rights*, vol. 1, April–June 1979, pp. 31–42.

Gordon, D. 'Sustaining Economic Reform in Sub-Saharan Africa: Issues and Implications for USAID', Working Paper no. 6 in *Implementing Policy Change* (Washington, D.C.: Management Systems International, 1994).

Government of India *Economic Survey 1992/93* (Delhi: Indian Ministry of Finance, 1993).

Graham, C. *Safety Nets, Politics and the Poor: Transitions to Market Economies* (Washington, DC: Brookings Institution, 1994).

Gramling, E. and W. Freudenberg 'Opportunity, Threat, Development and Adaption: Towards a Comprehensive Framework for Social Impact Assessment' in *Rural Sociology*, vol. 57 (1992) pp. 216–34.

Green, Reginald H. 'The IMF and the World Bank in Africa: How Much Learning?' in Thomas M. Callaghy and John Ravenhill (eds) *Hemmed In: Responses to Africa's Economic Decline* (New York: Columbia University Press, 1993)pp. 54–89.

Grindle, Merilee S. 'The New Political Economy: Positive Economics and Negative Politics', *Policy, Planning and Research Papers*, WPS 304 (Washington, DC: World Bank, December 1989).

Gulhati, R. 'Imposing Conditions on Aid' in Uner Kirdar and Leonard S. Silk (eds) *A World Fit For People* (New York: New York University Press, 1994) pp. 200–210.

Bibliography

Haggard, S. *Pathways from the Periphery: The Politics of Growth in the NICs* (Ithaca: Cornell University Press, 1990).

Haggard, S. and R. Kaufman 'The Challenges of Consolidation' in *Journal of Democracy*, vol. 5, no. 4 (1994) pp. 5–16.

Haggard, S. and S.B. Webb (eds) *Voting for Reform: Democracy, Political Liberalization, and Economic Adjustment* (New York: Oxford University Press, for the World Bank, 1994).

Hartford, Kathleen 'Reform or Retrofitting? The Chinese Economy Since Tiananmen' in *World Policy Journal*, vol. 9, no. 1 (1991) pp. 36–66.

Helleiner, Gerald K. 'The IMF and Africa in the 1980s', Essays in International Finance, no. 152 (July 1983) Princeton University, Department of Economics monograph series.

Helleiner, Gerald K. 'Africa's Adjustment and External Debt Problem: Issues and Options – An Unofficial View' in I.G. Patel (ed.) *Policies for African Development: From the 1980s to the 1990s* (Washington, DC: International Monetary Fund, 1992).

Helleiner, Gerald K. 'The IMF, the World Bank, and Africa's Adjustment and External Debt Problems: An Unofficial View' in *World Development*, vol. 20, no. 6 (June 1992) pp. 779–92.

Helleiner, Gerald K. *From Adjustment to Development in Africa: Conflict, Controversy, Convergence, Consensus* (New York: St Martins Press, 1994).

Hiemenz, U. and R.J. Langhammer 'Liberalization and the Successful Integration of Developing Countries into the World Economy' in G.T. Renshaw (ed.) *Market Liberalization, Equity and Development* (Geneva: International Labour Organisation, 1989) pp. 105–39.

Howard, Rhoda 'The "Full Belly" Thesis: Should Economic Rights Take Priority Over Civil and Political Rights? Evidence From Sub-Saharan Africa' in *Human Rights Quarterly*, vol. 5, no. 4 (1983) pp. 467–90.

Human Rights Watch *Indivisible Human Rights: The Relationship of Political and Civil Rights to Survival, Subsistence and Poverty* (New York: Human Rights Watch, 1992).

Huntington, Samuel P. *The Third Wave: Democratization in the Late Twentieth Century* (Norman: University of Oklahoma Press, 1991).

Husain, Ishrat and Rashid Faruquee *Adjustment in Africa* (Washington, DC: World Bank Regional and Sectoral Studies, 1994).

Jayawardena, L. 'The Bretton Woods Institutions and the Development Problems of the Poorer Developing Countries' in Bretton Woods Commission, *Bretton Woods: Looking to the Future* (Washington, DC: Bretton Woods Commission, 1994) pp. C–121–C–132.

Jaycox, E.V.K. *Capacity-Building: The Missing Link in African Development* (Reston, VA: African American Institute, 1993).

Johnson, J.H. and S. Wasty 'Borrower Ownership of Adjustment Programs and the Political Economy of Reform', *World Bank Discussion Paper no. 199* (Washington, DC: World Bank, 1993).

Johnson, O. 'Managing Adjustment Costs: Political Authority and the Implementation of Adjustment Programs, with Special Reference to

African Countries' in *World Development*, vol. 22, no. 3 (March 1994) pp. 399–411.

Jordan, Lisa and Peter van Tuijl *Democratizing Global Power Relations* (The Hague: Institute of Social Studies, 1993).

Juma, C. and R. Ford 'Facing Africa's Ecological Crisis' in A. Seidman and F. Anang (eds) *Twenty-First-Century Africa: Towards a New Vision of Self-Sustainable Development* (Trenton, South Africa: Africa World Press and African Studies Association Press, 1992) pp. 183–201.

Khan, Mohsin S. and Malcolm D. Knight 'Fund-Supported Adjustment Programs and Economic Growth', *Occasional Paper no. 41* (Washington, DC: International Monetary Fund, 1985).

Killick, Tony 'Structural Adjustment and Poverty Alleviation: An Interpretive Survey' in *Development and Change*, vol. 26 (1995) pp. 305–31.

Killick, Tony *The Adaptive Economy: Adjustment Policies in Small, Low-Income Countries* (Washington, DC: The World Bank, 1994).

Killick, Tony 'Issues Arising from the Spread of Obligatory Adjustment' in Graham Bird (ed.) *Third World Debt: The Search for a Solution* (Aldershot: Edward Elgar, 1989) pp. 78–117.

Killick, Tony, Tony Addison and Lionel Demery 'Poverty, Adjustment and the IMF' in Khadija Haq and Uner Kirdar (eds) *Human Development, Adjustment and Growth* (Islamabad, Pakistan: North–South Roundtable, 1987) pp. 112–37.

Kingsbury, D. *Compensatory Social Programs and Structural Adjustment: A Review of Experience* (Washington, DC: USAID, 1994).

Kiwanuka, R.K. 'Developing Rights: The UN Declaration on the Right to Development' in *Netherlands International Law Review*, vol. 35, no. 3 (1988) pp. 257–72.

Koch, E. 'Real Development or Rhetoric? The Potential and Problems of Ecotourism as a Tool for Rural Reconstruction in South Africa' mimeo, 1993.

Kohli, A. 'Democracy and Economic Orthodoxy: Trends in Developing Countries' in *Third World Quarterly*, vol. 14, no. 4 (November 1993) pp. 668–89.

Krueger, Anne O. 'Interactions between Inflation and Trade Regime Objectives in Stabilization Programs' in William R. Cline and Sidney Weintraub (eds) *Economic Stabilization in Developing Countries* (Washington, DC: Brookings Institution, 1981) pp. 83–117.

Lal, D. *The Poverty of Development Economics* (Cambridge, MA: Harvard University Press, 1983).

Landell-Mills, Pierre and Ismail Serageldin 'Governance and the External Factor' in *Proceedings of the World Bank Annual Conference on Development Economics, 1991* (Washington, DC: World Bank, 1991) pp. 303–20.

Mathieson, D. and L. Rojas-Suarez 'Liberalizing the Capital Account' in *Finance and Development*, vol. 29, no. 4 (December 1992) pp. 41–3.

Milor, V. *Changing Political Economies: Privatization in Post-Communist and Reforming States* (Boulder: Lynne Rienner, 1994).

Mkandawire, Thandika 'North-South Links and Democratization in Africa' in *Development*, vol. 3, no. 4 (1991) pp. 39–41.

Moore, M. 'Declining to Learn from the East? The World Bank on "Governance and Development"' in *Institute for Development Studies (IDS) Bulletin*, vol. 24, no. 1 (January 1993) pp. 39–50.

Moore, M. and M. Robinson 'Can Foreign Aid Be Used to Promote Good Government in Developing Countries?' in *Ethics and International Affairs*, vol. 8 (1994) pp. 141–58.

Morrison, Christian, Jean-Dominique Lafay and Sebastian Dessus 'Adjustment Programmes and Politico-Economic Interactions in Developing Countries: Lessons from an Empirical Analysis of Africa in the 1980s' in Giovanni A. Cornia and Gerald K. Helleiner (eds) *From Adjustment to Development in Africa: Conflict, Controversy, Convergence, Consensus* (New York: St Martins Press, 1994) pp. 174–91.

Moser, C. 'Gender Planning in the Third World: Meeting Practical and Strategic Needs' in R. Grant and K. Newland (eds) *Gender and International Relations* (Bloomington: Indiana University Press, 1991) pp. 83–121.

Mosley, P., J. Toye and J. Harrigan *Aid and Power: The World Bank and Policy-Based Lending* (London and New York: Routledge, 1991).

Murphree, M. 'Communities as Institutions for Resource Management', Paper presented at the National Conference on Environment and Development, Maputo, Mozambique, October 7–11, 1991.

Mussa, M. 'The Adjustment Process and the Timing of Trade Liberalization', National Bureau of Economic Research, Working Paper Series, no. 1458 (September 1984).

Nelson, Joan M. (ed.) *Economic Crisis and Policy Choice: The Politics of Adjustment in the Third World* (Princeton: Princeton University Press, 1990).

Nelson, Joan M. *Encouraging Democracy: What Role for Conditioned Aid?* (Washington, DC: Overseas Development Council, 1992).

Nelson, Joan M. 'Poverty, Equity and the Politics of Adjustment' in Stephen Haggard and Robert R. Kaufman (eds) *The Politics of Economic Adjustment: International Constraints, Distributional Conflicts and the State* (Princeton: Princeton University Press, 1992) pp. 221–69.

Nelson, Joan M. 'Consolidating Economic Adjustment: Aspects of the Political Economy of Sustained Reform' in Paul Mosley (ed.) *Development Finance and Policy Reform: Essays in the Theory and Practice of Conditionality in LDCs* (New York: St Martins Press, 1992) pp. 105–28.

North–South Roundtable *The United Nations and the Bretton Woods Institutions: New Challenges for the 21st Century* (New York: Society for International Development, 1993).

Onis, Z. 'Redemocratization and Economic Liberalization in Turkey: The Limits of State Autonomy' in *Studies in Comparative Economic Development*, vol. 27, no. 2 (Summer 1992) pp. 3–23.

Organization for Economic Cooperation and Development (OECD) *Development Co-operation in the 1990s: Policy Statement by DAC Aid Ministers and Heads of Agencies* (Paris: OECD, 1989).

Oxfam *Africa, Make or Break: Action for Recovery* (London: Oxfam, 1993).

Patnaik, Prabhat *Post-War Capitalism and the Problem of Transition to Socialism* (Shimla: Indian Institute of Advanced Study, 1993) mimeo.

Patnaik, Prabhat 'International Capital and National Economic Policy: A Critique of India's Economic Reforms' in *Economic and Political Weekly*, vol. 29, no. 12 (March 19, 1994) pp. 683–9.

Patnaik, Prabhat 'Development Planning: The India Experience' (New Delhi: Centre for Economic Studies and Planning, Jawaharlal Nehru University, 1994) mimeo.

Pereira, Luiz C.B. 'Economic Reforms and Economic Growth: Efficiency and Politics in Latin America' in Luiz C.B. Pereira, Jose A. Maravall and Adam Przeworski (eds) *Economic Reforms in New Democracies: A Social-Democratic Approach* (Cambridge: Cambridge University Press, 1993) pp. 15–76.

Perrson, T. and G. Tabellini 'Is Inequality Harmful for Growth?' in *American Economic Review*, vol. 84, no. 3 (June 1994) pp. 600–21.

Pickel, A. 'Authoritarianism or Democracy: Marketization as a Political Problem' in *Policy Sciences*, vol. 26, no. 3 (1993) pp. 139–63.

Please, Stanley *Hobbled Giant: Essays on the World Bank* (Boulder: Westview Press, 1984).

Please, Stanley 'Beyond Structural Adjustment in Africa' in *Development Policy Review*, vol. 10, no. 3 (September 1992) pp. 289–307.

Please, Stanley 'From Structural Adjustment to Structural Transformation' in Willem van der Geest (ed.) *Negotiating Structural Adjustment in Africa* (London: James Curry, 1994) pp. 14–24.

Popper, Karl *The Poverty of Historicism* (London: Routledge and Paul Kegan, 1957).

'Proceedings of the January 1994 Meetings of the American Economic Association' in *The American Economic Review*, vol. 84, no. 2 (May 1994) pp. 211–65.

Pronk, Jan P. 'Triggering Debt Relief' in Jan Joost Teunissen (ed.) *Europe and Third World Debt Reduction: The Role of the Netherlands* (The Hague: Forum on Debt and Development (FONDAD) 1991) pp. 9–18.

Ramachandran, V.K. 'Notes on Kerala' (1993) mimeo.

Rahnema, M. 'Participation' in W. Sachs (ed.) *The Development Dictionary, A Guide to Knowledge as Power* (London: Zed Books, 1993) pp. 116–31.

Ramphele, M. 'Participatory Research: The Myths and Realities' in *Social Dynamics*, vol. 16, no. 2, (1990) pp. 1–15.

Reisen, Helmut 'Financial Opening and Capital Flows' in C. Bradford (ed.) *Mobilising International Investment for Latin America* (Paris: OECD, 1992) pp. 143–52.

Reisman, W. Michael 'Through or Despite Governments: Differentiated Responsibilities in Human Rights Programs' in *Iowa Law Review*, vol. 72, no. 2 (1987) pp. 391–9.

Remmer, K. 'Democracy and Economic Crisis: The Latin American Experience' in *World Politics*, vol. 42, no. 3 (April 1990) pp. 315–35.

Rich, B. *Mortgaging the Earth: The World Bank, Environmental Impoverishment and the Crisis of Development* (Boston: Beacon Press, 1994).

Rickson, R. 'Impacts of Rainforest Preservation on Rainforest People and their Communities' in *Impact Assessment Bulletin*, vol. 9, no. 4 (1991) pp. 41–55.

Rickson, R. and S. Rickson 'Assessing Rural Development: The Role of the Social Scientist' in *Environmental Impact Assessment Review*, vol. 10, no. 1/2 (1990) pp. 103–12.

Rickson, R., J. Western and R. Burdge 'Social Impact Assessment: Knowledge and Development' in *Environmental Impact Assessment Review*, vol. 10, no. 1/2 (1990) pp. 1–10.

Rock, M. 'Transitional Democracies and the Shift to Export-Led Industrialization: Lessons from Thailand' in *Studies in Comparative International Development*, vol. 29, no. 1 (Spring 1994) pp. 18–37.

Rosales, O. 'An Assessment of the Structuralist Paradigm for Latin American Development and the Prospects for Its Renovation' *CEPAL Review*, no. 34 (April 1988) pp. 19–36.

Ross, H. 'Community Social Impact Assessment: A Framework for Indigenous Peoples' in *Environmental Impact Assessment Review*, vol. 10, no. 1/2 (1990) pp. 185–93.

Rueschemeyer, D., E.H. Stephens, and J.D. Stephens *Capitalist Development and Democracy* (Chicago: University of Chicago Press, 1992).

Ruggie, John G. 'Political Structure and Change in the International Economic Order: The North–South Dimension' in John G. Ruggie (ed.) *Antinomies of Interdependence: National Welfare and the International Division of Labor* (New York: Columbia University Press, 1983) pp. 423–87.

Sachs, J.D. 'Strengthening IMF Programs in Highly Indebted Countries' in C. Gwin and R. E. Feinberg (eds), *Pulling Together: The International Monetary Fund in a Multipolar World* (New Brunswick, NJ: Transaction Books, 1989) pp. 101–22.

Sandbrook, Richard 'Taming Africa's Leviathan' in *World Policy Journal* (Winter 1990) pp. 673–701.

Schmitz, Gerald J. and David Gillies *The Challenge of Democratic Development* (Ottawa: North-South Institute, 1992).

Schoultz, Lars *Human Rights and United States Foreign Policy Toward Latin America* (Princeton: Princeton University Press, 1981).

Seidman, G. 'Shafted: The Social Impact of Down-Scaling on the Free State Goldfields' in *South African Sociological Review*, vol. 5, no. 2 (1993) pp. 14–34.

Sen, A.K. 'Public Action and the Quality of Life in Developing Countries' in *Oxford Bulletin of Economics and Statistics* (Oxford: Oxford University Press, 1981) p. 43.

Sen, A.K. 'Markets and Freedoms: Achievements and Limitations of the Market Mechanism in Promoting Individual Freedoms' in *Oxford Economic Papers*, vol. 45 (October 1993) pp. 519–41.

Senghaas, D. 'European Development and the Third World: An Assessment' in *Review* (of the Fernand Bramdel Center for the Study of Economics, History, and Civilizations), vol. 11, no. 1 (Winter 1988) pp. 127–40.

Serven, L. and A. Solimano 'Debt Crisis, Adjustment Policies and Capital Formation in Developing Countries: Where Do We Stand?' in *World Development*, vol. 21, no. 1 (1992) pp. 127–40.

Shafer, D.M. *Winners and Losers: How Sectors Shape the Development Prospects of States* (Ithaca: Cornell University Press, 1994).

Shihata, Ibrahim F.I. *Issues of 'Governance' in Borrowing Members: The Extent of Their Relevance Under the Bank's Articles of Agreement* (Washington, DC: World Bank, 1990).

Shihata, Ibrahim F.I. *The World Bank in a Changing World: Selected Essays* (Dordrecht and Boston: Martinus Nijhoff Publishers, 1991).

Shihata, Ibrahim F.I. 'The World Bank and Non-Governmental Organizations' in *Cornell International Law Journal*, vol. 25 (1992) pp. 623–41.

Singer, Hans W. 'Terms of Trade: New Wine and New Bottles' in *Development Policy Review*, vol. 9, no. 4 (1991) pp. 339–52.

Skalnes, T. 'The State, Interest Groups and Structural Adjustment in Zimbabwe' in *Journal of Development Studies*, vol. 29, no. 3 (April 1993) pp. 401–28.

Soludo, Charles 'Growth Performance in Africa: Further Evidence on the External Versus Domestic Policy Debate', *Development Research Papers Services*, no. 6 (Addis Ababa: UN Economic Commission for Africa, November 1993).

Spiegel, A. 'The Anti-Politics Machine: Development, Depoliticization and Bureaucratic Power by James Ferguson' in *Social Dynamics*, vol. 18, no. 2 (1992) pp. 101–4.

Steer, Andrew and Ernst Lutz 'Measuring Environmentally Sustainable Development' in *Finance and Development*, vol. 30, no. 4 (1993) pp. 20–3.

Stern, E. 'Introduction' in V. Thomas (ed.) *Restructuring Economies in Distress: Policy Reform and the World Bank* (Oxford: Oxford University Press, 1992).

Stewart, Frances 'Should Conditionality Change?' in Kjell J. Havenevik (ed.), *The IMF and the World Bank in Africa* (Uppsala: Scandinavian Institute of Africa Studies, 1987) pp. 29–45.

Stewart, Frances 'Many Faces of Adjustment' in P. Mosley (ed.) *Development Finance and Policy Reform: Essays in the Theory and Practice of Conditionality in LDCs* (New York: St Martins Press, 1992) pp. 176–231.

Stiefel, M. *A Voice for the Excluded: Popular Participation in Development: Utopia or Necessity?* (London: Zed Books, 1994).

Streeten, P. 'Structural Adjustment: A Survey of the Issues and Options' in *World Development*, vol. 15, no. 12 (December 1987) pp. 1469–82.

Summers, L. and L. Pritchett 'The Structural Adjustment Debate' in *American Economic Review*, vol. 83 (May 1993) pp. 383–9.

Summers, Lawrence H. and Vinod Thomas 'Recent Lessons of Development' in *World Bank Research Observer*, vol. 8, no. 2 (July 1993) pp. 241–54.

Taylor, Lance *Varieties of Stabilization Experience: Towards Sensible Macroeconomics in the Third World* (Oxford: Clarendon Press, 1988).

Thomas, V. *Best Practices in Trade Policy Reform* (New York and Oxford: Oxford University Press, 1991).

Ul Haq, Mahub. 'From Dialogue to Action' in K. Haq and U. Kirdar (eds) *Human Development, Adjustment and Growth* (Islamabad, Pakistan: North-South Roundtable, 1987) pp. 14–20.

United Nations Conference on Trade and Development *International Monetary and Financial Issues for the 1990s: Research Papers for the Group of Twenty-Four, Volume II* (New York: United Nations, 1993).

United Nations Development Programme *Human Development Report 1991* (New York and Oxford: Oxford University Press, 1991).

United Nations Development Programme *Human Development Report 1992* (New York and Oxford: Oxford University Press, 1992).

United Nations Development Programme *Human Development Report 1993* (New York: Oxford University Press, 1993).

United Nations Economic Commission for Africa *African Alternative Framework to Structural Adjustment Programmes for Socio-Economic Recovery and Transformation* (Addis Ababa: UNECA, 1989).

United Nations Economic Commission for Africa *Economic Report on Africa 1990* (Addis Ababa: UNECA, 1991).

United Nations Economic Commission for Africa *Strategies of Financial Resource Mobilization for Africa's Development in the 1990s*, Document E/ECA/CM.19/5 (Addis Ababa: UNECA, April 1993).

Wade, Robert *Governing the Market: Economic Theory and the Role of Government in East Asian Industrialization* (Princeton: Princeton University Press, 1991).

Wai, Dunstan M. 'Governance, Economic Development and the Role of External Actors', paper delivered at the Conference on Governance and Economic Development in Sub-Saharan Africa, Oxford University, May 1991.

Walton, J. and D. Seddon *Free Markets and Food Riots: The Politics of Global Adjustment* (Oxford and Cambridge: Basil Blackwell, 1994).

Weaver, A. 'Integrated Environmental Management: Some Practical Considerations', Paper delivered to the World Environment Day Symposium, Johannesburg, South Africa, June 4, 1992.

Weaver, James H. 'What is Structural Adjustment?' in Daniel M. Schydlowsky (ed.) *Structural Adjustment: Retrospect and Prospect* (Westport: Praeger, 1995) pp. 3–17.

Webster, E. 'Participatory Democracy or Utopian Blueprint?' in *Business Day* (March 16, 1994).

Weingast, B.R. *The Political Impediments to Economic Reform: Political Risk and Enduring Gridlock* IPR Working Paper Series, no. IPR68 (Washington, DC: Institute for Policy Reform (IPR), January 1994).

West, P. and S. Brechin (eds) *Resident People and National Parks: Social*

Dilemmas and Strategies in International Conservation (Tucson: University of Arizona Press, 1993).

Williamson, John 'In Search of A Manual for Technopols' in John Williamson (ed.) *The Political Economy of Policy Reform* (Washington, DC: Institute of International Economics, 1993) pp. 9–28.

Woodward, D. *Debt, Adjustment and Poverty in Developing Countries* (New York: St Martins Press, 1992).

World Bank *Accelerated Development in Sub-Saharan Africa: An Agenda for Action* (Washington, DC: World Bank, 1981).

World Bank *Sub-Saharan Africa; From Crisis to Sustainable Growth: A Long Term Perspective Study* (Washington, DC: World Bank, 1989).

World Bank *Adjustment Lending Policies for Sustainable Growth*, Policy and Research Series no. 14 (Washington, DC: World Bank, 1990).

World Bank *China: Between Plan and Market* (Washington, DC: World Bank, 1990).

World Bank *Report on Adjustment Lending II: Policies for the Recovery of Growth* (Washington, DC: World Bank, 1990).

World Bank *World Development Report 1990* (Oxford: Oxford University Press, 1990).

World Bank *World Development Report 1991* (Washington, DC: World Bank, 1991).

World Bank *Adjustment Lending and Mobilization of Private and Public Resources for Growth*, Policy and Research Series no. 22 (Washington, DC: World Bank, 1992).

World Bank Portfolio Management Task Force *Effective Implementation: Key to Development Impact* (Washington, DC: World Bank, 1992).

World Bank *World Bank Structural and Sectoral Adjustment Operation: The Second Operations Evaluation Department Review* (Washington, DC: World Bank, 1992).

World Bank *Implementing the Bank's Poverty Reduction Strategy: Progress and Challenges* (Washington, DC: World Bank, 1993).

World Bank *Poverty Reduction Handbook* (Washington, DC: World Bank, 1993).

World Bank *The East Asian Miracle: Economic Growth and Public Policy* (New York: Oxford University Press, 1993).

World Bank *The World Bank Annual Report 1993* (Washington, DC: World Bank, 1993).

World Bank *Adjustment in Africa: Reforms, Results and the Road Ahead* (Oxford: Oxford University Press, 1994).

World Bank *Financial Flows and The Developing Countries: A World Bank Quarterly* (Washington, DC: World Bank, February 1994).

World Bank *Global Economic Prospects and The Developing Countries* (Washington, DC: World Bank, 1994).

World Bank *Governance: The World Bank's Experience* (Washington, DC: World Bank, 1994).

Yagci, Fahrettin, Steven Kamin and Vicki Rosenbaum 'Structural Adjustment Lending: An Evaluation of Program Design', *World Bank Staff Working Paper no. 735* (Washington, DC: World Bank, 1985).

Bibliography

Zingle, J.G. 'Social Assessment' in CSIR, *Environmental Impact Assessment: Eastern Shores of Lake St Lucia*, vol. 1, Specialist Reports, Chapter 9 (Pretoria: CSIR Environmental Services, 1993).

Zingle, J.G. and S. Bekker 'Community Life and Social Services' in CSIR, *Environmental Impact Assessment: Eastern Shores of Lake St Lucia*, vol. 2, Reports on the Key Issues, Chapter 8 (Pretoria: CSIR Environmental Services, 1993).

Notes on Editors and Contributors

Jo Marie Griesgraber is Project Director for the Rethinking Bretton Woods project at the Center of Concern where she has worked on issues related to Third World debt and global economic justice since 1989. Her most recent publications include contributions to Lowell S. Gustafson (ed.), *Economic Development Under Democratic Regimes: Neoliberalism in Latin America* (Westport, CT: Praeger, 1994) and 'In Quest of Systematic Hope: Rethinking Bretton Woods', *Theology & Public Policy*, vol. 4, no. 2 (Washington, DC: Churches' Center for Theology and Public Policy, Winter 1994) pp. 19–33.

Bernhard G. Gunter has worked with the Rethinking Bretton Woods project as an intern at the Center of Concern. He is a Ph.D. candidate in Economics at The American University, Washington, DC, a member of Pax Christi, Germany, and has focused on global justice since 1980. His most recent publication is 'Financial Crises and the Great Depression in Germany, 1927–1933: A Review With Some New Facts and Arguments' in *Essays in Economic and Business History*, vol. 13 (1995) pp. 55–70.

C.P. Chandrasekhar is an Associate Professor at the Centre for Economic Studies and Planning at Jawaharlal Nehru University in India. His interests include macroeconomic, industrialization and planning issues in developing countries – areas in which he has written and published widely. He has been actively involved in the debate on the effects and efficacy of stabilization and structural adjustment in India and the rest of the developing world, and his latest publication is 'The Macroeconomics of Imbalance and Adjustment' in Prabhat Patnaik (ed.), *Themes in Indian Economics:*

Macroeconomics (New Delhi: Oxford University Press, forthcoming). The author gratefully acknowledges comments by Chandra Hardy and H.W. Singer on an earlier draft of this chapter.

Jacklyn Cock is Professor of Sociology at the University of the Witswatersrand in South Africa. She has been involved in struggles around human rights, feminism, the environment and militarism for some time, and has written and spoken widely on these subjects. She has co-edited *War and Society: The Militarization of South Africa* (Cape Town: David Philip, 1989; New York: St Martin's Press, 1989) and *Going Green: People, Politics and the Environment in South Africa* (Cape Town: Oxford University Press, 1991). Her most recent publications include *Colonels and Cadres: War and Gender in South Africa* (Cape Town: Oxford University Press, 1991); and *Women and War in South Africa* (London: Open Letters, 1992; Cleveland: The Pilgrim Press, 1993).

Barend A. de Vries is retired from 35 years as an economist with the IMF (1949–55) and the World Bank (1956–84). Before joining the IMF, he worked with the Cowles Commission for Research in Econometrics at the University of Chicago. From 1984–6, he was a Guest Scholar at the Brookings Institution, and from 1986–90 lecturer at Georgetown University. He continues to write and speak about economic development and poverty alleviation. Other publications by Dr de Vries include *Champions of the Poor: The Economics and Ethics of Fighting Poverty* (Washington, DC: Georgetown University Press, forthcoming) and a chapter in *Remaking the World Bank* (Washington, DC: Seven Locks Press, 1987).

David Gillies is Policy Coordinator at the International Centre for Human Rights and Democratic Development in Montreal. He has served as a consultant for the North–South Institute, the Canadian International Development Agency, and the Canadian Council for International Cooperation. He has published numerous articles on issues of humanitarian intervention and state sovereignty; the application of human rights and democratic norms to the activity of the World Bank; and the integration of human rights and democratic governance in the work of the Organization for Economic Cooperation and Development. Recent publications with the International Centre are: 'Human Rights, Democracy and Development', commissioned by the UN Centre for Human Rights, and 'A Long Road to Uhuru: Human Rights and Political Participation in Kenya'.

Daniel C. Milder is an independent consultant specializing in research on comparative economic development and North–South relations. He has been a Visiting Lecturer in political science at Texas A&M University and the University of Vermont. His chapter in this book condenses the analysis and findings of his forthcoming Ph.D. dissertation at the University of Michigan, entitled 'Economic Policies as Political Tools in Structural Adjustment'.

Owodunni Teriba has been Chief of the Socio-Economic Research and Planning Division of the United Nations Economic Commission for Africa (UNECA) in Addis Ababa, Ethiopia, since 1989. From 1984–9, he was UNECA's Senior Regional Economic Adviser. He taught economics for nearly 20 years at the University of Ibadan, Ibadan, Nigeria, and has written extensively on Africa's development problems and issues, including: 'Financing Growth and Development in Africa: Outlook and Issues – A View from the UN Commission on Africa' in I.G. Patel (ed.) *Policies for African Development: From The 1980s to the 1990s* (Washington, DC: International Monetary Fund, 1992) pp. 171–87; 'The General Framework for Industrial Development in Nigeria' in Teriba, O. and M.O. Kayode (eds) *Industrial Development in Nigeria: Patterns, Problems and Prospects* (Ibadan, Nigeria: Ibadan Unviersity Press, 1977) pp. 11–31. He is also co-editor (with Adebayo Adedeji, and Patrick Bugembe) of *The Challenge of African Economic Recovery and Development* (London: Cass, 1991). The author is grateful for the comments and assistance of Karamo Sonko, J.K. Thisen and Eloho Otobo in the preparation of this chapter. The views expressed here do not necessarily reflect or represent those of UNECA.

Eddie C. Webster is Professor and Head of the Department of Sociology at the University of the Witswatersrand in South Africa, where he is also the Director of the Sociology of Work Unit. He has been involved in the struggle for a democratic labor movement since the early 1980s, publishing widely in the field of work and industrial relations, including 'Managerial Resistance to the Unionization of Black Metal Workers in South Africa, 1973–1977' ,*Labour, Capital and Society*, vol. 17, no. 1 (April 1984) pp. 67–96; and 'Two Faces of Black Trade Union Movement in South Africa', *Review of African Political Economy*, no. 39 (September 1987), pp. 33–41. He is a founder and editor of the *South African Labour Bulletin* and past president of the Association of Sociologists of South Africa.

Rethinking Bretton Woods

PROJECT SPONSORS

Charles Abugre
Third World Network
GHANA

Adebayo Adedeji
African Centre for Development and Strategic Studies
NIGERIA

Peggy Antrobus
Development Alternatives with Women for a New Era
(DAWN)
BARBADOS

Tissa Balasuriya
Centre for Society and Religion
SRI LANKA

David Barkin *
Lincoln Institute of Land Policy
Cambridge, MA (MEXICO)

Leonor Briones
Freedom from Debt Coalition
PHILIPPINES

Edward Broadbent and **David Gillies**
International Centre for Human Rights
and Democratic Development
CANADA

Salvie D. Colina
Asian Center for the Progress of Peoples
HONG KONG

Sarath Fernando
Devasarana Development Centre
SRI LANKA

Susan Fleck and **Bernhard Gunter**
Economics Graduate Student Union, The American University
Washington, DC USA

Louis Goodman
Dean, School of International Service, The American University
Washington, DC USA

J. Bryan Hehir *
Harvard University
Cambridge, MA USA

Gabriel Izquierdo, SJ
Centro de Investigacion y Educacion Popular (CINEP)
COLOMBIA

Fatima Mello
Federation of Organizations for Social and
Educational Assistance (FASE)
BRAZIL

Guy Mhone
Southern Africa Regional Institute for Policy Studies
ZIMBABWE

Luis Peirano and **Humberto Campodonico**
Centro de Estudios y Promocion del Desarrollo
(DESCO)
PERU

Sebasti L. Raj, SJ
Indian Social Institute
INDIA

Jorge Sabato *
Centro de Estudios Avanzados
ARGENTINA

Francisco Sagasti
Grupo de Analisis para el Desarrollo (GRADE)
PERU

Tom Schlesinger
Southern Finance Project
Philomont, VA USA

Kavaljit Singh
Public Interest Research Group
INDIA

Rob van Drimmelen
World Council of Churches
SWITZERLAND

Peter van Tuijl and **Augustinus Rumansara**
International NGO Forum on Indonesian Development
INDONESIA / THE NETHERLANDS

Layashi Yaker
United Nations Economic Commission for Africa
ETHIOPIA

Noel Keizo Yamada, SJ
Sophia University
JAPAN

* Personal Capacity, organization listed for identification only.

PROJECT ADVISORY GROUP

Nii Akwuettah
Africa Development Foundation

Nancy Alexander
Bread for the World Institute

Steven Arnold
Professor, School of International Service
The American University

Ambassador **Richard Bernal**
Embassy of Jamaica

Daniel Bradlow
Professor, Washington College of Law
The American University

Robert Browne
Economic Consultant

Margaret Crahan
Luce Professor of Religion, Power and Political Process
Occidental College, Los Angeles

Maria Floro
Professor, Department of Economics
The American University

Louis Goodman
Dean, School of International Service
The American University

Jo Marie Griesgraber
Project Director, Center of Concern

Chandra Hardy
International Development Training Institution

James E. Hug, SJ
Director, Center of Concern

Constantine Michalopoulos
The World Bank

Moises Naim
Senior Fellow, Carnegie Endowment for International Peace

Ambassador **Margaret Taylor**
Embassy of Papua New Guinea

Marijke Torfs
Friends of the Earth

Index

For acronyms see list on pp. xi-xii. Figures and Tables are given in **bold**. *Italic* page numbers refer to the Glossary.

231

Index by Auriol Griffith-Jones